THE MOUNTAIN WHITE-CROWNED SPARROW: MIGRATION AND REPRODUCTION AT HIGH ALTITUDE

Martin L. Morton

Biology Department
Occidental College
Los Angeles, California

Studies in Avian Biology No. 24
A PUBLICATION OF THE COOPER ORNITHOLOGICAL SOCIETY

Cover drawing of female Mountain White-crowned Sparrow (*Zonotrichia leucophrys oriantha*)
attending her nest by Maria Elena Pereyra

STUDIES IN AVIAN BIOLOGY

Edited by

John T. Rotenberry
Department of Biology
University of California
Riverside, CA 92521

Artwork by
Maria Elena Pereyra

Studies in Avian Biology is a series of works too long for *The Condor,* published at irregular intervals by the Cooper Ornithological Society. Manuscripts for consideration should be submitted to the editor. Style and format should follow those of previous issues.

Price $27.00 including postage and handling. All orders cash in advance; make checks payable to Cooper Ornithological Society. Send orders to Cooper Ornithological Society, % Western Foundation of Vertebrate Zoology, 439 Calle San Pablo, Camarillo, CA 93010.

ISBN: 1-891276-32-8

Library of Congress Control Number: 2002104020
Printed at Allen Press, Inc., Lawrence, Kansas 66044
Issued: June 12, 2002

CONTENTS

DEDICATION vi

ABSTRACT 1

PREFACE 4

CHAPTER 1: Introduction 9

   THE *ZONOTRICHIA* 10

   FEATURES OF MONTANE ENVIRONMENTS 15

   THE STUDY AREA 16

CHAPTER 2: Migration Arrival 23

   ARRIVAL SCHEDULE 24

   ALTITUDINAL MOVEMENTS 28

   FORAGING 30

CHAPTER 3: Social System and Behavior 33

   TERRITORY ESTABLISHMENT 34

   PAIRING 34

   BETWEEN-YEAR BREEDING DISPERSAL 35

   COPULATIONS 38

   MATE GUARDING 39

   MATE SWITCHING 39

   MATES PER LIFETIME 40

   AGE OF MATES 40

   FLOATERS 41

   POLYGYNY 42

   AGGRESSION 43

   VOCALIZATIONS 45

CHAPTER 4: Demography 51

   LIFE TABLE 52

   AGE STRUCTURE OF BREEDING POPULATION 53

CHAPTER 5: Gonadal Condition 57

   GONADAL CHANGES 58

   INCUBATION (BROOD) PATCH 59

   ROLE OF ENVIRONMENTAL CUES IN ANNUAL CYCLES 60

   PHOTOPERIOD EFFECTS 62

Non-photoperiod Effects   64

Gonadal Hormones   70

CHAPTER 6: Body Size and Body Condition   75

Wing Length and Sex   76

Wing Length and Age   77

Seasonal Changes in Body Mass   78

Daily Changes in Body Mass   82

CHAPTER 7: Nests and Eggs   87

Nests   88

Egg Laying   94

Description of Eggs   96

Egg Dimensions   96

Egg Volume   98

Weight Loss of Eggs During Incubation 106

Clutch Size 108

Incubation 113

CHAPTER 8: Nestlings and Fledglings 121

Hatching 122

Brood Reduction 125

Hatching Asynchrony 127

Sex Ratio 131

Cowbird Parasitism 131

Provisioning Rates 132

Nest Sanitation 133

Patterns of Parental Care 134

Growth and Thermoregulation in Nestlings 135

Natal Dispersal 144

CHAPTER 9: Nest Failure 149

Predation 150

Desertion 152

Storms 153

Renesting 157

CHAPTER 10: Reproductive Success 165

Annual Reproductive Success of Nests 166

ANNUAL REPRODUCTIVE SUCCESS OF INDIVIDUALS 167

LIFETIME REPRODUCTIVE SUCCESS 168

SNOW CONDITIONS 170

CHAPTER 11: Late-season Events 179

GONADAL PHOTOREFRACTORINESS 180

MOLT 183

TIMING OF SEASONAL BREEDING 192

PREMIGRATORY FATTENING 193

MIGRATION DEPARTURE 197

THE STIMULUS FOR MIGRATION 198

STOPOVER MIGRANTS AND THE MIGRATION SCHEDULE 199

CHAPTER 12: Concluding Remarks 205

ACKNOWLEDGMENTS 209

LITERATURE CITED 210

DEDICATION

This monograph is dedicated to Barbara Blanchard DeWolfe with admiration and respect for her pioneering field studies of White-crowned Sparrows and for her career-long support and encouragement of young scientists.

ABSTRACT

The reproductive biology of a migratory passerine, the Mountain White-crowned Sparrow (*Zonotrichia leucophrys oriantha*) was studied for 25 summers in the Sierra Nevada of California at Tioga Pass. Data were obtained on individuals of known age and sex from time of arrival at subalpine breeding meadows to departure for wintering areas in Mexico about four months later. During the summer season many aspects of the reproductive cycle were examined. These included the social system, nesting habits, seasonal and lifetime reproductive success, gonadal development and hormone secretion rate, energy balance as measured by fluctuations in body mass and fat and by doubly-labeled water, molt, and migration departure schedules. Developmental changes in nestlings, along with their survival and dispersal were also investigated. The cardiovascular and respiratory systems of birds pre-adapt them for living at high altitude but achieving reproductive success in montane settings requires adjustments to unusual environmental conditions such as increased solar heating, low nocturnal temperatures, sudden intense storms, and large interannual variations in residual snowpack. Emphasis was placed, therefore, not only on the key features of migration and reproductive biology probably found in all passerine migrants, but also on how these were affected or altered in response to environmental variation. Special attention was paid to underlying physiological mechanisms and this approach, along with the unusual location, helps to distinguish this long-term field study from others.

Both sexes tended to return to previously occupied areas although site fidelity was greater in males than in females and mate switching between years occurred in 34.1% of returning pairs. Modal number of mates per lifetime was one and the maximum was six. Pairing usually occurred soon after arrival on the study area but it could be delayed by several weeks in years of deep snowpack. Although females were guarded by their mates, at least one-third of the nestlings were the product of extra-pair fertilizations. Females were aggressive and female-female conflicts sometimes delayed settling by one-year-olds, which were then often shunted to less desirable territories. Polygyny occurred in 3.5% of males, and the number of fledglings produced from their nests increased from 3.1 to 5.5 per season. Fitness in females was unaffected by engagement in polygynous matings.

Median time of survival, once one year of age was attained, was 1.9 years for both sexes and survival rate of adults was about 50% per year. This was not different from survival rates found in a sedentary conspecific (*Z. l. nuttalli*) so migration itself does not appear to induce extra mortality in White-crowned Sparrows.

Males arrived at breeding areas with partially developed testes, which continued to enlarge for about one month, no matter the environmental conditions. Plasma testosterone levels were high throughout this period although testis size and testosterone concentrations were greater in older adult males (age 2+ years) than in one-year-olds. Females of all ages, on the other hand, arrived with only slightly enlarged ovaries, which remained in this condition until shortly before nesting began. This could be a month or more in heavy snow years when nesting sites were covered and unavailable. If nesting sites were provided to such delayed females by avalanche-deposited trees or by investigators, however, they built nests and ovulated within four days. Thus, availability of nesting sites was shown at times to exert proximate control over the reproductive schedule.

Body mass varied greatly in females during the nesting cycle. They gained quickly in the three days preceding their first ovulation then lost during laying and, slowly, during incubation. During the day or so that it took for a brood to hatch females lost about 8% of their body mass. It was hypothesized that this occurred because females were spending maximum time on the nest, even at the expense of self maintenance, in order to minimize hatching asynchrony.

Eggs were laid at dawn at 24-hour intervals and did not vary in size with clutch size or female age. No consistent pattern with laying order was discovered although last-laid eggs were most frequently the largest. Egg size seemed to be affected by prevailing ecological conditions and it varied interannually in individuals and in the population. Clutch size decreased steadily with calendar date despite large interannual variations in habitat conditions, including vegetation development. This response was likely due to a photoperiodically controlled down-regulation in ovarian function as females progressed gradually toward the condition of complete photorefractoriness.

Hatching asynchrony was considered at length and was suggested to be the by-product of a mechanism that has evolved to turn off a physiological phase of reproduction (ovulation) while simultaneously turning on a behavioral one (full-time incubation). A model of this response, the "hormonal hypothesis," is presented.

Nestlings grew rapidly (with more feedings being provided by the female parent than the male), reached thermal independence by Day 7 of age, and fledged on Day 9. Logarithmic growth rate constants, obtained during the first four days after hatching, increased with hatching order and with brood size. The hatching order effect was attributed to brooding behavior by females; they tended to sit tightly until all eggs had hatched, and as a result first-hatched chicks were not maximally provisioned. Small broods (one or two chicks) tended to be produced at the end of the season when arthropod food supplies were probably dwindling and large broods (5 chicks) only when unusually favorable trophic conditions existed; in most cases (87%) brood size was three or four chicks.

More than half of the nests (53%) failed to fledge young. About 30% of nests were consistently lost to predators, the remainder to investigator impacts and to storms. Despite the stochasticity of storm occurrence and severity, and even in the face of multiple nesting failures, reproductive output was maintained because of vigorous renesting efforts.

Individuals were known to be engaged in reproduction at up to nine years of age and the number of fledglings produced per season did not vary with age (experience) or sex. Mean lifetime reproductive success was not different for the sexes, being 8.14 fledglings for males (range = 0–26) and 7.10 fledglings for females (range = 0–23). These lifetime numbers are relatively high for passerines and indicate that *Z. l. oriantha* is well suited for reproducing in montane environments.

Postnuptial or prebasic molt lasted for about seven weeks in individuals and began about five days earlier and lasted about three days longer in males than in females. Data from females showed clearly that molt did not begin until they had become photorefractory; they never laid eggs once molt was under way. Still, molting overlapped with the period of parental care in more than 70% of adults of both sexes.

Premigratory fattening required about nine days in both juveniles and adults and the shift in weight-regulation set point (induction of hyperphagia) was found to occur within the span of a single day. Fattening began as molt ended although the two events were not coupled physiologically. On average, juveniles left on migration three days earlier than adults.

In addition to providing a large data base on life history parameters and reproductive physiology, this study revealed a variety of responses that promoted survival and reproductive success in conditions encountered at high altitude. These conditions and the responses to them were: *(1) Deep snowpack.* In heavy snow years *oriantha* terminated migration at the appropriate latitude but tended to stage in foothill areas in Great Basin shrub-steppe rather than ascend to the breeding habitat. Because of this, arrival at the subalpine was sometime delayed by days or weeks. Once settled on the breeding area they exploited an array of foraging niches, including the snow surface itself, and they were euryphagic. If energy balance could not be maintained they flew back down to the staging areas, as shown by radio tracking, and remained there, usually for several days before ascending again. This sequence of movements was repeated several times if necessary. Females compensated somewhat for delays in nesting imposed by late-lying snow by altering their choice of nest sites. Rather than wait for completely thawed locations on the ground they built in the tops of short, shrubby pines and even in the branches of unleafed willows. During the wait for nest sites to appear (which could be as much as two months) testicular growth was completed. In contrast, and probably to save energy, ovaries remained small but on the brink of development during this time. *(2) Storms.* Early in the season, before clutches were started, *oriantha* often responded to storms by moving to lower altitudes. However, if snow cover had diminished and clutches were being produced, females tended not to move; rather, they remained and defended their nests. If a nest was lost to weather, or to any other factor, renesting was initiated at once and usually took only five days even though the complete sequence of courtship behaviors was repeated. Temporal efficiency of this response was abetted by pair-bond and territory retention and as many as five nesting attempts per season were known to occur. *(3) Solar heating.* Females protected eggs and nestlings from solar radiation by shading them with their bodies. Uncovered nestlings, even on the day of hatching, were capable of panting and neonatal down may also have acted as a parasol. *(4) Cold nights and thermolytic winds.* Early in the season, before nesting had begun, *oriantha* roosted on the periphery of meadows in lodgepole pines and pairs were sometimes located in the same tree. Presumably trees provided more favorable microclimates than undeveloped meadow vegetation. Nests were often placed on the lee side of shrubbery and those built above the ground had thicker floors and more densely woven, wind-resistant walls than those built on the ground. Body temperature of incubating females, as shown by egg temperature, drifted down as air temperature decreased, especially in above-ground nests. At the coldest air temperatures this trend was reversed, presumably by shivering. *(5) Rapid onset of winter conditions.* In order to prolong breeding without risking exposure to seasonally deteriorating weather conditions while still allowing time for molting and premigratory fattening, *oriantha* adults saved time by molting while still engaged in parental care. And juveniles from late nests compensated by molting at a relatively early age.

Because many individuals were handled soon after their arrival on the study area, as well as just prior to departure some four months later, it was possible to discover characteristics of physiology and behavior associated with migration itself. These involved the following: *(1) Migration schedule.* Males tended to arrive before females and older birds before yearlings. Since a higher percentage of older males were known to breed, it was suggested that early male arrival is important to territory acquisition and retention. As a group, juveniles tended to leave on fall migration ahead of adults so their primary directional tendencies must be genetic rather than learned. Although White-crowned Sparrows gather into flocks on winter areas, the arrival and departure data from *oriantha* indicate that migration occurs independently or, at most, in small flocks. *(2) Hyperphagia.* Only the very earliest of arriving birds, adult males all, still had fat deposits. Furthermore, autumnal premigratory fattening occurred quickly and obese birds left immediately. This suggests that presence of large fat stores may activate migration behavior and that the altered metabolic states associated with fueling migration, namely hyperphagia and its energy storage correlates, are regulated to match rather precisely the period of migration. Hyperphagia was also exhibited by stopover migrants (*Z. l. gambelii*). *(3) Hematocrit.* Contrary to initial expectations, packed blood cell volume or hematocrit was high in newly arrived birds then decreased during the summer while they were in residence; it increased again in those preparing to depart in the fall. Increased hemopoietic activity appears to be another feature of migration physiology.

It appears that environmental adaptation in migratory passerines occurs mainly through flexibility in their behavior and physiology and that sometimes these responses can involve trade-offs in energy costs and in survival.

Key Words: clutch size, dispersal, hatching asynchrony, high altitude, migration, molt, reproductive success, snow conditions, White-crowned Sparrows, *Zonotrichia leucophrys.*

PREFACE

This monograph describes a long-term study of the reproductive biology of a migratory sparrow at one of its high altitude breeding areas in the Sierra Nevada Mountains of California. The study's inception is probably best marked by a June afternoon in 1968 when our field crew arrived at Tioga Pass for the first time. There were four of us in that initial group, three Occidental College undergraduates, Judy Horstmann, Janet Osborn, and David Welton, and myself, at that time a young Assistant Professor. Guided by Dick Banks' recently published doctoral dissertation on geographic variation in White-crowned Sparrows (*Zonotrichia leucophrys*), we had been searching the Sierra for a potential study site. We wanted a location that was accessible and that held a robust population of the subspecies designated as the Mountain White-crowned Sparrow (*Z. l. oriantha*). Being a careful scientist, Banks had scrupulously listed the collection sites for the museum specimens he had been studying. We reasoned that those areas that had yielded the most specimens would likely have the largest populations. But this strategy had not been working out. Kaiser Pass, on the western slope, for example, was well-represented in museums, but in an extensive search of the area, only one pair of white-crowns was located. I suspected that over-grazing by cattle had altered the habitat so much in the intervening years that it had become unsuitable for our birds, but the students had another hypothesis. They kept suggesting, sometimes rather slyly I thought, that the museum collectors had simply shot them all! Now, however, as we drew near Tioga Pass, excited murmurs rose from within the vehicle. Large expanses of subalpine meadows, just emerging from beneath the melting snowpack, were coming into view. Here was undisturbed habitat of the type we were looking for and lots of it. As soon as we pulled over and stepped out, White-crowned Sparrows, with their distinctive black-and-white striped heads, could be seen and heard all around us. We fanned out across a meadow, peering into and beneath the leafing-out willows. Almost immediately, Jan discovered a nest. By the end of the afternoon a total of 12 had been located, all of them either fully constructed and ready for laying or already with one or more eggs.

In the following days and weeks we continued to find nests and began to capture and band the breeding adults. The surrounding countryside was explored on foot as well as other areas within easy driving range such as Lundy Canyon, Virginia Lakes, and Sonora Pass. Gradually it became clear that the meadows near Tioga Lake and along upper Lee Vining Creek, when linked together, would make a fine study area. So, after obtaining permission from the U. S. Forest Service, we settled into a nearby campground and began to study the reproductive biology of Mountain White-crowned Sparrows in earnest.

There were many motivations behind this decision: the need to establish a research project that would generate the enthusiasm and participation of undergraduate students, getting my children out of Los Angeles for the summer, being able to live in a beautiful outdoor setting, but mostly this direction was chosen because I was sure it would be interesting and productive. As a research assistant for my Master's thesis adviser, L. R. Mewaldt, I had learned a great deal about conducting field studies and about the habitat preferences of White-crowned Sparrows and their allies. Later, again as a research assistant, this time for my doctoral dissertation adviser, D. S. Farner, I spent a summer in Alaska doing field work which included collecting, dissecting, and fixing sparrow brains for neurosecretion studies. Several publications came from that one summer of work, but the enduring message for me from the Alaskan experience was that very few good field studies had been done in North America on the reproductive biology of migrants, and practically nothing at all on their migration schedules, mating systems, molt, or premigratory fattening responses. The biology of juveniles, particularly after fledging, was also poorly understood. In fact, this whole area of avian biology, of passerine migrants on their summering grounds, especially in locations where large variations in environmental conditions occurred, seemed open to investigation and I was stimulated to pursue it. The initial plan was to spend three summers at Tioga Pass, but the area proved to be so interesting that this eventually was stretched to three decades, and came to include studies of Belding's ground squirrels (*Spermophilus beldingi*) and Yosemite toads (*Bufo canorus*), as well as White-crowned Sparrows.

Exceptional progress in our understanding of avian biology occurred during the second half of the 20th century. Among the numerous reasons for this was the development of new techniques, many of them adapted from molecular biology, new theory, and increased computational and statistical powers. This growth in knowledge was also aided by an increase in the number of scientists willing to devote themselves for prolonged periods to the investigation of a single population or species under natural conditions, in other words, to engage in long-term field studies. For practical reasons, including investigator interest and availability of study areas, these have often centered on the reproductive biology and behavior (social systems, especially) of passerines. Some prominent examples would be those conducted on Florida Scrub-jays (*Aphelocoma coerulescens*; Woolfenden and Fitzpatrick 1984), Pinyon Jays (*Gymnorhinus cyanocephalus*; Marzluff and Balda 1992), Black-capped Chickadees (*Poecile atricapillus*; Smith 1991), European tits (*Parus* spp; Perrins 1979), Northern Wheatears (*Oenanthe oenanthe*; Conder 1989), Dunnocks (*Prunella modularis*; Davies 1992), Meadow Pipits (*Anthus pratensis*; Hötker 1989), Prairie Warblers (*Dendroica discolor*; Nolan 1978), Indigo Buntings (*Passerina cyanea*; Payne 1989), Song Sparrows (*Melospiza melodia*; Nice 1937, Hochachka et al. 1989), and Red-winged Blackbirds (*Agelaius phoeniceus*; Orians 1980, Searcy and Yasukawa 1995).

Long-term studies have contributed new information to a broad spectrum of ideas and hypotheses, but most, by necessity, have been limited in scope. And often they have had a similar approach, one that has combined and applied principles of ecology, evolution, and behavior through multiple annual cycles or seasons. In so doing investigators, like those cited above, have advanced avian biology and they have also helped to form and stimulate the sub-discipline of behavioral ecology.

This study shares characteristics with theirs and many others in that it has involved the accumulation of natural history and life history data (age and size at maturity, longevity, number, size, and sex ratio of offspring, etc.; Stearns 1992). Its focus is different, however, in that it tends to emphasize physiology more than behavior or ecology.

Avian physiology has traditionally been studied mostly in the laboratory, often with domesticated species. A significant component, however, especially with regard to photoperiodic, metabolic, and endocrine responses, has involved wild birds, mainly passerines. And recent technological advances utilizing radioisotopes and miniaturization of transmitters, for example, have allowed expansion of this work on physiological principles in field situations.

A major strength of long-term field studies is that they invariably reveal a great deal about the natural histories of organisms, and through the aid of permanent markers, such as numbered leg bands, these histories can sometimes span the lifetimes of individuals. More than 400 years ago, dating at least to Francis Bacon, it was already understood that natural history was the base upon which other scientific disciplines were built. Not so quickly grasped, however, was just how difficult it can be to obtain reliable, interpretable data of this type. They may, for example, vary with time, with characteristics of individuals, such as sex and age, with weather, and with trophic conditions, and this multitude of variables can act individually or in concert. Thus, natural history data often seem imprecise, unreliable, and non-replicable. Yet they can instruct us about the realities of the organism's life (of great importance to understanding ecosystem function and to conservation efforts) and fulfill one of the necessities of good science—the development of the right questions (Evans 1985). Such questions and the investigations and theory they inspire, when addressed to naturally oscillating systems, can contribute heavily toward achievement of one of modern biology's primary goals—translation of the real world into mathematical models (Rand 1973, Schaffer 1974). Another strength of field studies is that they inevitably assess phenotypes, the physical manifestations of genetic systems interacting with the environment. Phenotypes are the targets of selection and they are crucial to understanding its focus and process (Dean 1998).

In the minds of some ecologists, long-term studies are rarely well planned from the outset and have inescapable problems because their interpretations and conclusions are often based on correlations (Dunnet 1991). Most recognize their value to population and community ecology, however (Krebs 1991), and the data sets have considerable intrinsic value when it comes to understanding the frequency, duration, and amplitude of natural variations in ecological systems (Dunnet 1991). This approach to science can be cast as being in conflict with the experimental or hypothetico-deductive method (Taylor 1989), but actually the two are complementary. Furthermore, experiments are an inevitable and valuable part of long-term studies. These can be ones designed to work under field conditions, but there are also natural experiments that occur because of large fluctuations in environmental conditions. The latter are individually unrepeatable, of course, but they can add significant new dimensions to the research. Choice of study site is important here because some locations are more naturally endowed than others with environmental gradients or variation. As one ascends to the tops of mountains or toward polar regions, for example, environmental variation increases. Thus, high altitude and high latitude locations are ideal for studies of environmental adaptation.

CHAPTER 1: Introduction

THE *ZONOTRICHIA*

The genus *Zonotrichia* contains five species: *Z. capensis,* the Rufous-collared Sparrow; *Z. albicollis,* the White-throated Sparrow; *Z. querula,* the Harris's Sparrow; *Z. leucophrys,* the White-crowned Sparrow; and *Z. atricapilla,* the Golden-crowned Sparrow (American Ornithologists' Union 1998). Members of the genus can be found almost anywhere in the Americas, from the subarctic slopes of Canada and Alaska in the north to Cape Horn in the south. *Zonotrichia capensis,* which has multiple subspecies, occurs from the highlands of Middle America southward through much of South America and may well be the most widely distributed bird of that part of the world (Johnson 1967). The other four species live solely in North America and all five have at least some populations that are migratory. From data on allozymes, morphometrics, and mitochondrial DNA profiles, Zink (1982) and Zink et al. (1991) concluded that speciation within the *Zonotrichia* probably occurred in the Pleistocene, but before 140,000 yr ago. The oldest living member appears to be *Z. capensis,* and since it resides at low latitudes the genus may have originated in the Neotropics.

Information on the four North American species has now been compiled for *The Birds of North America* series and it is apparent that many features are shared by the group. For example, they prefer wintering habitat (most of which occurs in the U.S.) that includes elements of thick, shrubby cover mixed with open ground. Thus, they are likely to be found in weed patches, hedgerows, brushy ravines, and along the edges of forests and cultivated fields. Breeding takes place mostly in Canada and Alaska and, again, the preferred habitat often contains shrubby, patchily distributed vegetation. Forest openings, parklands, meadows, and tree clumps near tree line are used by *Z. albicollis* (Falls and Kopachena 1994); birch-willow shrublands and wet sedge meadows by *Z. querula* (Norment and Shackleton 1993); boreal forest, tundra, alpine meadows, and coastal scrub by *Z. leucophrys* (Chilton et al. 1995); and shrubby tundra at or above tree line by *Z. atricapilla* (Norment et al. 1998). All of these species tend to be omnivorous, eating seeds, fruits, buds, flowers, grass, and terrestrial arthropods, the latter being the major food source for dependent young.

The *Zonotrichia,* especially *Z. albicollis* and *Z. leucophrys,* have been widely used in both laboratory and field investigations of avian biology due, in part, to their abundance and ease of maintenance in captivity. Because the present study was based on a population of *Z. leucophrys,* an expanded discussion of their characteristics follows.

White-crowned Sparrows

Zonotrichia leucophrys are said to be sexually monomorphic although females are slightly smaller than males and as adults their head markings are usually not as bold. The plumage of adults has the same appearance year around and its most distinctive feature is a black- and white-striped head; a pair of black stripes in the crown is separated by a white median stripe and bordered by white eyebrow or superciliary stripes. In juveniles that have completed the postjuvenal (first prebasic) molt the head stripes are brown instead of black and buffy instead of white.

Like *Z. capensis,* this is a polytypic species with five generally recognized

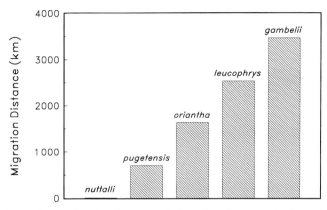

FIGURE 1.1.   Approximate migration distances of subspecies of *Zonotrichia leucophrys*, as measured from the middle of summer and winter ranges (*Z. l. nuttalli* is nonmigratory).

subspecies that are fairly distinct in their distributions, including very little overlap of breeding areas. These are *Z. l. leucophrys, Z. l. oriantha, Z. l. gambelii, Z. l. pugetensis,* and *Z. l. nuttalli.* Only *nuttalli* is sedentary; the others are migratory with *pugetensis* being the weakest and *gambelii* the strongest migrant (Fig. 1.1). Both summer and winter ranges of all five subspecies are confined to the North American continent and their distributions have been carefully mapped (Chilton et al. 1995, Dunn et al. 1995). Dunn et al. (1995) have also described in detail the nuances of morphology that distinguish the subspecies and have included high-quality photographs and drawings of both adults and juveniles.

The subspecies can be separated using morphological traits such as length of tarsus, bill, wing and tail; color of the back, rump and bend of the wing; and extent of the white superciliary stripe. This stripe extends to the bill, including the lores, in *nuttalli, pugetensis,* and *gambelii,* but is interrupted by black lores at the anterior corner of the eye in *leucophrys* and *oriantha.* In areas where white- and black-lored forms are sympatric, intermediates are common (Banks 1964, Lein and Corbin 1990). Banks (1964) felt that the two black-lored forms should be merged into one subspecies but Godfrey (1965) did not agree. He described differences in coloration of ventral parts (breast, flanks, and undertail coverts) in the two that seemed to warrant their continued separation. For the purposes of this treatise, *oriantha* will be considered distinct from the nominate form.

Although *leucophrys* and *oriantha,* the two red-backed, black-lored subspecies, can be difficult to distinguish in the museum tray, their breeding ranges are sep- arated by more than 1,500 km of unsuitable habitat (Cortopassi and Mewaldt 1965). It is possible, however, that the two may mingle on wintering areas in northeastern Mexico (Friedmann et al. 1950).

Rand (1948) speculated that subspeciation occurred in White-crowned Spar- rows when their range was invaded by glaciers during the Pleistocene. He sug- gested that four populations survived in refugia, one in the southeast (*leucophrys*), one in the Yukon-Bering Sea area (*gambelii*), one in the Rocky Mountains (*or- iantha*), and another along the Pacific Coast (*nuttalli-pugetensis*). Post-Pleistocene range expansion from these refugia then led to secondary contact between *orian- tha* and *gambelii* in southwestern Alberta, an area where considerable genetic introgression, detectable in both song and plumage phenotypes, has occurred (Lein and Corbin 1990). Recent data on rates of evolution in mitochondrial DNA in 35 species of North American passerines has thrown into doubt many of these old ideas about fragmentation of ancestral species into refugia by glacial advances (Klicka and Zink 1997). If the molecular clock used by these investigators is correct, then a great many of these species originated much earlier than the late Pleistocene.

The Pacific coastal complex of White-crowned Sparrows consists of a linear series of populations, often residing no more than a few hundred meters from the beach, that extends on its south-north axis some 1900 km from California to British Columbia. The southern-most breeding populations are *nuttalli* and these intergrade to the north with those of *pugetensis,* the latter being largely migratory (Grinnell 1928; Blanchard 1941, 1942; Mewaldt et al. 1968, Mewaldt and King 1978, DeWolfe and Baptista 1995). *Gambelii,* the most widely distributed of the subspecies, breeds from the Cascade Mountains near the northern border of Washington to above the Arctic Circle in Canada and Alaska (Farner 1958a, Banks 1964). *Leucophrys* breeds in eastern subarctic Canada, primarily in Manitoba, Ontario, and Quebec (Dunn et al. 1995). The various subspecies tend to winter between 20° and 45° N latitude with *leucophrys* being restricted mostly to the eastern half of the U.S. and the other groups to the western half as well as Mexico. Wintering *gambelii* occur in many of the western states of the U.S. as well as several of those in northern Mexico, including Baja California. About 0.3% of the individuals in wintering *gambelii* flocks sampled in Kern County, California were actually *oriantha* (Hardy et al. 1965).

The Mountain White-crowned Sparrow

The specific population investigated by us belongs to that subspecies designated as *Z. l. oriantha,* the Mountain White-crowned Sparrow. It breeds in montane regions of the western U.S., primarily along two major axes, one being formed by the Rocky Mountains to the east and the other by the Sierra Nevada and southern Cascades to the west. The Great Basin lies between these cordilleras and within it there are small, isolated mountain ranges that also harbor breeding *oriantha.* The northern limits of their distribution in the Rocky Mountains extends slightly into southern British Columbia, Alberta, and Saskatchewan, and the most northerly of the Sierra Nevadan populations is succeeded by populations still further to the north in the Cascades of Oregon.

Subalpine meadows at elevations of 2,500 to 3,500 m are selected most often as nesting habitat in both the Sierra Nevada (Morton et al. 1972a) and Rocky Mountains (Hubbard 1978). Sometimes alpine tundra is utilized, such as at Independence Pass in Colorado (3,680 m) and Beartooth Pass in Montana (3,350 m). Hubbard (1978) has shown that tree islands (krummholz) supply important protection for *oriantha* that nest in the alpine. They are known to nest at considerably lower elevations than this, however, especially at the highest latitudes of their summer range: for example, 1,500 m in northern Montana (King and Mewaldt 1987), and even down to 800 m in southern Saskatchewan (Banks 1964). Breeding populations are often disjunct and can be separated at times by hundreds of kilometers, as in the northern Great Plains of Montana where they are a component of insular montane avifaunas (Thompson 1978, Lein 1979). Inter-populational gene flow has not been studied in *oriantha,* but it seems possible that they function as a metapopulation over at least some of their range.

In an 800-km transect of habitat occupied by territorial or breeding *oriantha* in the Sierra Nevada and Cascade ranges, DeWolfe and DeWolfe (1962) concluded that five habitat components were common to all areas containing nesting birds: grassland, bare ground, shrubbery, fresh water, and tall conifers. Although lush subalpine meadows are often preferred sites for reproduction, a population of more than 40 pairs did occur at one time at 1,830 to 1,890 m on Hart Mountain in southeastern Oregon near a small riparian area in a generally arid landscape dominated by aspen (*Populus tremuloides*) and big sagebrush (*Artemesia tridentata*; King et al. 1976, King and Mewaldt 1987). Summering *oriantha* are also abundant in sagebrush flats of the Warner Mountains of northeastern California (T. Hahn, pers. comm.). Based on personal travels to many montane settings containing reproductively-active *oriantha,* I would add to the description of DeWolfe and DeWolfe (1962) that although water is always present at breeding areas, its forms can vary from thin sheets of snowmelt to permanent bodies such as streams and lakes, alone or in combination. Furthermore, tall conifers are sometimes absent, but it seems highly important for shrubbery to be present and that at least some elements of it be dense and low to the ground. Tall willows, for example, can sometimes be sufficient, but not when their lower branches have been heavily browsed by ungulates.

During their survey, DeWolfe and DeWolfe (1962) found that meadows suitable for *oriantha* were usually patchily distributed and sometimes so small that they contained only one to a few breeding pairs. We found the same thing a decade later while doing a 500-km transect confined to the Sierra Nevada and undertaken for the purpose of recording *oriantha* songs. Eight or fewer males were found at nine of the 14 sites sampled (Orejuela and Morton 1975). In the high country near Tioga Pass there are many small, wet meadows scattered near tree line, often in association with cirques or tarns, that hold breeding pairs, but not in every year. This intermittent use of small pieces of habitat may represent a microcosm of what can happen on a much larger scale, even at the massif or mountain range level. For example, King and Mewaldt (1987) documented the demise of the population at Hart Mountain whereas Balda et al. (1970) discovered the establishment of another in the San Francisco Mountains of Arizona. Local extinctions and colonizations would seem to be a normal part of *oriantha* biology, a trait that is typical of insular populations in general (King and Mewaldt 1987).

Friedmann et al. (1950) considered the primary wintertime distribution of *oriantha* to be from southern areas of California, Arizona, New Mexico, and southwestern Texas, throughout Baja California, and down to latitude 20° N in mainland Mexico (Fig. 1.2). Much of their information on wintering birds was probably obtained from collections made by Chester C. Lamb in the 1930s and 1940s. Twenty-seven of Lamb's specimens are deposited in the Moore Laboratory of Zoology at Occidental College. Five individuals were taken at or near sea level in Sinaloa, and the other 22 (from eight additional states) at elevations between 1,000 and 2,000 m. In December 1993 Maria E. Pereyra and I attempted to revisit many of Lamb's original collecting sites in mainland Mexico, but saw no *oriantha,* nor even very much of what could be considered suitable habitat. Nearly everything had been overgrazed by domestic livestock or placed under tillage.

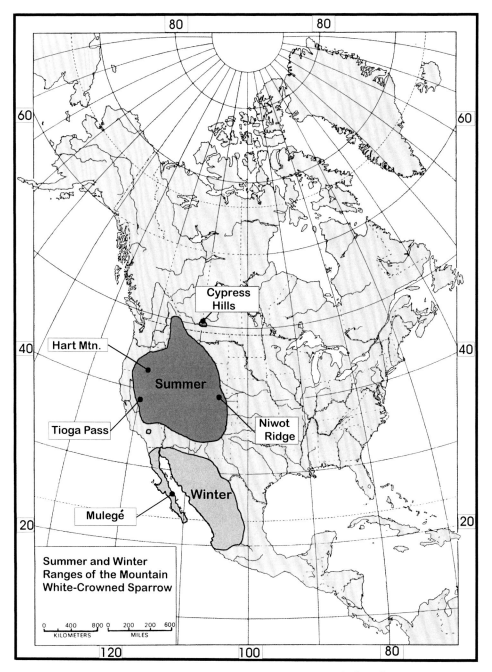

FIGURE 1.2.   Summer and winter ranges of *oriantha*. Locations marked on the summer range are where studies have been conducted: Tioga Pass, California (the present study); Hart Mountain, Oregon; Cypress Hills, Alberta and Saskatchewan; Niwot Ridge, Colorado. Range outlines taken from Banks (1964) and L. R. Mewaldt (pers. comm.). The winter range location, Mulegé, Baja California, is where a wintering *oriantha* from Tioga Pass was recovered in 1997 (see text).

Recently, however, new information was obtained on where the study population might be overwintering. On 7 March 1997 one of our banded birds, a four-year-old male, was captured and released near Mulegé, Baja California, Mexico by Robert C. Whitmore of West Virginia University (see Fig. 1.2). This same bird (band no. 138117256) was subsequently captured on our study area, some 2,100 km to the north, on 5 May 1997. White-crowned Sparrows appear to be abundant on agricultural lands in the Mulegé area during the winter months (Whitmore and Whitmore 1997).

FEATURES OF MONTANE ENVIRONMENTS

The large seasonal changes in environmental conditions, capricious weather, low oxygen tensions, and relatively simple habitat structure of the alpine and subalpine regions of the North Temperate Zone renders them inhospitable for year-around occupancy to all but a few species of vertebrates. Among birds, winter residents mainly include a few parids and corvids that are caching specialists, but diversity increases in summer when migrants from a wide array of taxa arrive for their reproductive seasons. A key problem for these migrants, of course, is to synchronize their arrival time and subsequent reproductive effort with the availability of food. The solution to this problem of temporal phasing can be expected to be the product of intensive natural selection on migration schedules and on mechanisms that initiate and terminate reproduction—an ideal natural system for investigating proximate or ecological factors (Chapter 5).

Three primary climatic variables change substantially in association with changes in altitude: temperature, moisture, and wind (Krebs 1972). Air temperature (T_a) decreases and wind velocity increases as one goes up a mountain. In accordance with the universal gas law and the adiabatic lapse rate, air rising in an elevational gradient will tend to accumulate water vapor until it is saturated; condensation then occurs leading to cloud formation and to precipitation (Rosenberg 1974). Large diurnal fluctuations in T_a occur, but its biotic impact appears to have reduced significance at high elevations because differences between microclimates tend to be already exaggerated (Swan 1952). The high winds, decreased availability of soil moisture due to freezing, and variable snowpack greatly influence the phenology and distribution of plants (Griggs 1938, Weaver 1974, Owen 1976, Weaver and Collins 1977). And climatic factors can combine to cause powerful summer storms, with precipitation in the form of rain, hail, or snow, that are potent selective events on annual productivity. Small mammals that have emerged from hibernation can suffer high mortality (Morton and Sherman 1978) and there may even be localized extinctions of some insect species (Ehrlich et al. 1972). Such storms can be non-density dependent disasters to breeding birds and cause high mortality in eggs, young, and even in adults (Morton et al. 1972a, Eckhardt 1977, Gessaman and Worthen 1982).

Seasonality of environmental factors also comes strongly into play at high altitude. For example, the residue of winter precipitation, the snowpack, as well as other factors such as soil temperature, T_a, and daylength can strongly affect plant phenophases such as seed germination; seedling, leaf and shoot growth; and flowering and fruiting. In addition, late-lying snow shortens the growing season (Weaver 1974, Weaver and Collins 1977, Ostler et al. 1982). The earlier phenophases, leaf and shoot growth for example, tend to be the ones most affected; for every 10% increase in snowpack above the long-term average, they are delayed up to eight days (Owen 1976). Certain plants can "catch-up" somewhat, but the condensation or telescoping of their development can lead to substantial decreases in annual productivity (Billings and Bliss 1959, Scott and Billings 1964, Weaver 1974, Owen 1976, Weaver and Collins 1977). One might safely assume, therefore, that snowpack could influence avian reproduction by modifying the availability of vegetation used for nesting sites, and/or by affecting the abundance of plant and insect food. It, and other seasonally variable events such as the swing in T_a, must have been key components in the evolution of migration and reproduction schedules in birds that are seasonal breeders in montane settings.

Birds are generally well suited for coping with the low partial pressures of oxygen encountered at high elevation. Their lung/air-sac system is efficient for gas exchange, myoglobin concentrations increase with physical conditioning, their hemoglobin has a very high affinity for oxygen (Faraci 1991), and many species have mixed types of hemoglobin, which gives them flexibility in the range over which oxygen can be bound and released, a decided advantage for making large altitudinal movements (Stevens 1996). They also have enhanced cardiovascular conditioning; their hearts (and stroke volumes) are large compared to mammals of similar size, and, unlike mammals, their cerebral circulation is maintained even during hypoxia-induced hypocapnia. They are alert and behave normally at 6,100 m, an altitude that renders mice comatose (Faraci 1991). Additional adaptation has occurred within the passerines because heart and lungs are larger in highland-dwellers than in lowland ones, and seasonal altitudinal migrants, such as those in the present study, closely resemble highland birds in their morphological and physiological characters (Norris and Williamson 1955, Carey and Morton 1976).

Despite the potential hazards of montane habitats, they can be favorable locations for reproduction. Even though summer is relatively brief, possessed of uncertain temporal boundaries, and can often include violent storms with high winds and sub-freezing temperatures, it is also a time when there is a rich pulse of plant and insect food that can be used to rear offspring.

The events that transpire during the few months that a migrant is on its breeding ground encompass the defining moments of the bird's life, the time when it does or does not pass its genes to a new generation. A manifestation of this is that the timing and duration of breeding seasons vary substantially, both among and within species, and even among members of the same population. Because of environmentally-related differences in selection pressures, the control systems that regulate gonadal function vary in sensitivity to the cues that affect them (Wingfield et al. 1992). Therefore, if the variation expressed in avian breeding systems is to be grasped, and the outcome of environment-reproduction schedule interactions predicted, it is necessary to understand not only the underlying biological systems, but also how they operate within a context of environmental variability. These problems can be pursued productively through the medium of the long-term study at locations such as high altitude.

THE STUDY AREA

The study contributing to this monograph was conducted during 25 yr, the last 20 being consecutive: 1968–1970, 1974, 1976, 1978–1997. The study area was located on the upper slopes of Lee Vining Canyon in the Sierra Nevada Mountains

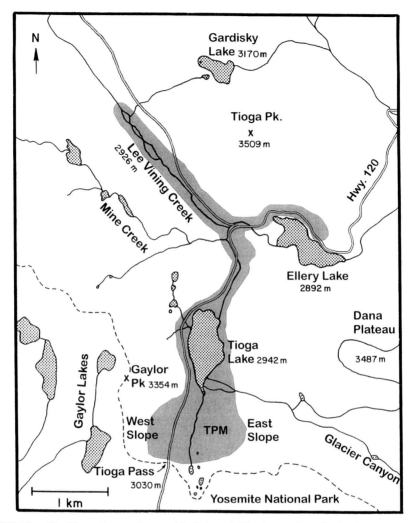

FIGURE 1.3.   The Tioga Pass study area (shaded area). Nesting studies of *oriantha* were conducted primarily along Lee Vining Creek, toward the north end of the study area, and on Tioga Pass Meadow (TPM), which lies between Tioga Lake and the boundary of Yosemite National Park at the south end of the study area.

near Tioga Pass, Mono County, California, at about 37.8° N latitude and 119.2° W longitude. Throughout its length Lee Vining Canyon, like many canyons of the eastern Sierra Nevada, has been carved and shaped by uplift, fluvial down-cutting, and repeated glaciations. Its upper branches often begin as cirques and its lower terminus is marked by a broad alluvial fan that extends into Mono Lake. California State Highway 120 follows the canyon bottom, or along the northern wall, from its junction with Highway 395 near the canyon's mouth, up to Tioga Pass then downward into Yosemite National Park.

   Once the final vestiges of glacial ice disappear (about 13,000 yr ago in upper Lee Vining Canyon) it still takes considerable time for mature vegetation to become established on the ice-scoured rock and glacial till that is left behind (Pielou

TABLE 1.1.   Mean Monthly Air Temperature and Precipitation Obtained at Ellery Lake, CA, 1931–1987

| Month | Temperature (C) | | | Precipitation (cm) |
	Daily	Maximum	Minimum	
January	−4.93	1.91	−11.78	10.51
February	−5.08	1.91	−11.97	9.50
March	−2.89	4.17	−10.13	7.56
April	−0.19	6.86	−7.19	4.42
May	3.52	10.19	−3.21	2.47
June	7.97	14.69	1.09	1.64
July	12.75	19.86	5.67	1.90
August	12.29	19.36	5.17	1.78
September	8.76	15.79	1.69	2.05
October	3.97	10.19	−2.34	3.43
November	−0.39	5.62	−6.59	7.09
December	−3.75	2.43	−9.93	10.36

Source: National Oceanic and Atmospheric Administration, Carson City, Nevada.

1991). Stabilization of the climate in its present form occurred about 4,000 to 4,500 yr ago, in the late Holocene (Grayson 1993), so modern community patterns have emerged only within the last few thousand years (Graham et al. 1996). This means that *oriantha* have probably been at Tioga Pass for only that period of time, or less.

In present times subalpine meadows in the upper portions of Lee Vining Canyon are kept green in summer by the melting snowpack, and a series of these were incorporated into our study. They are bounded by mature stands of lodgepole pine (*Pinus contorta*) and contain sedges, grasses, several species of willow (*Salix*), and a fair number of young, scrubby lodgepoles, a vegetational assemblage that is common in the Sierra Nevada at this elevation zone (Chabot and Billings 1972). The study area is irregularly shaped, tending to follow the streams that flow in the canyon bottom for about 7 km between elevations of 2,900 m at Ellery Lake to 3,000 m at Tioga Pass. The total area involved is about 280 ha, although most of the birds and most of our efforts were confined to a series of

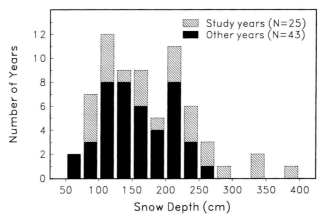

FIGURE 1.4.   Frequency distribution of snow depths measured 1 April on TPM by State of California Snow Survey crews (1927–1994); 65 yr of data, from State of California Bulletin 120, Water Conditions in California.

TABLE 1.2. SNOW CONDITIONS ON TIOGA PASS MEADOW MEASURED ON OR ABOUT 1 APRIL DURING THE YEARS OF THE STUDY

Year	Snow depth (cm)	Water content (cm)	Snow density (%)
1968	113.5	41.7	36.7
1969	342.1	143.8	42.0
1970	176.3	71.1	40.3
1973	204.2	70.6	34.6
1976	79.0	28.7	36.3
1978	263.4	116.3	44.2
1979	227.1	86.4	38.0
1980	262.6	114.0	43.4
1981	173.0	56.4	32.6
1982	294.4	119.6	40.6
1983	375.7	159.3	42.4
1984	205.0	93.7	45.7
1985	145.8	53.3	36.6
1986	243.3	116.3	47.8
1987	113.3	33.5	29.6
1988	121.2	46.7	38.6
1989	158.0	67.1	42.4
1990	90.9	33.5	36.9
1991	167.4	51.3	30.7
1992	108.2	38.9	35.9
1993	227.1	88.9	39.1
1994	94.0	32.0	34.1
1995	327.7	130.6	39.8
1996	230.1	96.8	42.1
1997	210.3	83.1	39.5

Notes. Water content is determined from snow mass. Snow density is water content ÷ snow depth × 100.

stream-side meadows on the upper, northerly end of Lee Vining Creek, and especially on a single subalpine meadow bounded by Yosemite National Park on the south and Tioga Lake on the north (Fig. 1.3). This was called Tioga Pass Meadow, or TPM, and, more than any other location, it was the focal area of the study.

There is considerable annual variation in T_a and precipitation at high altitude and, fortunately, many years of data for these parameters were available from a site at the northeast end of the study area (Ellery Lake). They show that May through October were the warmest and driest months (Table 1.1). These were, in fact, the only months when mean T_a was above freezing, and the same months of the year when *oriantha* were likely to be present at Tioga Pass. Precipitation from 39 storms was recorded by us with rain gauges on TPM during the study.

Data on snowpack depth and snow density were also available. These were gathered on a regular schedule each winter from a transect set up on TPM by State of California employees for the purpose of predicting water runoff from the Lee Vining Canyon watershed. Measurements taken on or about 1 April can be used as an indicator of the winter's maximum snow depth or snowpack because melting usually exceeds accumulation beyond that date. The 1 April data show that maximum snowpack varied interannually about five-fold at Tioga Pass during the 68 years that snow depth was measured (Fig. 1.4). Mean depth was 172.1 cm

(SD = 66.4 cm). Note that the four years of deepest snowpack: 1969, 1982, 1983, and 1995 (Table 1.2), all occurred during the time of our study.

The subalpine meadows making up the study area were in good condition. They are part of the Inyo National Forest and were not grazed by domestic livestock nor traversed by off-road vehicles during the study period.

CHAPTER 2: Migration Arrival

When migrants travel from wintering to summering areas they accomplish a journey that can take them through unfamiliar and inhospitable terrain and sometimes into the path of dangerous storms. Clearly the successful navigation of such hazardous passages requires substantial direction-finding and energy-managing abilities (Alerstam 1990). In addition, they must recognize and stop at the correct final destinations and arrive there near the optimum time for beginning their seasonally-restricted reproductive efforts. These problems can only be magnified when the final destination is a small mountain meadow that may still be buried under snow. This key part of vernal migration biology, its termination at the breeding area, will now be considered.

ARRIVAL SCHEDULE

To determine when *oriantha* were first arriving, an attempt was made to reach the study area before them. Daily searches of the area were then performed and seed-baited live traps were set next to emergent vegetation and to lodgepole pines at meadow borders. Most birds seemed willing to enter traps and the dates of first captures of individuals were taken to be the equivalent of their arrival times. Early season access to the study area was impossible in many years because of road closures, but in 1988, 1995, 1996, and 1997 Tioga Pass was reached ahead of the birds and their arrival times were recorded. The arrival period for the study population during these four years was arbitrarily defined as beginning with the first capture of the season and ending when the first clutches were started.

The first individuals trapped were males and their mean dates of arrival were from 8 to 12 d earlier than those of females (Table 2.1). For all birds combined, mean arrival time was 9.7 d earlier in males (N = 144) than in females (N = 94, t = 8.28, P < 0.001). Note that the number of males in the sample exceeded that of females by 53%. This can be attributed to males being more numerous in the population, to females being more difficult to capture, and also to the fact that some of the early-arriving males that eventually settled near the study area, such as the East Slope (see Fig. 1.3), tended at first to remain on TPM, where the traps were located, and where more open terrain, suitable for foraging, was available. By the time females arrived the slopes were thawed somewhat and they could go directly to them, bypassing the TPM trapline altogether.

The dynamics of arrival varied greatly from year to year, depending upon the extent of the residual snowpack and the frequency of spring storms. For example, in 1995 the snowpack was deep and persistent and four storms occurred during the arrival period, three in May and one in June (Fig. 2.1, upper). These storms

TABLE 2.1.   TIME OF ARRIVAL (=FIRST CAPTURE OF THE SEASON) OF *Oriantha* AT TIOGA PASS MEADOW DURING FOUR YR

	Date of first individual's arrival		Mean difference for whole arrival period		N		
Year	Male	Female	Days	P[a]	Males	Females	First eggs
1988	3 May	13 May	7.8	0.004	34	21	5 June
1995	17 May	26 May	12.0	<0.001	32	27	7 July
1996	5 May	11 May	11.1	<0.001	42	23	10 June
1997	5 May	6 May	8.0	<0.001	36	23	1 June

[a] P-values for t-test of mean differences in arrival times between males and females.

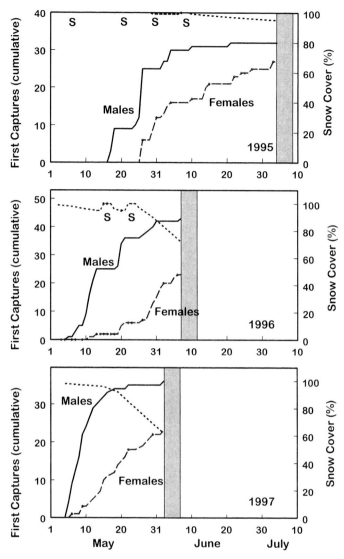

FIGURE 2.1.   Arrival schedules of *oriantha* at Tioga Pass Meadow for three yr. Dashed line indicates percentage of ground covered by snow and S the occurrence of a storm. Gray bars show when the first clutches were started.

tended to inhibit the influx of new birds to the study area, and plateaus in the incidence of arrival occurred when storms were in progress. There was no open ground in May of 1995, only a little in June, and females did not begin laying until 7 July at which time snow cover (the percent of ground covered by snow) was still about 95%. The first females were captured on 26 May so the interval between their arrival and the appearance of eggs was 42 days.

There was less snow in 1996 than in the previous spring and birds began to show up earlier on TPM; males first appeared on 5 May and females on 11 May (Fig. 2.1, middle). Once again storms occurred (two in May) that briefly inter-

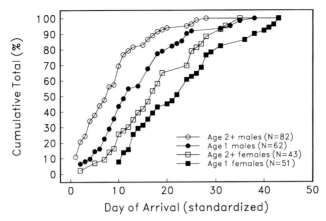

FIGURE 2.2.   Arrival schedules of *oriantha* at Tioga Pass Meadow by sex and age class. Data are for four yr (1988, 1995, 1996, 1997), and are standardized such that the date the first bird was captured each year was called day 1 of arrival for that specific year.

rupted the appearance of new birds. The first eggs were laid on 10 June, 30 days after the first females were present and when snow cover was about 70%.

Spring conditions were unusually mild in 1997 and there were no storms to impede the arrival schedule (Fig. 2.1, lower). Laying began on 1 June, 26 days after the first female was captured. Warm weather and absence of storms caused the snow to melt rapidly and snow cover had already decreased to about 60% when the first clutches were started. Aside from highlighting the variation that occurred in arrival schedules, the above data indicate that environmental conditions, storms and snowpack in particular, strongly influenced the reproductive schedules of *oriantha*. How they adapted to these conditions will be described more fully in later chapters. Note that Fig. 2.1 shows cumulative first captures only; it does not accurately represent how many birds were present at any particular moment during the arrival period because, as will be explained below, following their initial arrival individuals were sometimes absent from the breeding habitat for hours or days at a time.

Arrival varied with age as well as sex. As a group, older males (age 2+ yr) tended to arrive earliest, followed in order by one-year-old males, older females, and one-year-old females (Fig. 2.2). It seems that previous experience as an adult on TPM facilitated early arrival in both sexes. The standardized data displayed in Fig. 2.2 show that older males (N = 82) had a mean arrival time that was 5.4 d earlier than that of one-year-old males (N = 62, $t = 4.20$, $P < 0.001$), and that older females (N = 43) arrived 5.0 d earlier than one-year-old females (N = 51, $t = 2.51$, $P = 0.014$). No cohort arrived within a time period exclusive of the others, however, and by about 10 d after the first individuals had been trapped, members of both sexes and of all age groups were likely to be present (Fig. 2.2).

There have been no studies of *oriantha* in transit, but data from *gambelii* during both vernal (DeWolfe et al. 1973) and autumnal (Morton and Pereyra 1987) migrations suggest that each bird more or less follows its own schedule (as opposed to being obligately attached to a particular flock). They tend to dribble into stopover sites a few at a time then aggregate into small flocks while preparing for their next flight. The fact that only a few *oriantha* arrived at Tioga Pass on any given day also supports the idea that individuals were traveling alone or in small groups. Another similarity in migration biology shared by the various subspecies is that males tended to arrive ahead of females in both *gambelii* (Oakeson 1954, Norment 1992) and *pugetensis* (Lewis 1975b). Many other species, for example, Snow Buntings (*Plectrophenax nivalis*; Meltofte 1983), Savannah Sparrows (*Passerculus sandwichensis*; Bédard and LaPointe 1984), and American Redstarts (*Setophaga ruticilla*; Lozano et al. 1996) also exhibit the males-first pattern. And old males tended to show up earlier than young ones in all of these studies. On the other hand, male and female Harris's Sparrows arrived at about the same time at breeding areas in northern Canada (Norment 1992). Interestingly, this species does not seem to be highly philopatric, and site fidelity in adults decreased greatly in years following reproductive failure (Norment 1994). Sexual differences in wintering ground latitude have been linked to arrival patterns because males often winter farther north than females (Ketterson and Nolan 1976, Morton 1984); thus, a shorter migration distance may facilitate earlier arrival by males.

As far as timing goes, there should be selection for all migrants to arrive early enough to utilize fully the season favorable for reproductive activities, particularly at high latitudes and high altitudes where summer seasons are briefest. Beyond this, however, additional pressure may be exerted on males in areas where competition for optimal territories is intense (presuming that initial territory holders have an advantage over would-be usurpers).

Analyses of costs and benefits associated with arrival schedules show that early arrival enhances production of more and higher quality offspring (Barba et al. 1995, Aebischer et al. 1996, Lozano et al. 1996). But there is a cruel bind for early birds because they are also more likely to encounter a lack of food and shelter and thereby incur an increased risk of death due to starvation, exposure, and, possibly, predation. A good example is provided by Snow Buntings in arctic Greenland where high-quality breeding habitat is scarce. Males arrive in early April, six to eight weeks before nesting, and two to four weeks ahead of females. During this lengthy pre-nesting period they commonly experience severe storms and temperatures down to −30 C, and considerable mortality can occur. Yet year after year, males continue to arrive well ahead of the breeding season (Meltofte 1983).

In situations where selection is relaxed somewhat because the breeding habitat is uniform in quality or relatively abundant, one might expect males to arrive at about the same time as females. Judging from Norment's data on Harris's Sparrows, these same conditions may also promote a decrease in breeding site fidelity after reproductive failures. All of this indicates that the arrival schedule is the product of opposing selective forces that vary with breeding site characteristics, and that once its pattern is understood certain features of the breeding habitat, such as its degree of patchiness and/or saturation, might also be predicted.

Why do one-year-old *oriantha* tend to arrive later than the older birds? An obvious explanation is that the more experienced birds knew the migration route and they recognized the breeding ground area once they had reached it. Knowing where to fly must be of major importance to migrants, but knowing when to terminate the journey is not a trivial matter either. In many years at Tioga Pass, for example, the breeding habitat was still inundated by snow in May and large subalpine meadows, such as TPM, appeared to be nothing more than great, almost featureless, snowfields surrounded by forest. The older birds had been there be-fore, however, and although winter-like conditions still prevailed, they settled, usually in and around the pines at the border of a meadow nearest their previous years' territory. One-year-olds did not have the benefit of this experience although they may have picked up some useful information on habitat quality prior to migration in the previous autumn. They were highly philopatric, however, so somehow they were able to find their natal areas. Given the difference in habitat appearance in spring from that of the previous autumn, it may be that young birds require some homing cues, other than landmarks, in order to settle accurately. Perhaps these are provided by older birds, already in place, that the young birds can see and hear. If this is the case, it might explain why one-year-olds tend to lag behind older birds. Note that in the previous autumn, when they were juve-niles, these same young birds often left on migration toward the wintering areas *before* the older ones (Chapter 9).

The vernal migration period and its immediate aftermath can be a dangerous time for migrants, and storms, such as those experienced by *oriantha* and Snow Buntings, can be selective events. There are many observations of weather-related mortality occurring during migration (Gessaman and Worthen 1982). For example, Whitmore et al. (1977) found 569 individuals from 32 species dead after a violent spring storm in Utah. Those not killed outright were so hungry that they engaged in cannibalism and in scavenging the carcasses of others. Interestingly, these badly starved birds were found to be catabolizing their flight muscles for energy but not their gonadal tissues. Swanson (1995) discovered that Warbling Vireos (*Vireo gilvus*) had an elevated thermogenic capacity in spring and tolerated colder am-bient temperatures than they could in summer or fall. This increased ability to generate heat by shivering, using fat to fuel the rapidly twitching skeletal muscles (Marsh and Dawson 1982, 1989), may be an important adaptation in vernal mi-grants and it would be interesting to see how ubiquitous it is. Relevant to this characterization of physiological state is that hematocrits were at their seasonal highs in arriving *oriantha* (Morton 1994b).

ALTITUDINAL MOVEMENTS

Birds that inhabit open highlands in the Peruvian Andes are known to fly down the mountains when snowstorms occur (O'Neill and Parker 1978, Fjeldså 1991). It seems reasonable, then, that North American migrants living in mon-tane habitat, particularly in locations where the elevational gradients are steep, have this same option available to them; rather than confronting bad weather they could simply avoid it by retreating to lower elevations. Although it was suspected that *oriantha* were behaving in this way, proof did not come until a large storm moved into Tioga Pass on the night of 19 May 1987. A heavy downpour of rain was followed by snow that eventually accumulated to a depth of 15 cm. This storm continued through the evening of the 20th. On that day, at 15:30, a flock of 12 *oriantha* was observed in the lower end of Lee Vining Canyon, 10 km east of the study area and about 1 km lower in elevation. Al-though they were foraging together, members of this flock were expressing con-siderable hostility toward one another in the form of loud singing, physical displacements, and fighting. Nine members of the flock were trapped. They proved to be of both sexes, and five were banded individuals that had been handled up on the study area within the previous 12 days. Two other *oriantha* flocks containing four and five birds (all unbanded) were located nearby and another three unbanded individuals were mixed in with a flock of about 25 Dark-eyed Juncos (*Junco hyemalis*). At 11:30 on 21 May two males were heard singing on the West Slope above TPM and by the next morning most individuals were back on their previously occupied territories.

A female captured on the morning of 22 May 1987 on TPM weighed 26.4 g and her ovary had large (4–8 mm) atretic follicles that were being reabsorbed. On 19 May, just before the storm, this same individual had a fully constructed nest and weighed 29.2 g. Judging from that body mass, she would probably have ovulated on 20 May and laid her first egg on 21 May if the storm had not occurred. Eventually, this female recovered, built a new nest, and started her first clutch on 3 June. So the storm was responsible for setting back her nesting schedule by 13 days (21 May to 3 June).

Ojanen (1979) reported that more than 3,000 birds of 42 species died in a May storm in northern Finland. Because of the terrain, no downhill movements were possible in these heavily stressed populations but, interestingly, individuals that had been spaced out onto territories formed again into flocks during the cold period. Much the same type of response also occurs in Snow Buntings (Meltofte 1983), and flock formation after movement to lower elevations during May snow-storms has been observed several times in the present study in American Robins (*Turdus migratorius*) and Dark-eyed Juncos, as well as in *oriantha.*

Based on information obtained from transmitter-carrying individuals, however, many downslope movements of *oriantha* were completely solo and did not result in flocks being formed at lower elevations. Radiotelemetry studies were begun in 1995, a year when there was a deep, persistent snowpack and many spring storms (see Fig. 2.1, upper). It was quickly apparent that repeated altitudinal movements of individuals occurred in the pre-nesting period, even during good weather, between the study area and sites that were at least 1 km lower and 6 to 16 km east in the bottom of Lee Vining Canyon and beyond into the Mono Basin (Hahn and Morton 1995). Males tended to spend more time on the breeding area than females, but both sexes showed fidelity to just two sites, one at each of the two elevations. In 1996 a second group was fitted with transmitters and temporary downslope movements, similar to those of the year before, occurred during both of the May storms (see Fig. 2.1, middle). There were no flocks formed in either year. These data show that *oriantha* readily flew to lower elevations when storms occurred and when open ground, suitable for foraging, was in short supply. Descent to lower altitude during the pre-nesting period for protection and for maintenance of energy balance was not a rare event, but a regularly-expressed component of their behavioral repertoire.

These vertical migrations of transmitter-bearing *oriantha* and observations from other studies also provide a clue as to the whereabouts of individuals in years, such as 1995, when arrival at the breeding habitat is delayed. Taylor (1912), for example, noted the presence of *oriantha* in mid-May at low elevations in Nevada, prior to their movement up to breeding areas, and Hubbard (1978) found that they arrived in foothill areas in Colorado and loitered there for nearly a month before moving up slope to their breeding habitat. It seems likely that the migration route of the Tioga Pass population includes the low-altitude shrub-steppe of the

Great Basin where it abuts the eastern side of the Sierra Nevada, and a few lone individuals have indeed been observed there in May. Once the proper latitude is reached they may remain there until conditions favor ascension to the high meadows. If storms subsequently push them back down they gravitate for a time to familiar locations at the base of the range.

Similar movements occur in Yellow-eyed Juncos (*Junco phaeonutus*) in the Chiricahua Mountains of Arizona. These birds summer at about 2,500 m, approximately 1,000 m higher than and 15 km away from wintering areas. They usually move to breeding areas several weeks before nesting begins, but if bad weather occurs they return to their usual wintering sites until it subsides (Horvath and Sullivan 1988). The regulation of facultative responses to stressful conditions such as these may be mediated via secretion of hormones of the hypothalamus-anterior pituitary-adrenal cascade. These hormones, most notable corticosterone, are thought to be released in greater quantities in emergency situations and to orchestrate physiological and behavioral responses, such as gluconeogenesis and irruptive movements. These same hormones also promote recovery once the environmental stressor disappears (Wingfield and Ramenofsky 1997, Wingfield et al. 1998).

FORAGING

Zonotrichia are well known for the breadth of both their dietary choices and foraging modes, and they ingest a wide array of plant and animal materials (Morton 1967, Norment and Fuller 1997). These eclectic feeding habits served *oriantha* well during the pre-nesting period, especially in heavy snow years. They foraged on any kind of available open ground, such as talus slopes and knolls that were swept free of snow by the wind, and they satisfied their need for water by eating snow. Other preferred locations, which were among the first to come open early in the season, included the thawed edges of stream banks and wet patches of ground that appeared where streamlets flowed under the snowpack and melted it away. They sometimes appeared to be indiscriminately eating surface material, or "organic ooze," in these wet areas. They also foraged on small patches of ground that occurred next to heat absorbers and reflectors such as large rocks and tree trunks. Holes in the snow, 2 m or more in depth, sometimes formed next to trees due to reflected solar radiation (see Marchand 1987). Once these holes extended down to bare ground *oriantha* would drop into them to forage. They, along with other species on the study area such as Dark-eyed Juncos, Gray-crowned Rosy-Finches (*Leucosticte tephrocotis*), American Robins, and Mountain Bluebirds (*Sialia currucoides*), were also reliant at times on arthropods immobilized on the snow surface. Usually these were thinly scattered but they were observed at times in densities of about 15 per m^2. Arthropod fallout onto snow has been identified as an important source of food for birds in central Alaska (Edwards 1972, Edwards and Banko 1976), the Sierra Nevada of Spain (Zamora 1990), and a variety of other mountain ranges around the world (Edwards 1987).

At a site near Tioga Pass, Papp (1978) found that the fallout consisted mostly of Diptera, Hemiptera, and Homoptera, and because of the species involved, concluded that many had originated from cultivated fields lying at low altitude to the west in the Central Valley. In support of Papp's hypothesis concerning effects of prevailing winds, balloons bearing notes from schoolchildren in towns of the Central Valley were found several times by us on the study area. One balloon carrying an automobile advertisement came from Oakland, California, which is even further west.

CHAPTER 3: Social System and Behavior

As noted in the previous chapter, migrants, recently arrived at montane areas, are faced with finding the appropriate breeding habitat and surviving until conditions are favorable for beginning reproduction, a difficult task in some years because of lingering winter conditions and the occurrence of storms. But even in years when environmental conditions are mild there is a pause before nesting actually begins. During this pre-nesting period important elements of the social system are activated and expressed. These include establishment of territories and behaviors associated with mating, including pair formation, mate guarding, and copulation. Eventually, over many reproductive seasons a more comprehensive understanding of the social structure can be obtained as it becomes possible to measure mate fidelity, age of mates, frequency of polygamous pairings, and aggressive behaviors, as well as the functions of vocalizations.

TERRITORY ESTABLISHMENT

Almost immediately upon arrival most *oriantha* males began exhibiting preferences for specific locations. Forays, sometimes hundreds of meters in length, did occur but usually they sang from a few favorite spots and entered traps repeatedly at about the same place on the study area. In heavy snow years they showed preferences for certain clumps of large pines at meadow borders until patches of willows and small pines melted out. They then moved onto the breeding habitat proper. For returning males this was usually on or near their territory of the previous year. Gradually, over a period of two to three weeks as the vegetation developed, and after considerable singing and some chasing and fighting, firmly delineated territories were established.

PAIRING

Newly arrived females were sometimes observed occupying small willow patches by themselves, but within a few days they were usually being accompanied by a male. As in Northern Wheatears, pairing began even before all members of the population had arrived (Conder 1989). This pattern was typical only during moderate or light snow years, however. In heavy snow years pair formation could be much delayed. In 1995, for example, pairs were not present until 13 June. This was more than two weeks after the first females had arrived (see Fig. 2.1, upper). Radio transmitter data showed that during May and June of 1995 individuals, especially females, were regularly visiting lower elevations for several days at a time, and were ranging widely in search of food even on the breeding areas themselves. Not until enough vegetation had emerged from beneath the snow to give focal points for territories did they pair and remain at one location. Returning females, like males, tended to take up residence in the same general area as the year before (see below).

The greatest share of dispersal in passerines occurs prior to the first nesting effort, but successive nests are not usually placed in precisely the same location and the dispersal process continues as nesting is repeated throughout the bird's lifetime. If a breeder survives from one year to the next, the distance between its nests in successive years can be determined. This is the between-year breeding dispersal distance.

TABLE 3.1. BETWEEN-YEAR BREEDING DISPERSAL DISTANCES (M) IN *Oriantha* IN RELATION TO NESTING SUCCESS (FLEDGING AT LEAST ONE OFFSPRING) AND TO CHANGE OF MATES

	Males				Females			
Status	Mean	SD	N	P^a	Mean	SD	N	P^a
Successful								
Yes	115.2	121.1	72		137.2	120.8	74	
				0.684				0.638
No	104.6	73.7	17		112.9	88.1	24	
Mate change								
Yes	142.2	227.6	69		232.9	69.9	64	
				0.249				<0.001
No	82.9	63.8	31		77.8	60.0	30	

[a] P-value from test of medians (Mann-Whitney U).

BETWEEN-YEAR BREEDING DISPERSAL

In *oriantha,* as in most organisms that have been studied, dispersal distances were highly skewed; the greater the distance from the point of origin, the lower the density of individuals present. Yet there was often a year-to-year consistency in the pattern observed and the between-year breeding dispersal distance was no exception. No significant interannual variation in this distance occurred during 15 consecutive years of data collection (Morton 1997). The majority of birds of both sexes had their first nest of the season within 200 m of their first nest of the previous year. The between-year distance was greater in females, however, than in males (female median = 119.5 m, male median = 72.5 m; Kolmogorov-Smirnov 2-sample test: N_1 = 124, N_2 = 103, D = 0.339, P < 0.001). Strong site fidelity of this type might well be an alternative strategy to habitat quality reassessment at the time of spring arrival (Bédard and LaPointe 1984).

In a few cases, nests were located far from those of the year before. Along creeks, where territories were long and narrow, or where a lake arm bisected breeding habitat this distance could exceed 300 m. One female moved 750 m from her previous year's nesting spot because it was buried for too long under a deep snowpack (Morton 1997).

Between-year breeding dispersal in passerines is thought to occur because natural selection is operating on experience-based choices. For example, reproductive success promotes fidelity to a breeding site whereas failure promotes movement to a new site the next year (Darley et al. 1977, Nolan 1978, Freer 1979, Herlugson 1981, Gavin and Bollinger 1988, Bollinger and Gavin 1989, Pärt and Gustafson 1989). In *oriantha,* however, a failure to fledge young in one year did not affect their choice of breeding site the next year because dispersal distance did not change with reproductive success (Table 3.1). It did increase, however, particularly in females, when mates were changed between years (Table 3.1). This last effect could have occurred because of a tendency for passerine males to be more site-tenacious than females, to intra-sexual competition being more intense in females than in males, and/or because females were more discriminating than males when choosing a mate (Knapton 1979, Searcy 1979, Payne and Payne 1993). Any of these could lead to the result, consistently obtained in avian studies, that females tend to move greater distances than males (Darley et al. 1977, Nolan 1978, Gratto et al. 1985).

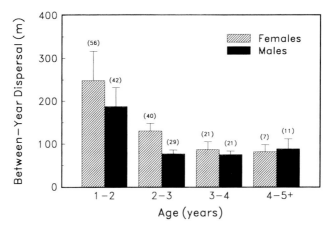

FIGURE 3.1. Between-year breeding dispersal distances in *oriantha* according to age. Bars show means (+ 1 SE); number of individuals in parentheses.

Another common pattern in passerines is that between-year breeding dispersal distances decrease with age (Greenwood and Harvey 1982, Payne and Payne 1993). At Tioga Pass, in agreement with this generalization, breeding dispersal distance was greatest in both sexes between their first and second seasons. It then decreased and remained stable thereafter (Fig. 3.1). The effect of age here was significant in females (Kruskal Wallis test, P = 0.014), but not in males (P = 0.380). There were some unusually long movements by females between their first and second years. In two cases females moved to completely different meadows, nearly 3 km away, something never observed in males. Greenwood and Harvey (1982) suggested that large movements between the first and second breeding seasons occur because one-year-olds often occupy territories of poorer quality than those of older birds. As two-year-olds they are able to move to better sites and thereafter dispersal is slight. The *oriantha* data fit this movement pattern, at least for females, but can it be shown that their behavior was related to territory quality?

Identifying variations in this parameter is a difficult problem. It is addressed here by letting the birds define territory quality through their nesting behavior. It was assumed that the more often an area was used for nesting over the years, the higher was its quality. In this case "area" was defined as being specific, individual hectares on TPM. These hectares could be identified from a detailed map overlain with horizontal and vertical 100-m grid lines. There were 44 one-hectare quadrats on which, over a period of 21 years, there was at least one *oriantha* nest. A total of 652 nests were involved and the number found per quadrat ranged from one to 67. For purposes of analysis, "low density" quadrats were arbitrarily designated as being ones that had held 30 or fewer nests. There were 38 of these and they accounted for a total of 385 nests. "High density" quadrats each held 31 nests or more. There were six of these and they accounted for a total of 267 nests.

The age distribution of breeding birds for the two quadrat types indicates that there was a tendency for one-year-olds to occupy low density areas whereas there were proportionately more older birds in the high density areas (Fig. 3.2). The age distributions in low density areas vs. high density areas was significantly

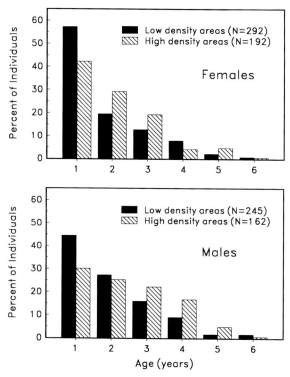

FIGURE 3.2.   Age distribution of breeding *oriantha* in relation to density of nests on 1-ha quadrats (see text). Sample sizes are for total number of nests.

different in both sexes (females: Kolmogorov-Smirnov Z = 6.155, P < 0.001; males: Z = 7.094, P < 0.001). The mean age of females nesting in low density areas was 1.80 yr (SD = 1.13 yr) and 2.02 yr (SD = 1.14 yr) in high density areas. For males, the comparable data were 2.01 yr (SD = 1.17 yr) and 2.43 yr (SD = 1.25 yr).

One possible prediction from these data is that when between-year breeding dispersal occurred, nests would sometimes be located in different quadrats. Furthermore, when such a shift did occur, it should be to a higher-quality territory. In other words, the birds should relocate to a quadrat that was habitually nested in more often than their original one. Data relevant to this hypothesis were obtained for 109 females and 98 males and they show that 30 females remained in the same quadrat and 79 moved to another one (Table 3.2). Of those that shifted, 29 moved to a lower density area and 50 to a higher density area, a significant difference (one-way Chi-square = 5.58, df = 1, P = 0.018). Females, therefore,

TABLE 3.2.   BETWEEN-YEAR BREEDING DISPERSAL IN *Oriantha* WITH RESPECT TO QUADRAT OCCUPANCY

Dispersal outcome	Females	Males
1. Remained in same quadrat	30	42
2. Moved to new quadrat	79	56
a. Lower density	29	24
b. Higher density	50	32

tended to move between years to higher quality territories. Males had similar tendencies but they were not statistically significant. Of those that moved, a larger number went to areas of higher density than lower density (32 vs. 24; one-way Chi-square = 1.143, df = 1, P = 0.285). These data also repeat the familiar theme of sex-specific mobility; a greater proportion of females than males moved to new quadrats between years (72.5% vs. 57.1%; Chi-square = 5.349, df = 1, P = 0.021).

Additional analyses were performed to see if territory quality, as assayed by low density vs. high density occupancy rates, affected reproductive parameters. The parameters chosen were settling date (as measured by first egg dates), clutch size, nest predation rate, nesting success (at least one fledgling produced), and mean number of fledglings produced per successful nest. There were no significant differences in any of these comparisons; the only difference found was the one on distribution of ages shown in Fig. 3.2. An apparent conundrum here is that the birds preferred to nest in certain areas even though this preference did not seem to enhance their reproductive success. If such an effect exists, perhaps it takes place over a longer time frame than we have evaluated, lifetimes rather than between years. On the other hand, the observed settling pattern might be nothing more than the one expected if the birds were following an ideal free distribution, as envisioned by Fretwell (1972).

Territory-quality may have affected female attentiveness because the incubation period was shorter in older females (age 3+ yr) than in younger ones (age 1 or 2 yr, Chapter 7). Perhaps living on a high quality territory spares more time for tending eggs because less time is required for foraging.

COPULATIONS

At the beginning of the season copulations began during the pre-nesting period, sometimes a week or more before the onset of nest building, and continued through the laying period. If nests were subsequently lost the courtship sequence, including copulations, was repeated, although over a more compressed time frame. Most copulations were observed in the morning hours, but there was not enough systematically gathered information to plot their diurnal frequency with confidence. Although copulation frequency in some avian species is often highest and mate guarding most intense in the hour or so after laying (Hankinson 1999), this close relationship between mating behavior and reproductive function is by no means uniform. Furthermore, timing of copulation may not be a reliable indicator of egg fertility (Adkins-Regan 1995).

Recently, M. E. Pereyra (pers. comm.) has observed that *oriantha* sometimes engage in flurries of copulations during the last few minutes of daylight, just before going to roost, a pattern also noted in Smith's Longspurs (*Calcarius pictus*; Briskie 1992). The ovum of birds must be fertilized during a small window of time that occurs immediately after ovulation because access by sperm is soon blocked by deposition of the perivitelline layer and albumen around the yolk (Howarth 1974). Ovulation of the next egg occurs about the same time as laying of the current one and *oriantha* lay in the early morning hours, soon after daylight (Chapter 6), so these late-evening copulations seem ill-timed as an insemination strategy unless fertilization is occurring, at least some of the time, from stored sperm. This is a distinct possibility given the efficacy of this mechanism (Birkhead 1992, Birkhead and Møller 1992).

MATE GUARDING

Females became paired soon after settlement and their mates began to exhibit guarding behavior. Males often watched from elevated perches and shadowed the female by moving along through the tree tops, terrain permitting. Most commonly, they guarded at close range, hopping alongside or slightly behind as the female moved about in her activities, driving off other males that came too near. Mate guarding appeared to lessen in intensity once incubation began, but it could be observed on the study area at almost any time in the summer because of the reproductive cycle being renewed in renesting pairs.

Guarding behavior appears to be stimulated by testosterone (Moore 1984) and its function, of course, is that it helps a male to assure his paternity by preventing other males from fertilizing his mate (Davies 1985, Montgomerie 1988). It may also help prevent the female from seeking fertilizations from extra-pair males (Gowaty and Plissner 1987, Gowaty and Bridges 1991, Møller and Birkhead 1991, Lifjeld et al. 1994).

Sometimes unmated (floater) males (usually one, although as many as six were observed) followed an *oriantha* pair and attempted to obtain copulations. When such processions occurred, the mated male positioned himself between the female and the other male(s). If the female quickly changed position by flying, skirmishing sometimes broke out as her mate tried to deal with the female's new exposure by chasing away the intruders. Floaters sometimes followed a pair for several hours at a time, especially when the female was soliciting copulations. The mated male could usually keep a lone follower away simply by maintaining an intermediate position on the ground or in vegetation, but the situation could destabilize quickly. For example, nearby territory-holding males sometimes flew straight toward the female. Her mate then usually launched aggressive, prolonged aerial chases of these intruders, leaving the female unguarded in the interim and potentially free to engage in extra-pair sexual activity. Although no extra-pair copulations were observed, electrophoretic analyses of four polymorphic loci showed that at least 34 to 38% of chicks hatched on the study area were not the offspring of one of the putative parents (Sherman and Morton 1988). Because females did not engage in brood parasitism, the mismatched young must have been the result of extra-pair fertilizations. In a much larger follow-up study on this same population, using microsatellites to determine paternity, MacDougall-Shackleton (2001) found that 41.2% of 342 nestlings were fathered by a male other than the social mate.

Oriantha have a monogamous mating system, as defined by Lack (1968), in that they form pairs and raise broods together. They behave similarly to most other so-called monogamous avian species, however, in that they do not maintain an exclusive mating relationship (McKinney et al. 1984, Birkhead 1987, Westneat et al. 1990). In actuality, as shown above, they are socially, not genetically, monogamous.

MATE SWITCHING

To detect continuity of pairings from year to year, there must be data on multiple-year nestings by females whose mates were known. Information of this type

TABLE 3.3. FREQUENCY DISTRIBUTION OF NUMBER OF MATES PER LIFETIME IN FEMALE AND MALE *Oriantha*

Number of mates	Frequency	
	Females	Males
1	194	121
2	43	40
3	7	19
4	1	5
5	0	0
6	1	0

on *oriantha* shows that half of the time (82 of 164 cases) the male from the previous year was still alive. In 54 of these 82 cases (65.9%) the two birds were paired again and in 28 they were not. The frequency of mate switching (also called the divorce rate by some investigators; see Ens 1992), therefore, was 34.1%. There were also three histories wherein a mated pair was together the first year, mated to new partners the second year, then re-mated to one another the third year.

MATES PER LIFETIME

Because small passerines, such as *oriantha,* usually live for only a short time, it was no surprise that the modal number of mates per adult lifetime for both sexes was one (Table 3.3). The average number of mates was 1.26 for females (SD = 0.60, N = 246) and 1.50 for males (SD = 0.47, N = 185). This imbalance between the sexes was significant (Chi-square = 17.96, df = 4, P < 0.001) and, when their distributions were modeled, was found to be due to proportionately greater numbers of females having had only one mate. Still the record, six different mates in a lifetime, was held by a female that nested for seven consecutive years on TPM (Table 3.3).

Natural mortality, along with mate-switching behavior, caused long-term pairings to be rare. There were only two cases wherein an uninterrupted sequence of pairings by the same two birds occurred for as long as four years; all other same-pair sequences were for two or three years. It is instructive that these long-term pairs were often found at locations where the breeding habitat was demarcated by well-defined boundaries. One such location, the southwest corner of TPM, contained a cluster of small pines that was suitable in size for only one territory and it was contiguous with only one other territory in most years. When both members of a pair survived that had used this corner of the meadow they could often be found there together again. The same pattern occurred in pairs that occupied the "vernal pool" territory, an isolated patch of habitat located on the West Slope. There, upon an expanse of dry hillside, encircling a spring, was a patch of willows that was used nearly every year as a nesting site. Thus, site fidelity contributes to re-pairing in *oriantha,* perhaps more so than mate fidelity.

AGE OF MATES

Although there was considerable turnover in mates, recall that if both members of a pair survived to the next breeding season about two-thirds of the time they were paired again. Thus, as individuals grew older the mean age of their mates

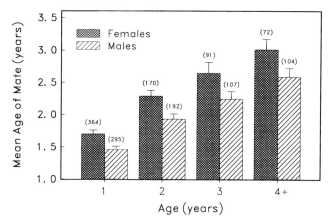

FIGURE 3.3.   Mean age of mates, according to age, in *oriantha*. Line shows 1 SE; sample sizes in parentheses.

increased (Fig. 3.3), a change that was highly significant in both sexes (females: ANOVA $F_{7,689}$ = 17.26, P < 0.001; males: ANOVA $F_{7,689}$ = 13.48, P < 0.001). The mates of one-year-olds (yearlings) were, on average, 1.5 yr old. At age two the interactions of mate retention and mate change resulted in both members of the pair being about the same age. Thereafter, the mates of older birds tended to be younger than they were (Fig. 3.3). Much the same pattern, and for the same reasons, occurs in Great Tits (*Parus major*; Greenwood et al. 1979). These age relationships are unexpected when mate choice is absent. In that situation, mean age of mates should not change with the age of an individual (Reid 1988). The tendency of mates of females to be comparatively older than those of males at the same age (Fig. 3.3) is probably the result of many yearling males (but not females) being unmated (see discussion on floaters below).

Mate choice in birds is often regarded as being within the purview of females and dependent upon two criteria: the genetic quality of the male and the quality of his territory. Since these should be positively correlated, the actual criteria applied by females when selecting males is operationally difficult to detect (Wittenberger 1976). Nonetheless, the *oriantha* data suggest that females, as well as males, have a strong affinity for their previously occupied breeding area. This preference for a specific location should, on average, lead to a reduction in mate quality, but this potential cost seems to be countered by engagement in extra-pair sexual activity.

FLOATERS

In both monogamous (Lack 1968) and polygynous passerines (Orians 1969) there is usually a readily observable population of floating, unmated males, whereas evidence for the existence of unmated females beyond the early part of the nesting season is slim. This general picture fits the *oriantha* data in that all females trapped during the nesting season were known to be associated with specific nests, or at least had a brood patch indicating that they had a nest somewhere. Although extra males were observed and females were not, there were indications that unmated females were present well after the breeding season was under way (also noted in Song Sparrows; Searcy 1984).

For example, on 30 June 1994 the female on the vernal pool territory disappeared and her four nestlings (Days 2 and 3) died that night. The male did not desert the area, however. He remained and began to sing for prolonged periods— as though advertising for a mate. On 10 July a new, unbanded female, presumably a yearling, started a two-egg clutch in the vernal pool willows and this newly-formed pair eventually fledged two chicks. The female had a just-developing brood patch, rather than a fully formed one, when she began to lay indicating that this was her first nest of the season. Also, on several occasions females were observed to insert late-season nests between or within pre-existing territories containing females that were already caring for nestlings. These inserting females were always yearlings and they did not bring a male with them; instead they paired with one of the territorial males already present and he fed the nestlings of both females. These data suggest that floating females do exist, at least during the first half of the season, and they also prompt discussion of two additional phenomena, polygyny and female aggression.

POLYGYNY

The scenario described above shows how polygyny sometimes developed but it also occurred in situations wherein the territories in question were established and maintained from the beginning of the season and the females involved were older than one year. Interestingly, in these latter cases the territories were often separated by a topographic feature such as a rocky knoll or grove of trees that may have been outside of both territories. In other words, the territories were adjacent, but not contiguous, and the females were probably not in close contact. Thus, female-female competition ordinarily may serve to decrease the frequency of polygynous matings.

Polygyny occurred in nine of the 17 years that mating patterns were carefully studied. Of the 429 males observed during that time, 15 (3.5%) were polygynous, and none for more than one season. Of these males, 13 were bigamous and two were trigamous. Note that polygyny was defined not on the basis of copulations, or known paternity, but by paternal care. A male that fed nestlings at two (or three) different nests, each one belonging to a different female, was declared to be polygynous. No more than one male was ever observed to feed nestlings at a given nest.

The mean age of males during the time that they were polygynous was 2.80 yr (SD = 1.52 yr, min = 1 yr, max = 5 yr), and their survival rate was high. Eleven of the 15 reappeared the year following the polygynous one, a return rate of 73.3%. Analysis of reproductive success in these males shows that they fledged more young during years when they were polygynous (mean = 5.47, SD = 2.53, N = 15) than in years when they were monogamous (mean = 3.07, SD = 1.25, N = 28), a significant difference (t = 3.45, P = 0.003).

There were 28 females involved in these polygynous matings, only one of them for multiple years, one year as the partner of a bigamous male and the other year a trigamous male. The mean age of females participating in polygynous relationships was 2.29 yr (SD = 1.44 yr, min = 1 yr, max = 5 yr). Of the 28 females, 15 were present again after the season of polygyny, a return rate of 53.6%. The mating pattern did not affect the number of fledglings produced by these females: with monogamous males their mean number of fledglings was 3.22 (SD = 1.75,

N = 32), with polygynous males it was 3.26 (SD = 1.84, N = 23; t = 0.086, P = 0.932). A few cases of polygyny have also been observed in *nuttalli,* and reproductive success of polygynous pairs was not different from that of normal pairs (Petrinovich and Patterson 1978). As in Savannah Sparrows (Wheelwright et al. 1992), female fitness in White-crowned Sparrows seems to be unaffected by mate sharing.

Polygyny was not age-restricted in *oriantha,* it did not appear to decrease survival (see Chapter 4), and reproductive success was unaffected in females and enhanced in males. Why, then, is this system not more prevalent? There are many factors to consider. Among these is that polygyny is advantageous to males so its occurrence may depend upon its effects on female success (Leonard 1990). This, in turn, hinges upon territory quality because polygyny is promoted by a high variance in quality among male territories (Pleszczynska 1978) and mating with a polygynous male on a high-quality territory may be more productive than mating with a bachelor on a low-quality territory (Verner 1964, Orians 1969). In addition, environmental conditions that promote polygynous matings could vary from year to year and there may be undetected consequences for lifetime reproduction as well. Cuckoldry rates could be higher in polygynous males, for example, and, lack of evidence from the present study notwithstanding, polygyny could be detrimental to male survival, especially if it is chronic. This is mentioned because although prolonged, high levels of testosterone in the blood are associated with polygyny (testosterone implants can induce it; Wingfield 1984a), Dufty (1989) found that this condition or manipulation significantly reduced survival.

Finally, the dynamics of intrasexual competition should be considered. For example, female-female competition appeared to prevent polygyny but this was sometimes circumvented as when yearling females did not settle until territory-holding females already had young. The aggressive tendencies of the latter were then starting to decrease and they sometimes let an unmated female become established and even share the resident male. House Wrens (*Troglodytes aedon*) exhibit a similar pattern (Quinn and Holroyd 1992). Note that the nests of females sharing a male in such instances will usually be out of synchrony making it unlikely that the male would need to feed two groups of dependent young simultaneously. On the other hand, the surplus of males may generate intense male-male competition for territories and mates, circumstances that tend to drive the system toward monogyny and that have probably caused the rate of polygyny to be stabilized at the rate observed.

Given the relative rarity and sporadic nature of polygyny in *oriantha* (and its conspecific, *nuttalli*), it seems reasonable to conclude that this permutation of their mating system is relatively unimportant and should be thought of as a facultative response. At the same time, the temporally separated clutch starts of male-sharing females tends to support the thesis of Slagsvold and Lifjeld (1994) that, due to competition for male help with dependent young, mated females may benefit from trying to prevent or delay settlement of other females, especially in poor years (Catchpole et al. 1985, Bart and Tornes 1989). Clearly, female aggression may have had a major role in the evolution of avian mating systems.

AGGRESSION

Most studies of aggression in passerines have focused on male-male interactions. These have been observed under uncontrolled field conditions and/or experimentally through the use of tools such as song playback and live or mounted conspecifics (decoys) placed upon the territory. Aggressive behaviors are not usually so overtly expressed in females as in males, and only recently has it become clear that females of many species compete not only for high-quality males, but also for limited resources such as food and nest sites (Hill 1986, Searcy 1988, Dunn and Hannon 1991, Slagsvold et al. 1992, Berglund et al. 1993, Slagsvold 1993, Cristol and Johnsen 1994, Liker and Szekely 1997).

In the Tioga Pass study the role of female aggressiveness in such important functions as mate selection and territory acquisition and defense were not specifically investigated, but some intriguing, relevant behaviors were noted. For example, returning females tended to settle on or near their previous territory regardless of the male that was present. As mentioned above, the strength of this site fidelity suggests that they discriminate much the way males are thought to do when it comes to territory choice and retention. Also, yearling females were sometimes unable to settle until the season was well along. Perhaps they could not find an unmated male with a suitable territory, but it could be that they were being excluded by other females. Females also expressed overt, classical types of aggression in that they sometimes sang vigorously during the pre-nesting period, much in the manner of males, and they were known to return from foraging trips and physically displace a conspecific adult near their nest.

These observations, and others, stimulated us to think about how aggression could be compared in males and females. Playback experiments using alarm or contact calls that are shared by the sexes could be used and so could the propensity to attack decoys. The method of using decoys was selected, then employed in a test that was objective and easy to conduct. It relied upon the observation that a bird in a trap often stimulated the territory holder to attack it through the trap wall. This response was exploited in an experimental paradigm that could be used to test aggressiveness simultaneously in both sexes.

In the period before nest building (pre-nesting), two four-cell traps were placed 5 m apart on an area occupied by a pair. One trap contained an adult female decoy (leaving three cells free for making captures) and the other trap contained an adult male decoy. Materials (snow, ice, rocks, dirt clods, vegetation) were placed, alone or in combination, against the sides and top of the cell containing the decoy so an attacking bird would likely be diverted into an open cell and thus be captured. No supplementary food, such as seed, was added and numerous direct observations verified that the territory holders were indeed attempting to attack the decoys. Each trapping session lasted for 20 min. Experiments like this were conducted during all stages of the nesting sequence except that, once the nest was built, the two traps were placed 5 m from it and from one another such that an equilateral triangle with 5 m sides was formed. A total of 144 experiments were performed in 1993 and 1994, 134 on birds engaged in their first nesting effort of the season and 10 on renesters. Seven different periods or stages were sampled: pre-nesting (before nest construction), pre-laying (nest constructed but not yet laid in), laying, incubation, nestlings present, fledglings present (first five d after fledging), and fledglings present (six to 10 d after fledging).

In the 134 experiments conducted on pairs engaged in their first nesting effort of the season, females were captured 63 times and males 54 times (Table 3.4, part A), a capture ratio that was not different (Chi-square = 1.23, df = 1, P =

TABLE 3.4. Frequency That Female and Male *Oriantha* Were Captured in Decoy Traps on Their Territories, in Relation to Stage of the Nesting Cycle

| | | Captures | | | |
| | | Females | | Males | |
Stage	Number of experiments	N	%	N	%
A. First nests					
Pre-nesting	25	7	28.0	17	68.0
Pre-laying	23	11	47.8	13	56.5
Laying	34	17	50.0	10	29.4
Incubation	19	14	73.7	7	36.8
Nestlings	17	10	58.8	5	29.4
Fledglings (days 1–5)	10	4	40.0	2	20.0
Fledglings (days 6–10)	6	0	0.0	0	0.0
B. Replacement nests					
Incubation	10	2	20.0	0	0.0

0.268). There was no evidence that the parent birds were affected by decoy sex. Females were captured 31 times with the female decoy and 32 times with the male decoy (Chi-square = 0.02, df = 1, P = 0.900). For males these same trapping frequencies were 21 and 33 (Chi-square = 2.67, df = 1, P = 0.102). On a few occasions an adult from a neighboring territory was captured, but those data were not included in Table 3.4.

Males were most sensitive to the presence of the decoys early in the season, before the nest was built (Table 3.4). Once the nest was in place, their capture frequency tended to decrease through the various nesting stages. In contrast, females strongly defended the immediate area of the nest and were captured with greater frequency as nesting progressed, with the peak rate occurring during incubation. By the time fledglings were more than five days out of the nest both parents had stopped reacting to the decoys. Even when decoy traps were placed near their fledglings neither parent was captured. Ten experiments were also conducted during the incubation period on pairs engaged in renesting efforts, and trapping success during incubation decreased substantially, although not significantly, from what it had been with first nests (Chi-square = 2.55, df = 1, P = 0.111; Table 3.4, part B).

These data show that territory or nest defense occurs in both males and females and that more information is needed on the relative roles played by the sexes in determining parameters such as territory configuration, settlement pattern, mate acquisition, and territory defense.

VOCALIZATIONS

The vocalizations of birds are an essential component of their social interactions, including sexual displays, and the study of song and other types of utterances has been an enormously productive line of inquiry into avian social systems. As a group, White-crowned Sparrows have had an important impact in this field because they are widely available and have vocal repertoires that are relatively easy to record and analyze. Their songs are composed of separable, distinctive, sequentially-arranged elements that can be quantified and compared (Fig. 3.4). In addition, they have dialects and the various components of songs often vary dis-

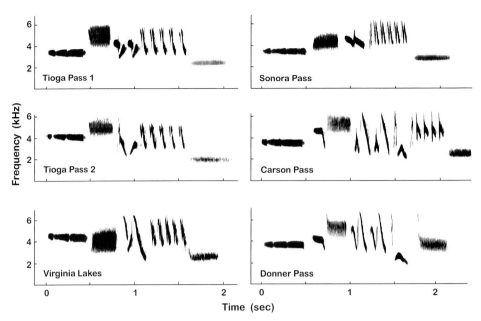

FIGURE 3.4.   Audiospectrograms of *oriantha* songs recorded at five different breeding areas in the Sierra Nevada. Two song types were encountered at Tioga Pass. The various notes have been described as whistles, buzzes, complex and simple syllables, and trills (Baptista and Morton 1982, 1988; Nelson et al. 1996). Audiospectrograms provided by Douglas A. Nelson.

tinctively from one geographic region to the next (Blanchard 1941, Marler and Tamura 1962; Baptista 1975, 1977). The possible function of these dialects in mate choice by females or as potential barriers to gene flow has been probed extensively, but results have been equivocal (Chilton et al. 1990, MacDougall-Shackleton 2001). Still they, and other features of White-crowned Sparrow vocalizations, have been the focus of many contemporary studies of song learning and sociality (Petrinovich and Patterson 1981; Baptista and Morton 1982, 1988; Baker 1983, Baker and Thompson 1985, Baptista 1985, Kroodsma et al. 1985, Chilton et al. 1990, Lampe and Baker 1994, Nelson and Marler 1994; Nelson et al. 1995, 1996; MacDougall-Shackleton 2001, MacDougall-Shackleton et al. 2001).

Non-song

The various vocalizations of *oriantha,* other than song, including their description, context of use, and possible functions, have been reported for a population in the Rocky Mountains of southwestern Alberta by Hill and Lein (1985). They found nine vocalizations expressed by adults that could be reliably identified. All nine were used by males and five were used by females. The five most commonly used calls were given the descriptors of *pink, whine, trill, flag,* and *sip.* The *pink* was a mobbing or scolding note used by both sexes when a disturbance or intrusion occurred on the territory (in our study this note was described as *chip*). The *whine* was used by both sexes and was associated with conflicts and with locomotor activity. The *trill* was also used by both sexes, but in quite different contexts. It was uttered by females when soliciting copulations and by males when they were involved in same-sex attacks and territorial disputes. *Flag* was used only by males and was associated with agonistic behavior. *Sip*, a quiet call, audible to the investigators only from close range, was given by males during non-ago-nistic encounters and by incubating females while flying back to their nests.

The non-song vocalizations in this Rocky Mountain population, and their social contexts, are mostly familiar to us, but they may be employed in a slightly dif-ferent manner in Sierra Nevada populations. For example, the *sip* call (*seep* to us) was used at Tioga Pass by incubating females when leaving the nest, as well as when entering it. If the call was not given by the departing female, the male appeared not to recognize her and would pursue her quite aggressively in an aerial chase until both birds finally landed, whereupon hostilities ceased. The *sip*, there-fore, appears to function as an identification or contact call between mates. In both wild and captive *oriantha* we have heard numerous calls or notes, often of low volume and given at close range to other birds, that were not mentioned by Hill and Lein (1985). Given the microgeographic variation present in the songs of *oriantha* (see below), it seems clear that additional studies of inter-populational variation in their non-song vocalizations should yield interesting comparative data.

Song

In 1969, during a search for *oriantha* populations to the north of the study area, it was discovered that males singing in meadows at Sonora Pass and at Carson Pass sounded quite different than the ones at Tioga Pass (Fig. 3.4). The following summer Jorge Orejuela recorded more than 1,000 songs from 142 males at 14 locations over a distance of 500 km along a north-south axis of the Sierra Nevada. Songs had a duration of about 2 sec in all populations, but substantial variation in their structure was evident, and 10 distinctly different patterns or dialects were identified. Furthermore, variation in song within populations was inversely related to habitat area, being less variable in large meadows than in small ones (Orejuela and Morton 1975). Twenty-six years later, in 1996, males were again recorded at some of the original sites and it was discovered that the local dialects had been retained except for some drift at the smallest, most frag-mented of the habitat areas (Harbison et al. 1999)

In another study of geographic variation in song types of *oriantha*, Baptista and King (1980) recorded songs from 18 populations scattered over six western states (California, Colorado, Idaho, Nevada, Oregon, Wyoming) and two prov-inces (Alberta, British Columbia). They found regional differentiation of song into types that shared elements in common with other subspecies (*nuttalli*, *pug-etensis*, and *gambelii*). It is well understood that White-crowned Sparrows learn their songs by copying those that they hear early in life (Marler 1970), so some *oriantha* juveniles appear to learn at least portions of their songs while in contact with other subspecies, presumably during migration or on wintering areas. In their survey, Baptista and King (1980) also discovered that a recently established pop-ulation in the San Bernardino Mountains of southern California was probably founded by birds from the central Sierra Nevada because their dialect was iden-tical to the one at Tioga Pass. Note that this speculation gains support from Harbison et al.'s (1999) demonstration that dialects are retained in an area over a considerable period of time. Lein (1979) was also able to use the concept of dialect persistence in *oriantha* to address another zoogeographic question. He found that birds in the Cypress Hills, a disjunct population (see Fig. 1.2), were probably not in contact with their closest neighbors, some 250 km away in the Rocky Mountains, because their dialects were quite different.

Singing by female songbirds, specifically the oscine passerines, is considered to be uncommon, but it does occur. The function of female song is unknown, but various suggestions have been made. For example, it may facilitate pair bonding in Northern Cardinals (*Cardinalis cardinalis*; Ritchison 1986), or signal intra-sexual aggression in Yellow Warblers (*Dendroica petechia*; Hobson and Sealy 1990). Among White-crowned Sparrows, captive *gambelii* females sing frequently while undergoing photostimulation (Morton et al. 1985) and *nuttalli* females sing year around in the wild, perhaps to advertise for a mate or to fend off other females from their territory (Baptista et al. 1993). Female *oriantha* were observed singing robust, male-like songs, but only at the beginning of the nesting season (Morton et al. 1985, Baptista et al. 1993). As yet, no adaptive value can be assigned to this behavior. It could be functioning in territoriality, but its apparent restriction to the early season in this subspecies suggests that it might simply be an epiphenomenon, the result of high, transient levels of sex hormones produced during a period of generally elevated steroidogenic activity.

CHAPTER 4: Demography

One of the most interesting questions about members of any study population is, "How long do they live?" For avian populations, despite a few drawbacks and assumptions, this question has been profitably addressed by affixing individuals with uniquely numbered bands (Farner 1955b). From banding returns it is then possible to accumulate demographic statistics that can be used for obtaining basic information on such parameters as age-specific survival and population growth rates and, eventually, to comparisons that can illuminate the relative hazardousness of events such as those involving migration flights and occupancy of different types of breeding habitat. A traditional method for consolidating demography data into a concise and standard format is the life table (Deevey 1947).

LIFE TABLE

A dynamic-composite life table was constructed for Tioga Pass *oriantha* by using data obtained from philopatric juveniles. That is, a cohort was assembled from juveniles, banded during the years 1978 to 1986, that returned as adults to nest on the study area. This method does not yield reliable information on survival during the first year of life (which is thought to be less than 30% in passerines; Newton 1989b), because there were probably many surviving one-year-olds that did not settle on the study area. Those that did settle there, however, were site-faithful with regard to their subsequent annual selection of breeding territories, so their survival statistics can provide a useful life table for individuals that lived for more than one year (Table 4.1). The sample size of males in this table was higher initially than that of females because females tended to be less philopatric than males (Morton 1992b, 1997). Median survival time for the individuals represented in Table 4.1 was 1.94 yr for males and 1.91 yr for females, and this was not different (Wilcoxon test: $W = 0.102$, $df = 1$, $P = 0.750$).

About half of the adult population, both males and females, survived each year (Table 4.1). This is similar to the rate obtained by Baker et al. (1981) for *nuttalli*, the sedentary subspecies, and is an interesting result because it suggests that migration may not be particularly hazardous for *oriantha*. Note that survival in *oriantha* has been computed in increments of one year, from one summer to the next, so the average bird is probably living about 0.5 yr longer than one might gather from looking at Table 4.1.

These data tend to support the hypothesis that passerines show a constant age-

TABLE 4.1. AGE-SPECIFIC LIFE TABLES FOR MALE AND FEMALE *Oriantha* BANDED AS JUVENILES AT TIOGA PASS

Age (yr)	Males				Females			
	n_x	d_x	l_x	e_x	n_x	d_x	l_x	e_x
1–2	134	71	1.000	1.49	80	44	1.000	1.40
2–3	63	28	0.470	1.60	36	16	0.450	1.50
3–4	35	17	0.261	1.49	20	10	0.250	1.30
4–5	18	10	0.134	1.42	10	7	0.125	1.10
5–6	8	3	0.060	1.55	3	2	0.038	1.45
6–7	5	2	0.037	1.19	1	0	0.012	2.50
7–8	3	2	0.022	0.64	1	0	0.012	1.50
8–9	1	1	0.007	0.43	1	1	0.012	0.50

Notes: n_x = cohort size, d_x = number of disappearances, l_x = the fraction of the initial cohort returning at each subsequent age class, e_x = the future life expectancy (see Deevey 1947, Stearns 1992).

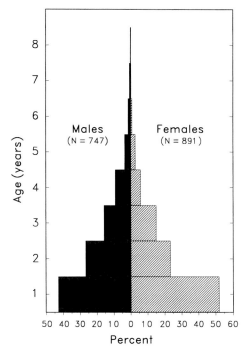

FIGURE 4.1.   Age distribution of *oriantha* males and females known to be engaged in reproduction at Tioga Pass.

specific mortality rate once they reach adulthood (Deevey 1947, Bulmer and Per-rins 1973). This evident lack of senility may be an artifact due to small sample sizes for older individuals found in most studies, or it may simply be that phys-iological time is scaled to body size (Lindstedt and Calder 1976). No generaliza-tion about survival chances seem possible, however, because significant declines have been demonstrated in several species, both short- and long-lived (Newton 1989b).

The maximum life span obtained for *oriantha* from the life table was eight years. This is not quite within the range of maximum longevities for four species of *Zonotrichia,* 9 to 13 yr, gleaned from banding records deposited with the Bird Banding Laboratory (Klimkiewicz and Futcher 1987). Interestingly, the oldest age reported, 13.3 yr, was for a *gambelii,* the subspecies of White-crowned Sparrow that migrates the greatest distances (Fig. 1.1).

AGE STRUCTURE OF BREEDING POPULATION

As would be expected in a small passerine, more one-year-old *oriantha* were engaged in reproduction in any given year than members of any other age class. The pyramid depicting the proportions of known-age breeders for each sex for all years of the study shows that 42.8% of the males and 52.0% of the females known to have nests were one-year-olds (Fig. 4.1). The maximum age attained by *oriantha* during this study was eight years (one male and one female), but it is worth noting that at the end of the study in 1997 there were three eight-year-old *oriantha* at Tioga Pass, two males and one female, and that one male and the

TABLE 4.2. AGES AND RETURN RATES OF *Oriantha* KNOWN TO HAVE NESTS

Age (yr)	Males		Females	
	N	% return	N	% return
1	320	—	463	—
2	199	62.2	208	44.9
3	117	58.8	134	64.4
4	68	58.1	52	38.8
5	26	38.2	24	46.2
6	11	42.3	7	29.2
7	5	45.5	2	28.6
8	1	20.0	1	50.0

female, then age nine, returned again in 1998 but not in 1999 (E. MacDougall-Shackleton, pers. comm.). Mean age of breeding individuals was 1.88 yr for females and 2.12 yr for males, a significant difference (Kolmogorov-Smirnov test: $N_1 = 891$, $N_2 = 747$, $D = 0.091$, $P = 0.002$). Sample sizes for the sexes were skewed somewhat by identification techniques because it was easier to prove that females were associated with nests than it was for males; females could be identified by their color bands when flushed from a nest (while incubating or brooding) or when bringing food to the nestlings, males only when bringing food. In addition, sitting females were sometimes driven off the nest into a mist net to obtain positive identification. About half of each age cohort depicted in Fig. 4.1 returned to the study area each year (Table 4.2).

These data are puzzling. The life table (Table 4.1) shows no difference in survival time for the sexes, yet among the breeders males were older. There could be at least two different reasons for this and they could be acting simultaneously. One is that mortality rates were actually higher in females than in males, although this was not shown in the life table because of small sample sizes. In fact, adult female passerines often die at a higher rate than males of the same age (Lack 1954), and this can happen both in early (Smith 1995) and late adulthood (McGillivray and Murphy 1984). Another reason is that a disproportionate number of the younger adult males, especially one-year-olds, did not gain territories and mates.

The age class with the lowest percentage of known nesters for both sexes was the one-year-olds (Table 4.3). Only 45.2% of the males and 63.3% of the females of that age were known to have nests. For reasons stated above, these numbers are underestimates (probably close to 100% of the older birds, especially the

TABLE 4.3. PERCENTAGE OF ADULT *Oriantha* OF VARIOUS AGES CAPTURED ON THE STUDY AREA THAT WERE KNOWN TO HAVE NESTS ON THE STUDY AREA

Age (yr)	Known to have nests (%)			
	Males	N	Females	N
1	45.2	520	63.3	474
2	50.5	223	74.3	187
3	60.7	107	80.5	82
4	66.0	50	75.5	49
5	68.2	22	73.3	15
6+	70.6	17	88.9	9

females, actually had nests), yet they undoubtedly reflect some biological realities. For example, unmated males were usually one-year-olds, and non-breeding adult males outnumbered females not only because males tended to outlive females, but also because some mated males were polygynous (Chapter 3). In a study of mortality in the Great Tit, Bulmer and Perrins (1973) also found that breeding males were older than breeding females. As in the case of *oriantha*, this was attributed to an excess of males caused by their lower mortality and to lower competitive abilities of younger males. Higher mortality rates in females are frequently associated with the energetic demands accompanying reproduction, and Sealy et al. (1986) have shown that female passerines are taken off their nests by predators, and that they sometimes die of exposure or starvation while trying to defend their nests during storms. No cases of death from starvation were known in *oriantha* females, but in a number of instances (three times in 1984 alone) feathers were found in and around disrupted nests, indicating that a predator had taken the tending female. Furthermore, females that nested late in the season were very lean and probably highly stressed. They were sometimes the sole providers of parental care, and often while undergoing molt (Chapter 11).

Table 4.2 does not have the legitimacy of a regular life table because the majority of the birds represented in it were handled for the first time on the study area as adults and were assumed at that time to be one-year-olds. And, like Table 4.1, its usefulness depends upon the adults being site-faithful. These caveats aside, among the birds known to be engaged in nesting, one-year-old females returned less often as two-year-olds than did males (Chi-square = 6.79, df = 1, P = 0.009). None of the other multiple contrasts of annual return rates of the sexes from age two to age six were significantly different (beyond that age sample sizes were too small to do valid Chi-squares). This is an interesting result because it mirrors what Smith (1995) found in Black-capped Chickadees. She discovered that males lived longer than females due to differential mortality during and immediately after the first breeding season. Females mated to young males were vulnerable because they were poorly provisioned by their inexperienced mates. Male *oriantha* are known to provision their mates, but only rarely (Zerba and Baptista 1980), and one-year-old *oriantha* females did have a higher percentage of one-year-old mates than females of any other age class (Chapter 3).

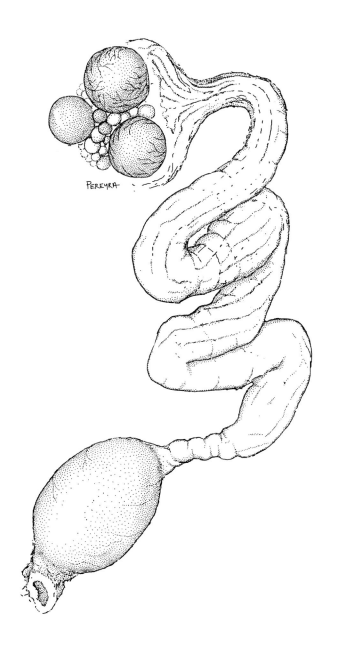

PEREYRA

CHAPTER 5: Gonadal Condition

Of central importance in the biology of migratory passerines is the great change that occurs seasonally in the size and functional status of their gonads. Enlargement of testes and ovaries from a regressed, quiescent condition begins while individuals are still on their wintering areas. Development continues apace during the vernal migration (King et al. 1966), but is often only partially completed when the birds arrive on their summering areas. What happens there, as the cycle continues to full sexual capability, is an opportune time for discovering how the energetic costs to the bird of migrating with enlarging gonads are traded off with the necessity of being able to breed without delay, and how social and ecological cues interact to affect the metamorphosis of the reproductive organs.

GONADAL CHANGES

There are several ways to characterize the annual cycle of gonadal growth or recrudescence. For example, its progress in male *oriantha* on the breeding grounds was assessed by measuring the length of the left testis during laparotomy as well as by the length of the cloacal protuberance (Fig. 5.1A). The latter contains the seminal vesicles and it allows sperm to be stored externally at lower than core body temperature (Wolfson 1954). Seasonal changes in these two structures were

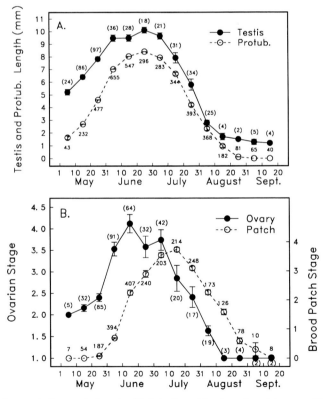

FIGURE 5.1.   Seasonal changes in length of left testis and in cloacal protuberance (A) and in ovarian and brood patch development (B) in *oriantha*. Sample sizes for gonadal condition are in parentheses and those for cloacal protuberances and brood patches are without parentheses. Testis lengths and ovarian stages were determined during nine different years (by laparotomy), protuberances and patches during 22 yr.

similar and highly correlated ($r^2 = 0.605$, df $= 401$, P < 0.001). In females the diameter of the largest ovarian follicles were measured during laparotomy and categorized by stages as follows. *Stage 1:* follicles in winter condition; 0.4 mm or less in diameter. *Stage 2:* follicles 0.5–1.0 mm. *Stage 3:* follicles 2–3 mm; no yellow yolk. *Stage 4:* follicles 4–10 mm; yellow yolk present. *Stage 5:* about to ovulate or egg in oviduct (Fig. 5.1B). The condition of brood patches was also defined by stages (see below).

Growth of the testes continued for about a month after males had begun to arrive at Tioga Pass. They reached maximum size in June, began to regress in July, and were near their wintertime minimum by early September (Fig. 5.1A). Cloacal protuberance length followed much the same pattern. Fluctuations in protuberance size provided a rough estimate of testicular secretory activity because growth of this structure is stimulated by testosterone (Witschi 1961), and its congruence with the testicular cycle, with a slight lag, is to be expected.

Ovarian follicles grew slowly during May then increased rapidly in size as females began nesting. Their collapse to minimum size was completed by mid-August, about the same schedule observed in males. Incubation or brood patch development and regression is a function of circulating estrogen levels (Kern 1979), so, like the cloacal protuberance, its status is an easily obtained measure of gonadal activity in the bird under examination. The seasonally consistent, two- to three-week lag of patch condition behind ovarian condition (Fig 5.1B) was probably a function of both ovarian secretion rates and the time it took for the extensive morphological changes involved in brood patch cycling.

Incubation (Brood) Patch

The incubation or brood patch of White-crowned Sparrows has been described in detail by Bailey (1952). He and Hinde (1962) point out that three notable changes occur in the ventral surface of female passerines when they prepare for incubation of eggs and, eventually, brooding of nestlings: defeatherization, vascularization, and edema. Loss of feathers from the ventral surface occurs four or five days before the first egg is laid. Immediately following defeatherization, blood vessels in the dermis of the ventral apterium begin to increase in size and number and vessels become large enough to be seen with the naked eye. Toward the end of laying and on through incubation the dermal tissue becomes edematous and thickened.

We found that this description only applied to first nests of the season, however. If a nest was lost during incubation the dermal fluid was withdrawn, exposing large blood vessels to view, and the patch became dry and wrinkled in appearance. It became edematous again if a new nest and clutch appeared.

Through the use of implants, Bailey (1952) was able to show that exogenous estrogen could induce brood patch formation in wintering females, and that if the birds were hypophysectomized, prolactin injections were synergistic. He deduced that estrogen stimulates increased vascularity in the dermis and, when estrogen is present, prolactin stimulates defeatherization and dermal edema. In a review of the endocrinology of patch formation, Jones (1971) suggested that patch formation is completed through the influence of escalating prolactin levels on the female's estrogen-primed skin.

The relationship of brood patch condition to the reproductive status of *oriantha* females was as follows. The first loss of feathers from the distal region of the abdomen (stage 1) occurred in females engaging in their first nesting effort of the season. It was observed in females that were building nests, had nests already constructed, or, in a few cases, had even begun to lay. A completely defeathered patch, with a trace of vascularity but without edema (stage 2), was found in laying birds and those in the first day or two of incubation. Sometimes edema was already present in individuals entering incubation and they were designated as being in a stage 3 condition. Stage 4, when the patch had accumulated enough fluid to be described as moderately edematous, was noted in some females making the transition to full-time incubation. The stage 5 patch, one that was highly vascularized and fully edematous, was found in females that were well into incubation or that had hatchlings.

As the season wore on, brood patch condition changed in accordance with nesting success and, eventually, the onset of postnuptial molt. The same classification system was used but the etiology of patch condition was different. For example, the partially defeathered condition (stage 1) occurred late in the season when the patch was being refeathered during the molt. Eventually it was completely obliterated by new feathers and became stage 0, the same condition observed early in the season before commencement of nesting activities. Females with fledglings had stage 2 patches because the fluid had been reabsorbed, and those that had recently lost a nest could be diagnosed because they had regressed to a stage 3 condition, and the rich vascular bed, normally present during stages 4 and 5 but obscured by the thick layer of fluid, was now highly visible.

ROLE OF ENVIRONMENTAL CUES IN ANNUAL CYCLES

Environmental influences on annual cycles, especially those portions involving reproduction, have intrigued avian biologists for many years. Early in its history this field of study benefited greatly from a theoretical framework envisioned by J. R. Baker (1938a, b). He described environmental factors as being either ultimate or proximate in their effects on the timing of reproduction. Ultimate factors or causes give survival value to the adjustment of the bird's cycle to that of the environment and proximate factors provide the actual timing that brings the adjustment into play (Thomson 1950).

The availability of an adequate food supply for the parents and young is nearly always identified as being the most potent of ultimate factors, but others such as competition, nesting conditions, predation pressure, and weather patterns can, under certain circumstances, exert ultimate control by selecting for a breeding schedule that will maximize the number of reproductively viable young produced (Immelmann 1971, 1973). Environmental events such as those listed above occur too late in the season, however, to serve as information for timing the onset of gonadal maturation (Immelmann 1973, Rand 1973). Thus, the need arises for proximate factors that can act through the endocrine and neuroendocrine systems to provide a finer control of the correct timing and temporal sequence of stages in the reproductive cycle. This input is essential because of intra- and interannual variations in ecological conditions on the breeding grounds, variations that can affect the most propitious fit between environmental and reproductive schedule by at least several weeks in birds summering at mid- to high latitude or at high altitude. This would apply to all species migrating to rigorous climes even though the mechanisms controlling their basic rhythm and preparation for migration and re-production might vary from being totally endogenous to one that is driven strictly by changes in daylength (see reviews by Marshall 1960, 1961; Farner 1964, 1975, 1983; Farner and Follett 1966, 1979; Lofts and Murton 1968, Farner and Lewis 1971; Immelmann 1971, 1973; Elliott and Goldman 1981, Meier and Russo 1985).

During the last five decades there have been numerous investigations of environmental cues that are presumed to affect avian reproduction, especially those that are proximate factors since they are more amenable to testing than ultimate ones. An undesirable side effect of all this research has been the generation of considerable overlapping, redundant, and confusing terminology. This was recti-fied in a series of papers that systematically organized and defined the roles of proximate information, particularly as it affects reproduction in passerines (Wing-field 1980, 1983; Wingfield and Kenagy 1991; Wingfield et al. 1992). These definitions are as follows:

Initial predictive information

These factors initiate gonadal development and other vernal phenomena in an-ticipation of the ensuing breeding season but are insufficient by themselves to initiate nesting. They may also cause, indirectly, gonadal regression at the end of the breeding season. The most important factors of this type would be the annual cycle of photoperiod or daylength and endogenous circannual rhythms that are themselves entrained by exogenous cues such as photoperiod or rainfall (Gwinner 1986).

Supplementary information

These factors, usually perceived through visual and auditory systems (Ball 1993), supplement initial predictive information and, acting as short-term predic-tors, initiate the final stages of gonadal development. They help correct for inter-annual variation in environmental conditions and are crucial for coordinating the nesting phase with local phenologic progressions. They can regulate behaviors such as arrival schedules, territory establishment, and pair bonding, as well as the final stages of gonadal maturation. Inhibition or acceleration of these events can occur depending upon the immediate situation. Specific examples of supplemen-tary factors are presence of a mate, availability of nesting sites, rainfall, ambient temperature, and nutritional plane. Together, the initial predictive and supplemen-tary factors regulate the seasonal cycle of gonadal maturation and regression.

Integrating and synchronizing information

These factors become important once reproduction is actually under way. They serve to integrate events of the reproductive cycle so that the correct temporal sequence of nest building, copulation, oviposition, incubation, and feeding of young occurs. They also affect synchronization of the reproductive effort between members of a pair. Examples would be visual and tactile cues from the nest and eggs and auditory cues from nestlings, as well as reciprocal behavioral interactions between mates. Note that these categories are not necessarily exclusive; some factors such as interactions between the sexes could be functioning as more than one type of information.

Modifying information

These factors cause disruption of the nesting phase at any stage and are restricted temporally, by definition, to the nesting phase. Good examples of such factors would be predation and storms.

Thus far, studies of proximate factors controlling avian reproduction in North America have been focused mainly on those that provide initial predictive information, especially the photoperiod. Studies of photoperiodic effects on the gonadal cycle and associated functions, such as premigratory fattening and molt, have been highly effective lines of inquiry; they can be conducted indoors under controlled conditions, are amenable to experimental design and hypothesis testing, and often provide excellent quantitative results. Photoperiod experiments on *Zonotrichia* have been particularly productive because exposure to long days appears to be an essential requirement in their annual cycle (Follett et al. 1975, Sansum and King 1976), as well as that of many other temperate zone-breeding passerines (Gwinner and Dittami 1985). Nonetheless, the length of day provides only initial predictive information and no species of wild bird, even of *Zonotrichia,* is known to breed strictly under the influence of the vernal photoperiod; fine tuning in the form of essential supplementary information is required.

Despite enduring interest among avian biologists in proximate and ultimate factors, and continued efforts to unravel their interactions and individual efficacies, it has been much easier to postulate their roles in wild populations than it has been to actually show how they operate; it is difficult to separate cause and effect relationships when numerous, uncontrolled biotic and abiotic variables are interacting simultaneously. Conducting long-term studies of breeding birds through many annual cycles at locations with markedly variable environmental conditions, as in the present study, is one approach toward solving this problem.

PHOTOPERIOD EFFECTS

Among White-crowned Sparrows, the role of photoperiod in the control of annual cycles, such as the one in gonadal function, has most often been studied in *gambelii.* In them (and other *Zonotrichia*) gonadal development in both males (Farner and Wilson 1957, Farner 1964, Farner and Follett 1966) and females (Farner et al. 1966, Morton et al. 1985) is stimulated by long days perceived via encephalic photoreceptors. Gonadotropic activity is thought to occur when there is coincidence between the environmental photophase (daylight) and the sensitive phase of an entrained circadian rhythm in photosensitivity (Farner et al. 1981). In captive males with fully regressed testes weighing only 2–3 mg, full reproductive development, including spermatogenesis, has been routinely induced by exposure to photoperiods of 16 hr or longer for only a few weeks (Farner and Follett 1966). Peak mean mass of the paired testes in these captives was about 300–360 mg (King et al. 1966, Lewis 1975a, Farner et al. 1980), not quite as high as the 440–460 mg reported for breeding *gambelii* in Alaska and Washington (King et al. 1966). Long days are also stimulatory to ovarian growth in *gambelii,* but only from an initial mass of 5 mg up to about 50 mg (Farner et al. 1966, Morton et al. 1985). This is an order of magnitude change but still far less than the two orders that occurs in males. And the photoperiodically-driven growth of ovaries stops well short of the mean mass of 326 mg reported for females breeding

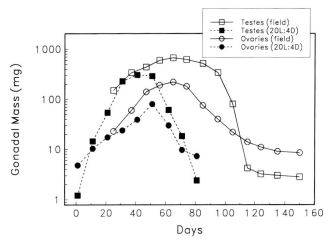

FIGURE 5.2. Mean gonadal mass in *oriantha* (log scale) collected between May and September at Tioga Pass (solid symbols) and in captives exposed to a 20L:4D regime (open symbols) beginning at day 0 of the abscissa. Sample sizes were 3–14 in the field and 2–5 in the lab.

in Alaska (King et al. 1966). So captive females, more so than males, ordinarily do not approach full gonadal development, as measured by changes in mass, when stimulated by photoperiod alone. There appears to be an initial phase of growth beyond which captives do not progress, at least during their first year after capture. Exposure to male song augmented ovarian growth rates in captive *gambelii,* but the final mean mass still did not exceed 50 mg (Morton et al. 1985). Life in the cage must be non-stimulatory for some reason, perhaps because of sensory deprivation and/or induction of fear (King et al. 1966). Furthermore, females are well known to be more strongly affected by modifying factors than are males (Farner and Lewis 1971). We have now learned more about how modifying and supplementary factors, all of which are non-photoperiodic, can operate in the natural setting. Next, we will pursue their importance, as revealed in our study of *oriantha,* with results from both the lab and field.

To test for the role of photoperiod, first-year *oriantha* were brought from the field to the laboratory on 30 September and placed in captivity on a short-day regime (8L:16D). On 11 December, well beyond the time required for them to become photosensitive (Farner and Mewaldt 1955), half were placed on long days (20L:4D), and the other half were retained on short days (8L:16D) as controls. For the next 40 to 50 days birds under long days exhibited gonadal growth (none occurred in the short-day birds). Involution then followed so that after 80 days of exposure, gonadal mass approached that of the controls (Fig. 5.2). Maximum mean mass of testes, achieved in the day 40 sample, was 305 mg, and of ovaries, achieved in the day 50 sample, was 80 mg (one ovary of 205 mg strongly influenced the mean).

Next to the data from these artificially photostimulated birds are juxtaposed those on gonadal mass, collected during four field seasons, at a place on the graph where gonadal size of captives and of field birds were similar. The data on field birds go from mid-May to late September and they illustrate about how much gonadal growth occurs after the birds reach their breeding areas. The mid-May means were 155 mg for testes and 23 mg for ovaries. Based on mean maximum masses recorded during the breeding season (see below), more than 75% of testicular growth and 90% of ovarian growth in *oriantha* was post-migrational. This suggests that selection has acted to minimize the biomass that is carried during the migration itself. Some support for this view can be found in a study by Brooke (1979) on Northern Wheatears that migrate in spring to Wales. He had no actual data on gonad condition, but thought that a three-week pause that occurred between arrival and egg laying was probably necessary for development of the reproductive organs rather than for a need to build up energy reserves for egg formation.

The field birds (Fig. 5.2) had been photostimulated by shorter days than the lab birds, but for longer periods of time, so comparisons of the growth and involution schedules of the two groups is difficult. Also, one-year-old males are known to have smaller testes than older ones at all times during the reproductive cycle (Morton and Allan 1990, Morton et al. 1990). Nonetheless, substantial differences exist here that might tell us something about non-photoperiodic influences.

First, gonads of birds in the wild population grew to much larger sizes than those in captivity. Maximum mean mass in the wild was 220 mg for ovaries and 670 mg for paired testes and masses observed in individuals could be much larger. For example, on 27 June 1968 three males with 820, 849, and 976 mg testes were collected. Second, maximum mass was not retained for very long in 20L:4D birds. It is typical of captives that the longer the days they are held on, the sooner they are likely to regress once the enlarged condition has been achieved. Based on the study of Moore et al. (1983) on this phenomenon, the Tioga Pass birds, due to their exposure to natural daylengths (which are shorter), should have shown testicular regression from the photostimulated state about 10 days later than the 20L:4D birds. It was actually about 40 days later (see Fig. 5.2), so about one additional month of retention at peak functional condition occurred in the field birds beyond that expected from a purely photoperiod effect. Clearly, engagement in reproductive activities is stimulatory to gonadal growth and maintenance. Just what would some of these stimuli be?

The history of this field suggests that the fine-tuning of reproduction is achieved via complex, reciprocal behaviors between males and females, along with responses to local environmental conditions, especially by females (Lewis and Orcutt 1971; Moore 1982, 1983). To develop some understanding of this complicated mélange of stimuli, correlates of both social and ecological cues will be discussed next.

Non-photoperiod Effects

Social cues: Males

There is abundant experimental evidence that the reproductive condition of passerine males can be affected by the behavior of females. For example, Gwinner (1975) found that an endogenously programmed readiness for sexual activity in captive male European Starlings (*Sturnus vulgaris*) was enhanced when they were in the presence of females. Testicular regression was also prevented. Moore (1983) found that solicitation displays, which normally ceased during egg laying, could be extended into the incubation period in female *pugetensis* by implanting them with estradiol. The mates of these females had significantly elevated plasma levels of testosterone and dihydrotestosterone. Moore (1983) also found that testosterone and luteinizing hormone increased in photostimulated captive males that were paired with estradiol-implanted females. These males copulated and also maintained enlarged testes for a longer time than control males paired with untreated, non-receptive females. Interestingly, males that had been maintained on short photoperiods also attempted to copulate when caged with implanted, soliciting females even though their testes were undeveloped and plasma testosterone and luteinizing hormone levels were basal. In a similar vein, Runfeldt and Wingfield (1985) found that testosterone was elevated and that territorial behavior was maintained for up three extra months in male Song Sparrows mated to females with estradiol implants. Gonadal activity and sexual behavior in male passerines, therefore, can be strongly affected by the behaviors of females.

Social cues: Females

As mentioned above, ovarian growth rates in *gambelii* were increased by exposure of females to male song during the initial phase of photostimulation (Morton et al. 1985), and it has now been shown that gonadotropin levels and ovarian development increase in *oriantha* females treated in a similar fashion (MacDougall-Shackleton et al. 2001). Aside from these studies on White-crowned Sparrows, however, there seems to be little evidence that social interactions with males affect gonadal function in females. To the contrary, the presence of a male enhanced neither estradiol secretion nor ovarian growth in photostimulated Great Tits (Jonsson 1994). Furthermore, Runfeldt and Wingfield (1985) found that although testosterone-implanted Song Sparrow males remained on territory and were responsive in song playback experiments well beyond the usual breeding season, their mates terminated reproductive activity at the regular time and went into molt. There are subtleties to the social cue-photoperiod interaction that need to be clarified, however. Specifically, a stimulatory effect of song on *gambelii* females was detectable when their schedule was 15L:9D, but not when it was 20L:4D. The latter was the same schedule used by Jonsson (1994) on Great Tits. It may be that very long photoperiods are so stimulatory to females that they swamp the relatively small effects that accrue from social input.

Ecological cues: Males

Berthold (1969) reported that testicular development was not affected in European Starlings exposed to bad weather at their breeding areas in Germany. On the other hand, exposure to prolonged spells of good weather caused advances in development of up to 10 days. He also found that testicular recrudescence was delayed in a Common Chaffinch (*Fringilla coelebs*) population prevented from arriving on their breeding area at the usual time by heavy snow conditions.

This last situation can also occur in *oriantha* when storms and deep snows converge to hinder their springtime occupancy of the breeding area meadows. In 1995, for example, we were present on the study area from 7 May onward, but no males were observed or captured until 17 May. Despite unfavorable environmental conditions, however, and unlike Berthold's chaffinches, testicular growth in these first arrivals was no different than that observed in 1988, a very mild

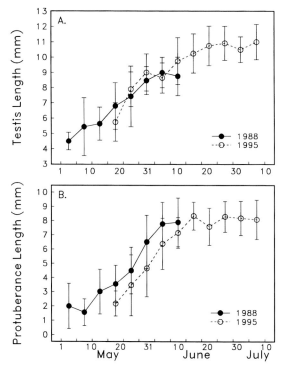

FIGURE 5.3.   Testis (A) and cloacal protuberance lengths (B) in a year of mild weather (1988) and in one of inclement weather (1995). Data stop at each year when clutches were started. Symbols indicate means ± 1 SE; sample sizes = 4–8.

year when males began arriving on 3 May (Fig. 5.3A). The data in Fig. 5.3A were plotted up to the time that egg laying began at Tioga Pass, which was early June in 1988 and early July in 1995. Since males are capable of breeding well before testes reached maximum size, as in 1988, the testicular growth that occurs after migration arrival may have more to do with sperm competition than sperm viability.

Although testes were the same size during the 25-d period of overlap in May and June shown for the two years in Fig. 5.3A, cloacal protuberances were not. They lagged behind by about a week in the 1995 males (Fig. 5.3B). This suggests that testosterone secretion was inhibited in years when unfavorable weather prevented early settlement onto breeding territories. This inhibition could have been the result of a decrease in the intensity or frequency of reciprocal sexual behaviors or to the deep snowpack and weather, or combinations thereof. No additional data for passerines could be found, but testicular development was unaffected in Least Auklets (*Aethia pusilla*) forced to wait for nesting sites because of overlying snow (Sealy 1975).

Ecological cues: Females

Was gonadal maturation in females affected by environmental conditions in the same way as males? Clearly not, if one assumes that completion of this process includes ovulation and laying, functions that will not occur unless a nest is present,

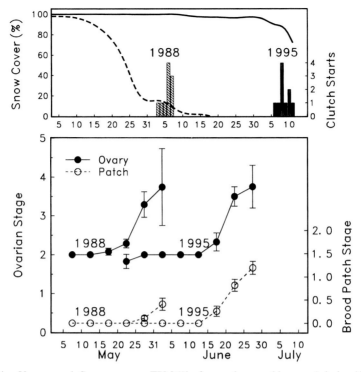

FIGURE 5.4. Upper panel: Snow cover on TPM (% of ground covered by snow) during 1988 (dashed line) and 1995 (solid line), along with dates of the first 10 clutch starts of the season on TPM for both years (histograms). Lower panel: Ovarian and brood patch development in 1988 and 1995; means ± 1 SE; sample sizes = 4–9. Data not shown beyond the time that first eggs were being laid (see upper panel).

which is an impossibility if all materials for building nests and places to hide them are buried under snow. Where then is development of the female tract arrested when breeding is long delayed? Again, the 1988–1995 comparisons are enlightening.

The schedules of snow melt-off and of the onset of egg laying for those years show that the much lighter pack in 1988 had mostly melted by early June, the time when females began to lay (Fig. 5.4, upper panel). Ovarian follicles in the 1988 females were at stage 2 in early and mid-May then began to enlarge as the time for nesting approached. Not until a few days before laying did their brood patches begin to develop (Fig. 5.4, lower panel). In 1995 the first females were not captured until 26 May and the first open ground available for nesting did not appear until the very end of June. Egg laying began almost immediately thereafter (Fig. 5.4, upper panel).

The 1995 data are important because they tell us what happens to females when nesting cannot proceed because of environmental conditions. It was pointed out previously that photostimulation causes ovaries to grow to about 50 mg in size with follicles that are usually 1 mm or less in diameter (a stage 2 ovary). This was the condition of females as they arrived on the breeding area in all years of the study, although a stage 1 was sometimes encountered. It appears that ovarian development was arrested at stage 2 for six or seven weeks in 1995 while the females waited for conditions to ameliorate. This is far different than the response of female Least and Crested (*Aethia cristatella*) auklets. They appear unable to halt follicular maturation when nesting habitat is unavailable and will eventually lay their eggs right on the snow (Sealy 1975).

Note that brood patches developed earlier with respect to onset of nesting in 1995 than in 1988 (Fig. 5.4, lower panel). This shows that the 50 mg ovary is capable of secreting enough estrogen to stimulate patch development. Furthermore, it is a functional platform from which females can very quickly initiate ovulation if the opportunity arises.

This was shown in an experiment conducted in 1995. On 22 June two small patches of open ground were discovered on TPM that had thawed out that morning where subnivean streamlets had caused the overburden of snow to melt and collapse. Pine boughs were immediately cut and stacked to a height of 1 m on each of these open areas. Two hr later both of the brush piles were already being occupied and investigated by *oriantha* pairs. Nests were being constructed on the following morning from dried grass stalks gathered from a nearby knoll and both females ovulated on 26 June, 4 days after the nesting sites were provided (their first eggs appeared in the nests on the morning of 27 June). This was 9 days earlier than the first clutch starts for nests built in naturally-occurring locations. The 50 mg ovary, therefore, is an active endocrine gland that can be transformed within just a few days to an ovulation-capable structure, providing that environmental conditions are favorable. In 1995 the availability of nesting sites was the last remaining factor crucial to this transformation, a clear demonstration of its importance as supplementary information.

In summary, long photoperiods stimulate testicular growth to about one-half, or less, of maximum mass. The remainder of growth and the prolongation of functional condition appears to be heavily reliant upon stimuli received from females. Ovaries are still quite small (50 mg) when photo-induced growth ceases, but at that point this gland is actually a well-organized structure, poised to carry out its hormone- and gamete-producing roles at the opportune moment. Once this stage of their cycle is reached, females do not appear to be especially reliant upon stimuli from males for continuation into the actual process of nesting. For that step to occur they must experience favorable feedback from ecological factors.

In terms of maintaining gonadal mass, the sexes also follow different strategies. Testes grow on the summering grounds to a size that is close to three orders of magnitude above mid-winter mass ($\sim$1 vs. 1000 mg), and they are maintained at that level until the shift to photorefractoriness begins (see Chapter 11). Ovarian mass can also vary seasonally by about three orders of magnitude ($\sim$5 vs. 5000 mg), but maintenance at maximum size is confined to the relatively brief period when a clutch is being produced. Immediately before and after that time it is about 50 mg. This must represent a considerable energy saving for females during both spring migration and the breeding season.

Ambient temperature

One would expect photoperiodically-induced gonadal growth to be modulated by ambient temperatures (T_a) if they are being utilized as supplementary information that is being transduced by the central nervous system to influence the appropriate endocrine axis (Chapter 1). But it is important to remember that T_a, unlike other types of supplementary information, has a biological counterpart, body temperature (T_b). Therefore, T_a has the potential to be both an environmental cue and, when it is low, if it causes T_b to decrease, an inhibitor of metabolism. In fact, T_b of captive *gambelii* decreased by 3 to 6 C when they were exposed to a T_a of -10 C, a saving of about 18% in metabolic cost (Paladino 1986). The point is that if low T_a induce hypothermia in the field, which is most probable at night because that is when T_a are lowest and the birds are roosting and least active, thermosensitive cell-division processes in the developing gonads could be decelerated. This potential interaction between photoperiod, T_a, and T_b has not been studied, however.

Full-time T_b data on *oriantha* were not obtained in this study, nor even reliable information on their exposure to T_a. They occupy numerous microclimates during their daily activities, some of which could even be at much lower altitudes (Hahn and Morton 1995). A start in monitoring microclimate usage by *oriantha* at Tioga Pass has been made, however, by Sockman and Hahn (1996). They found that early in the season transmitter-bearing mated pairs left their territories at night to roost in tall pines, sometimes in the same one, on the periphery of the meadows. Once the females had nests they roosted or sat in them, but males did not leave the trees and begin roosting on their territories until late June, by which time nocturnal T_a had increased substantially.

Although T_a effects in the field are difficult to assess, they could very well be providing important supplementary information that affects the final stages of gonadal maturation and implementation of reproductive effort. This probably occurred nearly every spring at Tioga Pass when escalating T_a caused the snow to melt and the vegetation to develop. In 1983, for example, a massive snowpack was quickly dissipated by unusually warm weather and nesting was delayed much less than had been expected.

The effects of T_a on gonadal development during photostimulation (but without concurrent information on T_b) has been tested in the laboratory in *gambelii, pugetensis,* and *oriantha,* with mixed results. Lewis and Farner (1973) found that testicular growth rates increased slightly with T_a in *gambelii* but ovarian growth was unaffected in both *gambelii* and *pugetensis* (male *pugetensis* were not tested). Subsequently, Wingfield et al. (1997) showed that testicular growth did not vary in *pugetensis* on various temperature regimes (5, 20, 30 C). Follicular and brood patch development were enhanced at 30 C but only if males were present in the environmental room. These investigators also found no evidence for a temperature effect on either the gonads or accessory structures in male and female *gambelii* (Wingfield et al. 1996). On the other hand, gonadal growth in *oriantha* was slower in both sexes on 5 than on 20 or 30 C (5 C is well below the thermoneutral zone of *oriantha*; Maxwell and King 1976). Despite this, there was no parallel change in luteotropic hormone; it was the same at all T_a (J. Wingfield et al., unpublished data). Maney et al. (1999) have discovered that these seemingly inconsistent gonadal responses of White-crowned Sparrows to T_a are mirrored by changes in their plasma prolactin levels. Since these levels appear to follow thyroxine secretion, Maney et al. (1999) have suggested that temperature information may act through thyroxine to increase prolactin. Prolactin, in turn, may mediate gonadal development (as in mammals) by increasing gonadotropin receptors at the gonad.

This would explain why a gonadotropic effect sometimes occurs even though luteotropic hormone levels do not change.

Relevant to the discussion of the role of T_a is a mathematical model developed by Wingfield et al. (1992) to assess the predictability of an organism's environment, and the relative roles of initial predictive information (such as photoperiod) and the more short-term supplementary information (such as T_a) with respect to this predictability. To apply their model to birds, they used data on the time of year when clutches were initiated to generate a measure of environmental predictability (*Ie*). *Ie* is the ratio of the fluctuations in resource levels across time (*M*) to the constancy of those resources (*C*). They suggest that when *Ie* values are low (near zero), the environment is relatively constant and initial predictive information should be sufficient to time gonadal maturation. When *Ie* values are near 1, *C* and *M* make equal contributions and individuals utilizing those environments may be required to integrate supplementary information. The more that *Ie* values exceed 1, the more important supplementary cues, such as availability of nesting sites and T_a, become in the regulation of breeding. They hypothesized that migrants, as well as other species with precisely timed breeding seasons, would be less responsive to supplementary cues than sedentary species and those with more flexible breeding times. A test of the model was made by looking at the effects of T_a on photoperiodically-induced testicular maturation in a variety of avian taxa. True to their prediction, low T_a tended to inhibit gonadal development more in resident birds than in migrants.

Ie values have now been calculated for four subspecies of White-crowned Sparrows (Wingfield et al. 1992; J. Wingfield et al., unpublished data) and, consistent with the environmental predictability model, the largest value, 6.3, was found for *nuttalli,* the sedentary subspecies, and the smallest, 1.1, for *gambelii,* the one that migrates the greatest distances. The value for *oriantha* was 2.1, suggesting that they should be sensitive to supplementary information, a prediction that is borne out by the inhibitory effects of low T_a on their gonadal development in captivity (noted above). Since the *Ie* value obtained for *pugetensis,* the short-distance migrant, was 4.3, an intriguing corollary emerges from these data: migration distance is inversely related to environmental predictability.

GONADAL HORMONES

Despite having only partially grown testes, the plasma concentrations of testosterone in newly arrived males were already near their seasonal high (Table 5.1). The averages through the nest-building period for all ages combined was about 3.3 ng/ml, about the same as those found in both *gambelii* (Wingfield and Farner 1978a) and *pugetensis* (Wingfield and Farner 1978b).

Testosterone remained high in mated males until nests had been built, then decreased steadily thereafter with successive stages of the nesting cycle, from parental care through molt and premigratory fattening. If a nest was lost, testosterone levels increased again in males as the pair resumed sexual activity (mean = 1.42 ng/ml, SD = 1.87 ng/ml, N = 7).

This profile of testosterone secretion to the bloodstream is the usual one found in male migrants and it is correlated with their behaviors. At first they interact aggressively while establishing territories and obtaining and guarding mates, then the social system becomes more stabilized, the frequency of aggressive encounters

TABLE 5.1. PLASMA HORMONE LEVELS IN ADULT *Oriantha* IN RELATION TO STAGE OF THE REPRO-
DUCTIVE SEASON

	Testosterone (males, ng/ml)			Estradiol (females, pg/ml)		
Stage	Mean	SD	N	Mean	SD	N
1. Arrival	2.98	3.60	111	84.6	52.8	34
2. Pre-nesting	3.32	3.46	41	82.8	34.6	18
3. Nest building	3.28	3.12	13	112.8	72.6	8
4. Pre-laying	1.89	1.92	8	112.9	125.1	16
5. Laying	1.13	1.46	30	88.6	51.9	40
6. Incubation	0.96	1.41	32	80.0	36.0	54
7. Nestlings	0.65	1.33	42	85.2	34.2	39
8. Fledglings	0.48	0.60	16	87.5	33.9	13
9. Molt	0.12	0.10	89	95.6	67.1	31
10. Fattening	0.19	0.19	23	83.0	26.9	8

Notes: Hormones were measured by radioimmunoassay (Wingfield and Farner 1975, 1976). Note that stages 3–8 in males could be
determined only in individuals that were known to be mated and engaged in reproductive activities.

diminishes, and the birds move into phases of parental care and self-maintenance
(Wingfield and Farner 1979; Wingfield 1984b, 1985; Wingfield et al. 1987, 1990;
Wingfield and Wada 1989, Wingfield and Goldsmith 1990, Wingfield and Hahn
1994).

The relationship of aggression to testosterone in male *oriantha* can be illustrated
by combining data from Tables 3.4 (responses to decoys) and 5.1 (testosterone
concentrations). Six stages of the reproductive cycle are shared in common in
these tables: pre-nesting, pre-laying, laying, incubation, nestlings present, and
fledglings present. A plot of means obtained for those stages indicates that the
two functions are related (Fig. 5.6). No statistics are given because the data are
for means and were gathered from different males in different years, but the tie
that is presumed to exist here between physiology and behavior is reinforced and
the method of using decoys for evaluation of aggressive tendencies is supported.

As stated above, testes and cloacal protuberances were both smaller throughout
the summer in one-year-old *oriantha* males than in older ones (Morton and Allan
1990, Morton et al. 1990), a disparity that has also been reported for Cassin's

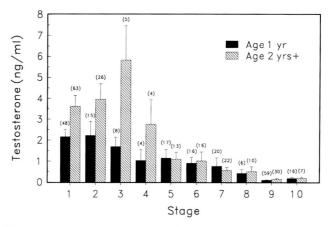

FIGURE 5.5. Mean plasma testosterone concentrations, according to age, in adult male *oriantha* in
sequential stages of the reproductive season (stages are defined in Table 5.1). Line shows 1 SE; sample
sizes in parentheses.

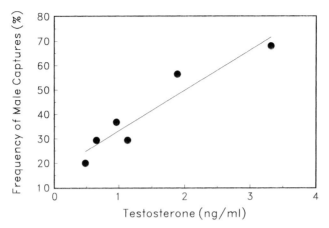

FIGURE 5.6.   Percent of time male *oriantha* were captured when decoys were placed on their territories in relation to plasma testosterone levels. Means obtained during six different stages of the reproductive cycle are shown (see text). Data taken from Tables 3.4 and 5.1.

Finches (*Carpodacus cassinii*; Samson 1976b), Dark-eyed Juncos (Ketterson and Nolan 1992, Deviche et al. 2000) and Great Tits (Silverin et al. 1997). Early in the season, as suggested by the data on protuberances, there was a hormonal correlate of this difference: testosterone levels tended to be lower in one-year-old males (Fig. 5.5), the difference being significant during the arrival and nest-building stages (t = 2.15, P = 0.034; t = 3.00, P = 0.012, respectively), but not the pre-nesting stage (t = 1.58, P = 0.122).

It seems likely that this age-related effect occurs because the smaller testes of immature birds, undergoing hypertrophy for the first time, have lower secretory capabilities than the larger, recrudescing ones of the older males. Intra-testicular testosterone levels may not have been affected because fertility, as measured by hatchability of eggs, did not vary with male age. But the lower peripheral (plasma) levels of testosterone in young birds may have had functional ramifications; it may have been the physiological basis for their reduced competitiveness and why relatively more of them were unmated. Just how various male-male and male-female behaviors might be affected by these lower testosterone levels, or vice-versa, has not been investigated although it is known that a positive relationship exists between song rates and testosterone levels in both European Robins (*Erithacus rubecula*; Schwabl and Kriner 1991) and Willow Tits (*Parus montanus*; Rost 1992). It would be interesting to know if singing frequency, as well as other behaviors that might affect territory and mate acquisition and defense, varies with male age in *oriantha*. It could also be that young males, as a group, lacked social stimulation from females because many of them were unmated and without territories. Diminished behavioral interactions with females has been suggested as the cause of age-class differences in testicular size in Dark-eyed Juncos (Deviche et al. 2000).

Plasma estradiol levels were quite low in females and did not vary with stage of reproduction (ANOVA $F_{9, 254}$ = 0.81, P = 0.688; Table 5.1). Wingfield and Farner (1978a) found that estradiol and estrone levels were both at or above 300 pg/ml in *gambelii* females engaged in courtship, nest building, and laying. They obtained similar results in *pugetensis* females for estrone, but estradiol levels hovered around 100 pg/ml (Wingfield and Farner 1978b), much the same as those observed in *oriantha*. Estradiol is metabolized readily to estrone (Common et al. 1968), and not having assayed for the latter, there is little we can say about total estrogen in relation to reproductive stages of females. Testosterone levels in females averaged 154 pg/ml of plasma during the pre-laying period (nest built and sitting empty), and between 50 and 100 pg/ml during the other stages. This variation was not significant (ANOVA $F_{9, 254} = 1.44$, $P = 0.11$).

CHAPTER 6: Body Size and Body Condition

Body mass is an easily obtained, non-invasive measure that can give immediate feedback on the health and general condition of the individual under scrutiny. It can be used to index the energy costs of specific life history events or stages, and to uncover productive avenues of investigation (Nice 1938). Sudden fluctuations in mass, especially when they are correlated with known behavioral or physiological conditions, can signal the presence of environmental stressors (Ricklefs 1974, Ricklefs and Hussell 1984) as well as altered, adaptive shifts in the regulation of appetite (Sherry et al. 1980) and of energy reserves (King and Farner 1959; King 1961a,b). In this chapter variation in wing length is related to sex and age and variation in body mass and fat class is related to reproductive status. This information is then used to pinpoint shifts in energy balance and in levels of stress as *oriantha* progressed through the complete cycle of nesting and rearing young.

WING LENGTH AND SEX

Banks (1964) found more sexual dimorphism in wing lengths of White-crowned Sparrows than in any other trait. Males were sufficiently larger than females in most populations such that this measurement could be used reliably to separate the sexes. Tioga Pass *oriantha* also exhibited this dimorphism. Wings of adult females (one-year-old or older) had a mean length of 75.67 mm (SD = 1.61 mm, min = 71 mm, max = 81 mm, N = 374), whereas mean length was 80.09 mm in adult males (SD = 1.81 mm, min = 75 mm, max = 85 mm, N = 449). This difference in means was 5.8% and highly significant (t = 37.0, P < 0.001). In *oriantha* captured at Hart Mountain, Oregon, the sex difference in wing length was 5.5% (Mewaldt and King 1986).

Wing lengths appeared to be normally distributed within the 1 cm range found for each sex, with some overlap between sexes occurring between 75 and 81 mm (Fig. 6.1). By themselves, therefore, they were not sufficient for determining sex in the live birds. Note that presence of a brood patch or cloacal protuberance or, if necessary, a laparotomy were used in this study to determine sex, not wing length. Nonetheless, this measure might be an effective way of determining population sex ratios if more positive means of identification were unavailable (Mewaldt and King 1986, Wheelwright et al. 1994). Wing length values might also

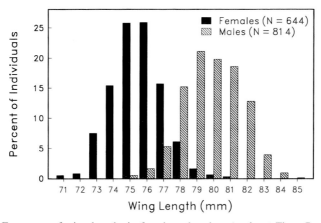

FIGURE 6.1.   Frequency of wing lengths in female and male *oriantha* at Tioga Pass.

TABLE 6.1. Wing Lengths (mm) of *Oriantha* According to Sex and Age

	Age (yr)	Males			Females		
		Mean	SD	N	Mean	SD	N
Juveniles	0	79.49	1.57	365	75.32	1.34	270
Adults	1	79.45	1.83	258	75.29	1.66	220
	2+	80.95	1.39	191	76.21	1.36	154

be useful as morphological correlates or predictors of migration behavior, especially if data are available from members of the same species with different migrational tendencies. In White-crowned Sparrows, for example, Banks (1964) found that subspecies that migrate the longest distances (*leucophrys* and *gambelii*) have wings that are about 7–8% longer than those that are sedentary or migrate only a relatively short distance (*nuttalli* and *pugetensis*).

WING LENGTH AND AGE

Change in wing length with age is a widely observed phenomenon in passerines. Specifically, wings frequently become longer at the end of the first postnuptial (prebasic) molt. This molt usually occurs in one-year-old adults immediately following their first breeding season (Van Balen 1967) and it is the first complete molt in many species. In a study that involved relatively small sample sizes of several passerine species, Stewart (1963) found the increase in wing length to be on the order of 2–3% in males, less in females. In a large, unsexed sample of *gambelii* this increase was 1.7% (Barrentine et al. 1993), and in *gambelii* of known sex the increase was 2.3% in males and 1.5% in females (Mewaldt and King 1986). In *oriantha* the increase was 1.9% in males (t = 9.92, P < 0.001) and 1.2% in females (t = 5.85, P < 0.001; Table 6.1). These differences were derived from wing lengths obtained from one-year-old adults during the breeding season (before their first postnuptial molt) and from two-year-olds, also during the breeding season. Wing lengths of juveniles (age 0 yr) measured after their primaries had grown in and before they departed on migration are also included in Table 6.1. The data indicate that mean wing lengths in young birds had not changed by the time they returned the next summer as one-year-old adults (males: t = 0.30, P = 0.759; females: t = 0.20, P = 0.842; Table 6.1). Frequency distributions of wing lengths also had not changed (Kolmogorov–Smirnov test; males: N_1 = 365, N_2 = 253, D = 0.065, P = 0.553; females: N_1 = 270, N_2 = 220, D = 0.092, P = 0.257). Thus, there was no evidence that directional selection on wing size occurred in *oriantha* during their first winter or first two migrations, although overwinter mortality has been shown to accentuate sexual size dimorphism in House Sparrows (*Passer domesticus*; Johnston and Fleischer 1981).

Wing lengths appeared to increase slightly with age in the older birds (Fig. 6.2), but the effect was not significant (males: ANOVA $F_{7, 813}$ = 0.73, P = 0.571; females: ANOVA $F_{7, 643}$ = 0.30, P = 0.910). Van Balen (1967) also found that one-year-old Great Tits had shorter wings than older birds and that wing lengths remained constant with age beyond the time of the first complete molt. He and others have suggested that growth of remiges might be restricted in young birds for nutritional reasons, but Alatalo et al. (1984) have pointed out that the one-year-old vs. older adult wing-length dichotomy is ubiquitous and most marked in

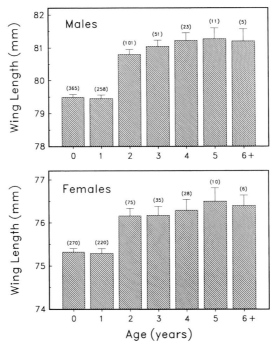

FIGURE 6.2.   Mean wing length (+1 SE) in *oriantha* of various ages at Tioga Pass. Age 0 individuals were juveniles with fully grown primaries. Sample sizes in parentheses.

species that do not change their primaries in the postjuvenal molt (such as White-crowned Sparrows). They suggested that young birds have shorter wings, not because of uncompleted growth, but because short wings give them increased maneuverability. Presumably this enhances survival when birds are inexperienced and particularly vulnerable to predation. The *oriantha* wing length data can be interpreted to support this hypothesis, and so does their autumnal behavior in the days or weeks prior to migration. At that time juveniles were in flocks and we often observed them engage in vigorous aerial pursuits of one another. These flights usually included many tight turns and abrupt changes in direction. Perhaps they were gaining strength and honing evasive skills, skills that are enhanced by short wings. Once individuals have survived a year the focus of natural selection, as it bears on wing length, might then switch to other factors, such as increased flying speed or simply to a larger body size, since wing length and total mass are closely correlated (Rand 1961, Van Balen 1967).

SEASONAL CHANGES IN BODY MASS

The seasonal highs and lows of mean body mass were congruent in the sexes. Lows, which occurred in late July, were 26.9 g for males and 25.0 g for females (Table 6.2). Highs, in early October, were 33.7 g for males and 29.9 g for females. This represented a change of 25.3% in males and 19.6% in females. During May, mass decreased slightly then increased on into mid-June as the population, on average, began to prepare for reproduction. Combining the early May data into a 10-d interval obscures the interesting fact that the very first males to arrive still

TABLE 6.2. Seasonal Changes in Body Mass (g) in Adult *Oriantha* at Tioga Pass, Pooled Over 18 Yr

	Males					Females				
	Mean	SD	N	Min	Max	Mean	SD	N	Min	Max
May										
1–10	28.3	2.0	26	25.3	33.4	26.2	1.6	7	24.2	28.2
11–20	27.8	1.3	84	25.2	30.8	25.6	1.6	33	24.2	28.3
21–31	28.8	1.6	173	25.5	32.5	26.8	2.1	133	24.0	30.7
June										
1–10	28.7	1.4	418	24.0	32.6	27.8	2.1	344	22.5	34.0
11–20	28.4	1.4	428	24.8	32.5	28.2	2.1	465	23.4	32.2
21–30	27.9	1.3	265	25.0	31.5	27.2	2.3	320	23.0	33.2
July										
1–10	27.3	1.3	218	25.0	32.0	26.4	2.5	234	22.5	35.0
11–20	27.0	1.5	285	22.5	30.6	26.2	2.6	305	22.3	34.7
21–31	26.9	1.4	261	22.5	30.5	25.0	1.7	232	21.3	34.0
August										
1–10	27.5	1.5	271	23.8	34.5	25.2	1.6	313	21.3	30.5
11–20	28.6	1.7	188	24.0	32.8	26.1	1.8	202	21.2	29.5
21–31	29.5	1.7	152	25.2	34.5	26.8	1.7	122	22.6	29.7
September										
1–10	29.6	1.8	176	25.0	33.4	27.3	1.8	135	23.0	34.5
11–20	31.8	3.1	220	26.1	39.8	27.9	2.9	204	21.8	36.5
21–30	31.6	2.8	170	26.5	39.2	29.2	3.0	187	23.5	37.5
October										
1–10	33.7	3.0	108	26.4	41.1	29.9	2.7	70	24.5	36.4

showed signs of migratory fattening. The earliest capture of a male was on 3 May and a total of five were captured before 6 May. This group had a mean mass of 31.1 g (SD = 1.3 g) whereas 21 males captured between 6 and 10 May weighed 27.5 g (SD = 1.2 g). These means were different (t = 6.41, P < 0.001), and the data suggest that hyperphagia, and the attendant obesity typical of migrants, was quickly terminated at the very end of migration. No fat newly-arrived females were ever captured, however. Male Willow Warblers (*Phylloscopus trochilus*) also arrived at breeding areas with extra fat (Fransson and Jakobsson 1998), and since the weather was usually favorable, the authors suggested that these reserves could be used for obtaining and defending a territory rather than as insurance against poor feeding conditions.

Other data of interest can also be gleaned from Table 6.2. For example, the heaviest adult male ever captured by us (in early October) weighed 41.1 g and the heaviest female (in late September) weighed 37.5 g. These individuals were obviously among those that had accumulated large amounts of fat in order to fuel their autumnal migration. Some very heavy females (34–35 g) were also present in July. These were laying females with greatly enlarged ovaries and oviducts.

Adults weighed the least from about mid-July to mid-August, with the lightest male being 22.5 g and the lightest female 21.2 g. This was also when their fat classes were lowest (Morton et al. 1973), and corresponded to the time when the majority were completing their season of parental care. When examined in the hand, many of these individuals, particularly the males, appeared to be very lean,

TABLE 6.3. FAT CLASSES IN *Oriantha* AS DETERMINED BY APPEARANCE OF SUBDERMAL FAT DEPOTS

	Fat depots		
Fat class	Claviculocoracoid	Lateral thoracic, subalar, and spinal	Medioventral, abdominal, and ischiopubic
0	None	None	None
1	None	Streaks	Streaks
2	Trace	Partially filled	Thin covering
3	Partially filled	Prominent, filled	Thick covering
4	Filled flush	Bulging	Bulging slightly
5	Bulging	Bulging	Bulging

and lacked even traces of subdermal fat (fat class = 0; Table 6.3). To find out what lean body mass actually was, we collected birds in June, weighed them, extracted their body lipids with petroleum ether in a Soxhlet apparatus, then subtracted the mass of lipid from the original body mass. Thus determined, lean body mass was 27.16 g in males (SD = 1.43 g, N = 20) and 24.59 g in females (SD = 1.46 g, N = 20). These data can be used as a reference point for judging relative leanness in live birds, plus they indicate that males were about 10% larger than females. According to information obtained with the doubly-labeled water technique, metabolic rate was about 10% higher in both males and females with nestlings than it was during the incubation period (W. Weathers et al., unpublished data). So the extremely low body mass relative to fat-free mass exhibited by adults toward the end of the parental phase suggests that some catabolism of non-adipose tissues, such as skeletal muscle, may have occurred to meet the costs of rearing young.

Mean body mass of both males and females began a steady increase in early August that continued until the last of them had departed from the study area in October (Table 6.2). During the first six weeks or so, this gain was due to restoration of tissues such as fat and muscle (Morton et al. 1973) and to an increase in blood volume that was associated with the growth of new plumage in the postnuptial molt (Morton and Morton 1990). The final portion of weight gain occurred as molt began to wane in September and was due solely to fat deposition.

To relate body mass and fat condition of *oriantha* more closely to their natural history than was possible from the data in Table 6.2, these two parameters were grouped in birds whose reproductive activities were known. Six stages or periods, each with its own biologically-coherent duration, were selected for this purpose. They covered the period from 10 days prior to ovulation to 10 days after fledging had occurred (Table 6.4).

TABLE 6.4. DURATIONS OF REPRODUCTIVE ACTIVITIES OF *Oriantha* ESTABLISHED FOR EVALUATING CHANGES IN BODY MASS AND FAT CLASS

Duration (d)	Description of activity
10	Pre-ovulating (courtship and nest building)
4	Ovulating (duration dependent upon clutch size)
12	Incubating
10	Nestlings present
20	Fledglings present
10	Post-parental (fledglings independent)

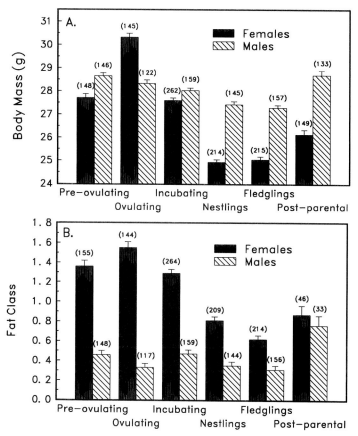

FIGURE 6.3. Mean (+1 SE) body mass (A) and fat class (B) in adult female and male *oriantha* in relation to various periods in the reproductive cycle (durations defined in Table 6.3). Sample sizes in parentheses.

Mean body mass of males (Fig. 6.3A) varied significantly between these six periods (ANOVA $F_{5, 756}$ = 19.19, P < 0.001). Their mass decreased once they began caring for nestlings (Scheffe's test, P = 0.034) and increased in the post-parental period (P < 0.001). Mean mass of females also varied significantly (ANOVA $F_{5, 1027}$ = 211.07, P < 0.001). Mass increased from the pre-ovulating period to ovulating period (Scheffe's test, P < 0.001), decreased from ovulating to incubating (P < 0.001), decreased again when they had nestlings and fledglings (P < 0.001), then increased during the post-parental period (P = 0.012). Once nestlings were present, mass decreased more in females (9.7%) than in males (2.1%). The pattern of change in body mass with stage was different for the sexes (two-way ANOVA, $F_{5, 1783}$ = 70.00, P < 0.001) and correlates with the observation that more parental care was provided by females than males (Chapter 8).

Changes in the amount of fat visible through the skin, as quantified by fat class scores (Table 6.3), closely mirrored the changes in body mass (Fig. 6.3B). Males were quite lean throughout the reproductive period and often had no visible fat. Once they had stopped caring for fledglings their fat scores rose significantly (Kruskal-Wallis H = 28.93, P < 0.001). Females carried more fat than males in

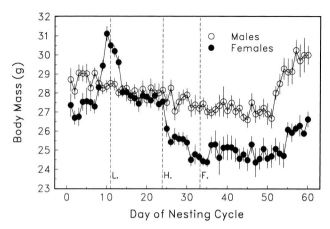

FIGURE 6.4.   Mean body mass ($\pm$ 1 SE) in *oriantha* by day of nesting cycle. Day 10 was day of first ovulation. Dashed line L shows when laying began, H when hatching began, and F when fledging occurred. Sample sizes 4–57 in females and 6–32 in males.

all six periods, particularly during the time before dependent young appeared (Fig. 6.3B), and the pattern of fat class with stage was different for the sexes (two-way ANOVA, $F_{5, 1777} = 27.14$, P $<$ 0.001). Females also exhibited considerable variation in their levels of fat between periods (Kruskal-Wallis H = 227.19, P $<$ 0.001).

DAILY CHANGES IN BODY MASS

Table 6.2 shows seasonal trends in body mass obtained from 18 different years. Body mass and fat class have been displayed in Fig. 6.3 according to the reproductive status of individuals known to be involved in breeding, but because they were compiled by calendar date or by various stages of involvement in reproduction, the data do not convey how body mass fluctuated day to day as the birds progressed through the nesting cycle. To see this, body mass data were normalized by using the day that females laid their first egg as a reference point. This was designated as being day 11 so the first ovulation was presumed to have occurred on the previous day, day 10. With the data thus set into synchrony, it can be seen that mass began to increase rapidly in females three days before their first ovulation (Fig. 6.4). Mean body mass on the morning of the first ovulation, 31.1 g, was the greatest measured on any one day of the nesting cycle. It then decreased slightly each morning thereafter until clutch completion, a reflection, no doubt, of a loss in ovarian mass as the largest follicles disappeared. Total mass loss during laying was about 3 g, or the equivalent of one egg. This shows that the resources required for a complete clutch were gathered both before and during laying, and that the patterns found in intraclutch egg mass variation (Chapter 7) could be either adaptive or constrained by nutrition, or combinations thereof (see Vinuela 1997).

During the 10 days following laying females were in full-time incubation, and they spent all night and 70–75% of the day on the nest, usually with their incubation patch applied to the eggs (Zerba and Morton 1983b). Based on calculations of heat exchange, Walsberg and King (1978) found that resting energy expenditure in an incubating *oriantha* at Hart Mountain, Oregon, was about 15% lower than expected for a bird perching outside the nest but exposed to the same microclimate.

Despite the advantage of being sheltered by the nest, body mass drifted down in females at Tioga Pass by about 0.5 g during the incubation period (Fig 6.4). This could have been due to resorption of the ovary and oviduct, but that should have occurred within the first few days after the onset of incubation (Ricklefs 1974). Furthermore, a sample of body weights taken from incubating females (1978 to 1981) showed that those with elevated nests were, on average, 5.1% lighter than those with ground nests (26.96 g, SD = 1.17 g, N = 20 vs. 28.40 g, SD = 1.39 g, N = 27; t = 3.77, P < 0.001). If changes in body mass of females reliably reflected changes in their energy balance, then it seems that it was more costly to incubate eggs in elevated sites where nests were exposed to convective cooling, than in those on the ground where they were tucked into more protected sites. Note, however, that fat scores were higher in females than in males even when their body mass was at its lowest (nestling and fledgling stages; Fig. 6.3)

Females began incubating before clutch completion, causing a hierarchy in embryo development and, eventually, asynchrony in hatching times. Hatching out of the total brood often took more than a day (Mead and Morton 1985) and the time frame for this process during the nesting cycle (Fig. 6.4) was from about day 24 to day 26. During this relatively brief period, body mass of females decreased by 8.0%, from a mean of 27.6 g to one of 25.4 g. Within the following few days mass decreased a bit more then stabilized at about 25 g for the next three weeks. Beginning at day 55, when fledglings were about 30 days of age, mass of females increased abruptly by about 6.5%. This gain may have been due to the release of females from parental duties because this was the age when young were known to achieve complete independence (Morton et al. 1972b).

Body mass of adult males decreased slowly but steadily from about 29 g to 27 g over a 50-d period (Fig. 6.4). Then, at day 52, they also showed an increase in mass, by about 8.5% over the next three days. As in females, this gain was likely related to cessation of parental care.

The pattern of body mass changes during the nesting cycle differed greatly in males and females except at the very end when both showed an increase. Before then females departed from males at two key times, once when they were synthesizing and laying eggs and again when hatching was taking place. That females should gain mass rapidly then lose it during production of the clutch whereas males, who do not produce eggs, remain at close to a steady state was no surprise. The large decrease in female mass that occurred during the hatching period seems less easy to explain, however. Why did females lose so much more than males during that two-day period and fail to gain it back? Observations of females at close range from blinds suggest that their mass loss was related to reduced food intake. While hatching was under way they usually sat very tightly, but also turned the eggs frequently, and sometimes stood up to assist an emerging chick by lifting off the eggshell and consuming it. They left for only brief intervals and returned with small bits of food for the chick(s). At some nests males began bringing food while hatching was still in progress and female behavior varied when this occurred. Sometimes they left the nest so the male could feed the young and sometimes they continued to brood, but took the food from the male and consumed it or passed it on to the hatchlings. Although activity at the nest was altered by these visitations, the usual degree of attentiveness associated with incubation (70% or more) was maintained during the hatching period (see Zerba and Morton 1983b, Table 3, incubation days 11 and 12). Attentiveness decreased immediately to about 50% once all chicks had hatched (Morton and Carey 1971). It seems that females lost mass during hatching because the time and energy devoted to foraging for hatchlings was subtracted from their own intake budget.

This tendency for females to be broody when hatching was still incomplete was carried to an extreme in nests wherein there was only one viable egg in the clutch. In these situations they spent so much time brooding unhatched eggs that the lone chick was stunted and did not survive.

A sudden decrease of mass in females, but not in males, when hatchlings begin to appear has been observed repeatedly in passerines (Freed 1981, Norberg 1981, Moreno et al. 1991, Woodburn and Perrins 1997), even when supplementary food was provided (Moreno 1991, Cavitt and Thompson 1997). Usually loss of mass in birds engaged in parental care has been attributed to energetic stress (Ricklefs and Hussell 1984), but some investigators have suggested that this is an adaptive, programmed response that has evolved because it reduces flight costs in the provisioning parents (Freed 1981, Norberg 1981, Jones 1994, Merkle and Barclay 1996). Freed (1981) discovered that female House Wrens lost about 13% of their body mass while feeding nestlings. Approximately half of the loss occurred before hatching was completed and the rest before food demands of the nestlings were greatest. Males provisioned at rates similar to those of females but showed no change in mass. Freed concluded that these patterns do not reflect stress (otherwise males would have lost mass too), and that the loss of mass in females saved them 23% in flight costs—a highly adaptive outcome. He does not explain why selection has favored acquisition of this supposed adaptation only in females, however. Not factored in either are the potential trade-offs or drawbacks of excessive weight loss to females. For example, desertion of clutches increased in Blue Tits (*Parus caeruleus*) when females were excessively lean (Merila and Wiggins 1997), so maintenance of good body condition would seem crucial to coping beyond the nesting phase with the high energy costs of feeding fledglings, with molting, and even to surviving (Slagsvold and Lifjeld 1989). Low body weights can also compromise a female's propensity to renest or double brood (De Laet and Dhondt 1989). Furthermore, field metabolism data indicate that maternal energy expenditure may not be tightly coupled to flight costs (Moreno et al. 1999).

The *oriantha* data are consistent with the hypothesis that mass loss occurs during parental care because it is energetically stressful; both sexes lost mass during the nesting cycle and gained it (and fat) immediately after their young became independent (Figs. 6.3, 6.4). Additional mass was lost in females at the time of hatching because incubation-levels of attentiveness were maintained and decreased self-maintenance (voluntary starvation) occurred as they attempted to facilitate hatching of all eggs in the clutch and, possibly, to minimize hatching asynchrony. The latter points to ultimate causation, to the reason that this response evolved in the first place. In addition, these brooding propensities probably caused differential growth rates early in nestling life that were dependent upon hatching order (see Chapter 8 for more discussion).

CHAPTER 7: Nests and Eggs

NESTS

Ancestral birds are thought to have first nested on the ground using an open cup that was molded to body size. This open-style nest may have evolved from a small pit wherein eggs were covered with debris and left for solar incubation. Once birds were able to maintain high nocturnal body temperatures, selection favored direct parental incubation because this served to shorten the period of development, a time when young are highly vulnerable. The acquisition of endothermy must also have facilitated radiation of birds into colder regions free from reptilian predators (Collias and Collias 1984). In species with precocial young, the nest is vacated soon after hatching—they are nidifugous. In other species, and this includes all of the passerines, the young are altricial and are heavily reliant upon parental care until they develop enough to fledge—they are nidicolous. Nidicolous species build the most well-formed nests of all birds (Collias and Collias 1984). Their nests must provide a microhabitat that is favorable for incubation of eggs, and also for the brooding and protection of nestlings. They must be hidden away from predators and still have properties of insulation and durability that are sufficient for prolonged occupation. Not surprisingly, environment plays a strong role in nest composition and location, and the type of nest is often species-specific and an indicator of evolutionary history. Well over one thousand nests were located in the present study, and their histories contribute to high altitude biology by providing reliable information on physiological and behavioral responses of breeding birds to environmental variation.

Construction

Early in the season the first behaviors associated with nest building were sometimes observed. Typically, these occurred when a foraging female interrupted her food gathering by grasping, manipulating, then dropping pieces of grass or other plant material. Handling of potential nest-building materials continued to be interspersed with feeding behavior at irregular intervals for a day or two. The female then began carrying these materials to the site chosen for nest construction. It was difficult to observe the process of nest-site selection, but in the days immediately preceding nest building, a female often spent considerable time hopping in and around the vegetation where the nest was eventually built. The male was usually close by at these times, exhibiting guarding behavior.

The method of nest construction varied somewhat, depending upon the site chosen. For nests built on the ground, females often first scratched out a hole in the usually damp soil or litter, then began adding twigs or coarse, wet stalks of grass. The nest was usually built from the top down with the first material being formed into a ring or rim around the hole, followed by the lining of the cavity walls and then the bottom. Lastly, finely-divided inner lining material was added. A few ground nests were built directly onto the undisturbed soil, rather than into an excavation, a position that may increase vulnerability to predation (Collias 1997). Their construction sequence was much the same: walls first, then bottom, followed by the lining.

In contrast, nests in elevated sites were constructed from the bottom up, especially those placed in pines and on large willow branches. First, a platform of cris-crossing twigs and/or grass stalks was placed to form the bottom of the nest.

TABLE 7.1. COMPOSITION OF *Oriantha* NESTS ACCORDING TO LOCATION

| | Nest location | |
| | Ground[a] (% of total mass) | Elevated[b] (% of total mass) |
Nest components		
Fine grass	18.9	15.7
Medium grass	50.9	23.1
Coarse grass	8.4	25.3
Twigs	4.8	16.1
Bark	1.5	2.8
Duff	10.4	5.5
Other	5.1	11.5

Note: Nests collected at Tioga Pass during laying or incubation (Kern 1984).
[a] Mean mass = 18.2 g, N = 5.
[b] Mean mass = 38.9 g, N = 17.

Walls were then built to their final height, and the inner lining was added as a last step. In some of the more densely leafed-out willows, walls were often built ahead of the bottom, as in ground nests, perhaps because they were held in place and supported more by the surrounding branches. In all types of constructions, females relied heavily on wet materials for the bottom and walls. After being put into position, these were molded and shaped by her body as she sat inside, scratching and moving from side to side. As the material dried it tended to hold to the shaped configuration. The innermost lining material was added dry, and the interior would take on a frayed, rather than smooth, appearance in a day or so unless the female revisited periodically and sat within. The total time spent by females constructing their nests was difficult to determine accurately, particularly since they tended to abort the effort if disturbed by an observer. Nonetheless, some crude data were accumulated (total building time determined to the nearest half-day).

Despite the lower volume of materials placed into ground nests as opposed to elevated nests, there was no difference in their construction times. What did vary, however, was the construction time for first nests of the season versus those built subsequently as replacements. First nests required a mean of 2.5 d (SD = 0.5 d, N = 23, min = 2 d, max = 3.5 d) whereas replacement nests required one d less (mean = 1.5 d, SD = 0.5 d, N = 14, min = 1 d, max = 2.5 d), a significant difference (t = 11.80, P < 0.001). Four first nests that were under construction at a time when snowstorms occurred were not included in these data. Usually snowed-upon, unfinished nests were abandoned, but in these four cases construction was resumed after a pause of three or four days, more than doubling the usual duration of construction. Direct observations of building females showed that effort devoted to first nests was discontinuous, and that when building bouts occurred, trips were usually three min or more apart. Renests, on the other hand, involved a more concerted effort. Trip frequency was sometimes one per min, even one per 10 sec, and in five of the 14 that were observed, the entire nest was built during one daylight period.

Nests built in elevated positions were much bulkier in appearance and weighed more than twice as much as ground nests (Table 7.1). From a thorough analysis of the composition, dimensions, and thermal properties of *oriantha* nests collected from our study area, Kern (1984) found that elevated nests had a greater propor-

TABLE 7.2.   DIMENSIONS AND THERMAL PROPERTIES OF *Oriantha* NESTS ACCORDING TO LOCATION

	Nest location		
	Ground	Elevated	P
Nest dimensions (cm)			
Height	5.9	8.7	<0.01
Depth of nest cavity	3.8	3.8	NS
Wall thickness	3.8	3.8	NS
Floor thickness	2.1	3.9	<0.05
Surface area of nest cavity (cm^2)	70.3	71.5	NS
Wind resistance (% of airstream penetrating)			
Walls	3.8	1.1	<0.05
Floor	1.8	0.6	NS
Thermal conductance (W · m^{-2} · °C^{-1})			
Walls	8.1	6.8	NS
Floor	4.1	3.0	<0.005

Note: Nests were collected during laying or incubation (Kern 1984). P-value from t-test of mean differences; sample size in Table 7.1.

tion of coarse grass and twigs than ground nests, thus accounting for their extra mass and bulk (Table 7.1). In both nest types the inner lining consisted mostly of very thin blades of bunchgrass (*Muhlenbergia* sp.).

Elevated nests had thicker floors, and thus had higher walls than ground nests, because the depth of the nest cup and its surface area were the same for the two types (Table 7.2). Uniformity in cup dimensions is to be expected because they were the product of female body size and not nest position. Nest cups were generally wider than deep, and their width increased in active nests due to the growth and movements of nestlings (Morton et al. 1972a, Kern 1984).

Thermal properties

Kern (1984) also found in the laboratory that elevated nests tended to be less penetrated by wind than ground nests and that their conductance (the reciprocal of insulation) was lower (Table 7.2). Porosity of walls, rather than their thickness, was a decisive factor here. Bear in mind that ground nests were usually located in highly sheltered positions and if thermal properties of nests had been measured *in situ* they might well have proven to be more effectively insulated than elevated nests. Indirectly, this is borne out by egg temperatures recorded from the two types of nests (Fig. 7.1). When ambient temperatures began to drop below 16 C, mean egg temperature began declining more rapidly in elevated than in ground nests. This trend was reversed when it was colder than 8 C, probably because females incubating in elevated nests began shivering in order to defend their body temperatures. Similar responses were observed in Dusky Flycatchers (*Empidonax oberholseri*) also nesting at Tioga Pass (Morton and Pereyra 1985).

These data suggest that the lower critical temperature of *oriantha,* the ambient temperature where shivering thermogenesis begins, is much lower in females sitting in their nests (about 8 C in elevated nests, and probably much lower in ground nests) than it is presumed to be in those perched outside the nest (about 23 C; Maxwell and King 1976).

Since the eggs and body of an incubating female form an integral thermal unit (Drent 1975), and since egg temperature is about three degrees cooler than core

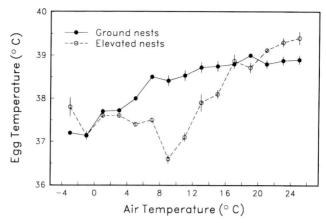

FIGURE 7.1.   Mean egg temperatures (± 1 SE) recorded during constant attentiveness by incubating female *oriantha*. Modified from Zerba and Morton 1983a).

body temperature in *oriantha,* core temperature at onset of shivering in females that were incubating in elevated nests must have been about 39–40 C; in other words, about three degrees above that of the eggs when they were first boosted upward (Fig. 7.1). Note that incubation patch temperature was found to be less than one degree cooler than core temperature (see below).

The increase in metabolism by females incubating in elevated nests may not have been trivial because temperatures at Tioga Pass were often below 8 C in the daytime, and nearly always so at night. Recall that body mass of females with elevated nests was about 5% lower than in those with ground nests (Chapter 6), another indicator that their energy expenditure was higher. It seems that females adjusted to the thermal environment of elevated sites by building in those locations nests with less-porous, better-insulated walls. But the walls were not thicker than those of ground nests, and despite being in a more tightly woven nest, the eggs, and by inference, the female's body, were susceptible to cooling. To overcome this, females had to expend more energy. This could have been prevented, one assumes, if elevated nests were larger and bulkier, but this would undoubtedly have made them more visible to predators. Thus, a trade-off seems to be present between predation avoidance and energy cost to the incubating female when she chooses to build above the ground. In a review of metabolic rates taken under field conditions, Williams (1996) concluded that incubation is not a time of reduced energy expenditure for birds, a result that tends to be supported by our data on body mass and egg temperatures of *oriantha* females striving to keep themselves and their eggs warm during the cold mountain nights, particularly when their nests were in exposed locations.

An additional interesting outcome of Kern's (1984) study was that the thermal conductance of elevated nests varied with their distance from the ground; the higher the nest was placed, the more conductance (and the poorer the insulation). It remains to be shown, but perhaps the amount and types of materials used is correlated with nest height and/or predation frequency. In a comparison of insulative properties of nests of 11 North American passerines, Skowron and Kern (1980) found that heat flux was fourth-lowest in *oriantha.*

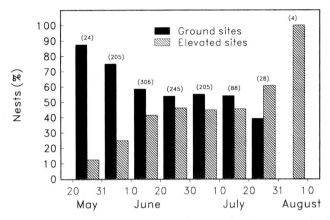

FIGURE 7.2.   Seasonal change in nest locations (on the ground or in elevated sites) for *oriantha* at Tioga Pass. Sample sizes in parentheses.

Nest sites

Nests are often in peril from predators and from fluctuations in microclimate and weather. As alluded to above, these forces seem to exert selection pressures on nest size that are in opposition to one another. A well-hidden nest, in a cavity under thick vegetation, for example, could be well protected from both of these factors. But when ground cover is sparse or when elevated locations are utilized, sites are less sheltered, and nests should be provided with more insulation. In other words, they should be larger and/or more densely constructed. However, predators would seem more likely to detect larger nests.

Nest sites utilized by *oriantha* ranged from those placed on the ground with little surrounding cover, other than short, dry grass, to elevated positions among thick pine boughs or crowns of willows. Data accumulated in every year of the study on nest positions indicate that both ground and elevated sites were used heavily but, overall, ground sites were preferred, 59.6% to 40.4% (N = 776 ground nests and 525 elevated nests, Chi-square = 48.4, df = 1, P < 0.001).

Because nest sites were tagged every year, and because many were highly familiar to us, such as those that might be in a particular grassy hummock or isolated pine, we were able to determine that some sites were used repeatedly by the same female and, over the years, by different females. Of 508 first nests of the season built on TPM, 29 or 5.7% were located under or within the same pine or willow as a previous nest. Eighteen of these 29, or 3.5% of the total, were thought to have been in precisely the same place as a nest from a previous year. We were certain of this because the spot had unique features or because the new nest was built on the remnants of an old one (most nests were destroyed every winter but sometimes material from an old nest did remain in place). One year an *oriantha* female built her nest inside a well-preserved American Robin nest from the year before.

Nests tended to be placed in different locations during the season. Ground sites were the most heavily utilized in May, but elevated sites were selected nearly half of the time in June and July, and in late July and August they were preferred (Fig 7.2). Nests in elevated sites were placed either in willows or pines. For the first

TABLE 7.3. Seasonal Change in Type of Vegetation Utilized by *Oriantha* Females for Nests Placed in Elevated Sites

Date	Vegetation utilized		N
	Pines (%)	Willows (%)	
20–31 May	66.7	33.3	3
1–10 June	56.9	43.1	51
11–20 June	51.6	48.4	126
21–30 June	50.0	50.0	114
1–10 July	34.8	65.2	92
11–20 July	25.6	74.4	39
21–31 July	12.5	87.5	16
1–10 August	0.0	100.0	4

month or so of the nest-building season, pines were utilized slightly more than willows. Thereafter, willow sites predominated (Table 7.3). The very last nests of the season were built almost exclusively in the crowns of fully leafed-out willows. The picture drawn here about nest locations is an average one, taken over many seasons. It does not convey accurately the extent of inter-seasonal variations that were linked to snow conditions and that illustrated environmental adaptation by nesting females (Chapter 10 and Fig. 10.7).

Through the use of transects, the heights of pines and willows on the TPM portion of the study area were sampled to characterize that aspect of vegetation structure (Table 7.4). These data show that *oriantha* tended to nest beneath plants that were shorter than the average for that type (i.e., pine or willow), and within plants that were taller than the average (Table 7.4). The functional significance of these propensities has not been pursued, but a study of nest-site microclimates through the whole season might be worthwhile.

Mean nest height for elevated nests was 59.6 cm (SD = 53.5 cm, N = 508), and height distribution of nests was quite different in pines and willows. Willows could provide hiding places even when quite small, and most willow nests were located below 50 cm (mean = 41.3 cm, SD = 24.0 cm, min = 4 cm, max = 180 cm, N = 279). Pine nests occurred over a wider range of heights, although most were built at or above 50 cm, and they often occurred at well over 100 cm (mean = 82.2 cm, SD = 68.9 cm, min = 12 cm, max = 650 cm, N = 229). The highest willow nests tended to be those built late in the season in the crown area whereas the highest pine nests occurred when deep snow was present and more traditionally used sites were scarce. When all elevated nests were compared, pine tree nests were significantly higher than willow nests (t = 8.58, P < 0.001).

The function of a bird's nest is to provide warmth and safety for the developing

TABLE 7.4. Height of Individual Pines and Willows (cm) on Tioga Pass Meadow as Sampled in Transects, and Nested Beneath (Ground Nests) or Nested Within (Elevated Nests) by *Oriantha*

	Plant height								
	Transects			Nested beneath			Nested within		
	Mean	SD	N	Mean	SD	N	Mean	SD	N
Pine	174.2	84.0	484	142.1	200.0	42	194.1	160.7	161
Willow	84.5	47.1	784	60.9	51.1	318	125.7	51.8	140

eggs and young (Collias and Collias 1984). Thus it should be built so as to counteract weather effects as well as those of predation, a supposition which is frequently borne out by field data (Lawton and Lawton 1980, McGillivray 1981, Martin and Roper 1988). Nest-site selection is a key behavior affecting reproductive success and it has presumably evolved in relation to a variety of factors. Among these are local availability of resources, including food and nesting materials, shelter or a favorable microclimate, and concealment from predators (Walsberg 1981, Collias and Collias 1984). Judged from the perspective of success, interaction of these factors would seem to have a similar outcome in ground and elevated *oriantha* nests: fledging success was 44.7% (335 of 750) in ground nests and 49.0% (245 of 500) in elevated nests, an insignificant difference (Chi-square = 2.26, df = 1, P = 0.132).

Although ground sites are thought to represent the primitive condition for birds, factors such as disturbance, predation, and competition probably led eventually to sites being selected off the ground, often in dense shrubbery (Preston and Norris 1947). A study of 233 nests of 26 open-cup nesters, utilizing 62 different plant species, showed that nest height varied directly with plant height (Gates 1979). As in the present study, first nests of the season were placed lower than later nests in response to growth and increased density of foliage as leaf emergence occurred. Presumably, this is an anti-predator response (Nice 1937, Walkinshaw 1939, Salt 1966). That view may be too simple, however, because microclimates can also change markedly with vegetation development. Horváth (1964) found, for example, that movement of hummingbird nests from low sites in spring to high ones in summer probably occurred because low sites were buffered from climate extremes and high sites were cooler because of evapo-transpiration from trees.

Concealment of nests from predators and protection from weather can both be accomplished if the nest is placed in the proper location, such as among thick boughs (Martin and Roper 1988). Still there are situations wherein elements of nest construction or orientation seem to be primarily in response to microclimatic factors. For example, the nest opening or entrance can be oriented toward the warming sun of early morning (Austin 1976), or away from the direction of prevailing winds and storms (McGillivray 1981, Böhm and Landmann 1995), especially in the alpine (Verbeek 1970, Norment 1993). In addition, nests may be situated beneath a plant canopy so as to create a favorable radiative environment, a situation found in Warbling Vireos (Walsberg 1981) and in *oriantha* (Walsberg and King 1978). *Oriantha* at Tioga Pass also tended to position their nests on the northeastern side of bushes, away from the southern winds that brought most of the cold air and storms onto the study area (Zerba and Morton 1983a).

Egg Laying

Many passerines make over a thousand trips in constructing their nest, so this endeavor requires a great deal of time and energy (Collias and Collias 1984). And once the nest is built females must also accomplish another energetically-expensive function, egg laying. The nest-ready interval, the interval between building and laying, will be examined next to learn more about the relative importance of physiological preparation and of energetic constraints in determining the temporal phasing of these events.

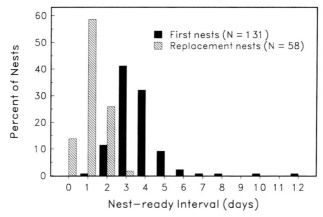

FIGURE 7.3. Nest-ready interval (days between nest completion and laying of first egg) in *oriantha* at Tioga Pass.

Nest-ready interval

During the first three years of this study, the average of the time between the end of nest construction and laying of the first egg was found to be 2.5 d (Morton et al. 1972a). Many more data are now available, and it appears that the duration of the nest-ready interval depends upon the nest's history. For example, first nests of the season usually sat empty for several days before laying began (mean = 3.63 d, SD = 1.40 d, min = 1 d, max = 12 d). Replacement nests, on the other hand, were empty for a much shorter time (mean = 1.16 d, SD = 0.67 d, min = 0 d, max = 3 d; Fig. 7.3), a highly significant difference (t = 16.42, P < 0.001).

In two of the 12 first nests of the season with a nest-ready interval of five days, and in all of the remaining seven nests wherein the interval was six days or more, the delay in laying could be attributed to intervention by snowstorms. Usually nests that had been constructed, but not yet laid in, were abandoned when covered by snow. In a few cases, however, the female returned after the thaw to begin laying, thus extending the interval to as long as 12 days (Fig. 7.3).

The physiological condition of females building these two types of nests must have been quite different. Since ovulation precedes oviposition by approximately 24 hr, it is clear that many of the renesting females finished their nests at just about the time they ovulated; 34 of 58 (58.6%) of the nests were empty for only one day (Fig. 7.3). There were even eight cases (13.8%) wherein the nest was built in entirety on the day before laying, yielding a nest-ready interval of zero days. In three of these eight, females were observed adding more nest lining material on the morning of the first egg, after laying had already occurred; one of them was moving the lining from her old nest to the new one, rather than gathering fresh material. Obviously some renesting females accomplished all or nearly all of their nest building while heavily engaged in vitellogenesis and even while carrying an egg in the oviduct. For first nests this situation was quite different. Females built them at a more leisurely pace and then usually did not lay until several days had elapsed. Judging from concurrent changes in body mass (see Fig. 6.4), the nest-ready interval coincided closely to the time (3–4 d) required to prepare physiologically and metabolically for laying. In these situations, nest building and rapid ovarian development did not overlap.

This temporal flexibility in the nest-ready interval, as shown by the influence of environmental conditions and by the difference between first nests and renests, strongly indicates that nest building and ovarian preparation for oviposition are controlled by different mechanisms. Furthermore, their co-occurrence in renesting females shows that neither function by itself exerts maximal energetic stress.

Laying times

Egg laying occurred in the early morning hours in *oriantha,* at about sunrise or shortly thereafter. By watching laying females from concealment or by frequent visits to their nests, we were able to show that mean time of laying was 05:44 (SD = 0.7 hr, N = 32) and that the time did not vary with egg order (Oppenheimer et al. 1996). In 16 instances for which laying times between successive eggs were known, it averaged 24.1 hr (SD = 0.9 hr).

Laying occurred, with few exceptions, on successive days until the clutch was completed. There was no effect on the laying schedule by conditions such as sub-freezing temperatures or storms unless the storm was severe enough to interrupt the nesting cycle altogether. In only four of many hundreds of nests monitored did it appear that the regular sequence of ovipositions was broken. In other words, a day of laying was skipped. In three cases the skip followed the first egg, in the other case the second egg. Our discovery of the nest could have disturbed the laying female and caused her to lay one egg somewhere away from the nest, but in these four nests we doubt this happened. More likely, the female failed to ovulate or the oviduct failed to capture the ovum.

DESCRIPTION OF EGGS

Oriantha eggs were pale blue with reddish brown spots. Spots were usually irregular in shape and ranged in size from tiny specks to 2 mm or more in greatest dimension. They could be distributed rather uniformly over the whole egg but usually they were concentrated toward the blunt end. Occasionally spots were condensed into a band or ring on the blunt end. In a long-term study of captive Village Weavers (*Ploceus cucullatus*), Collias (1984, 1993) found that the color and amount of spotting of eggs was constant throughout a female's lifetime. Eggs within *oriantha* clutches closely resembled one another in appearance and this resemblance carried over into consecutive clutches (a direct comparison of eggs could be made when a first clutch was deserted with eggs intact and the renest was found).

EGG DIMENSIONS

Eggs were numbered on their blunt ends throughout the breeding season according to laying order, if known, for 13 consecutive years, 1981 to 1993. Many were then measured with calipers to the nearest 0.01 mm to obtain maximum lengths and widths. A sample of 25 eggs from seven clutches was also weighed within two hr of laying in order to obtain the fresh egg mass. Maximum lengths and widths of these same 25 eggs were then entered into Hoyt's (1979) formula for determining egg volume: volume = 0.51 × length × width^2. The eggs had a mean mass of 3.20 g (SD = 0.12 g) and a mean volume of 3.20 cm^3 (SD = 0.13

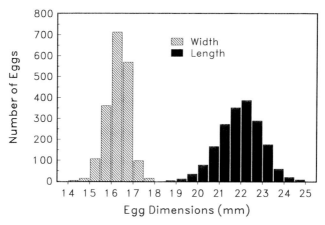

FIGURE 7.4.   Frequency distribution of width and length measurements of 2,030 *oriantha* eggs.

cm³). A regression of calculated volume on measured mass showed the two to be highly correlated (r^2 = 0.952, P < 0.001). It appears, therefore, that fresh egg mass can be reliably estimated from egg dimensions.

Length and width measurements were obtained on 2,030 eggs. Both measures were rather symmetrically distributed (Fig. 7.4). Mean width was 16.29 mm (SD = 0.51 mm) and mean length was 21.99 mm (SD = 1.00 mm), a length-to-width ratio of 1.35. Egg widths ranged from 14.05 to 17.88 mm and lengths from 18.46 to 27.50 mm, so, even at their extremes, these dimensions did not overlap. A single runt egg, 13.09 × 17.41 mm, that did not hatch was omitted from this analysis.

The fact that calculated volumes seemed to predict egg mass suggests that a regular relationship exists between egg length and width. To test this idea width was regressed on length for all 2,030 eggs in the sample. This gave the line, Y = 0.183X + 12.25, and an r value of 0.36, slightly below the one of 0.41 found for Hooded Crow (*Corvus corone*) eggs by Rofstad and Sandvik (1985). Egg volumes, as calculated from the linear measurements, were normally distributed in *oriantha* (Fig. 7.5). Mean volume was 2.98 cm³ (SD = 0.26 cm³) and, disregarding the lone runt egg, ranged from 1.95 to 3.83 cm³, almost a two-fold difference.

Egg size has been shown to be a highly heritable trait in a diverse array of avian species (Moss and Watson 1982, Byrkjedal and Kålås 1985, Wiggins 1990), and the major share of variation in egg dimensions is genetic (Ojanen et al. 1979, Van Noordwijk et al. 1980). There is little unequivocal evidence, however, that a positive relationship exists between egg size and offspring fitness in birds (Williams 1994). Still, egg size is an important determinant of reproductive investment (Flint and Grand 1996), and volumes are known to vary among years and between nesting sites as, for example, in American Pipits (*Anthus rubescens*) breeding at high altitude in Montana (Hendricks 1991). At Tioga Pass, egg volume in *oriantha* also varied significantly among the 13 years (ANOVA $F_{12, 1986}$ = 4.17, P < 0.001). Eggs averaged the smallest in 1991, 2.92 cm³ (N = 230), and the largest in 1984, 3.07 cm³ (N = 175), a 5.1% difference.

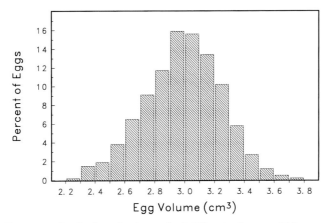

FIGURE 7.5.   Frequency distribution of volumes for 2,030 *oriantha* eggs. Volumes were determined from Hoyt's (1979) formula.

EGG VOLUME

The characteristics of eggs, especially their size and number, provide useful information for quantifying reproductive investment. In a long-term study, furthermore, it is possible to evaluate this investment within a context of environmental variability and also in relation to clutch size and to traits of individuals such as age, body size, and body condition. This sort of information can then be used to test models and hypotheses that address differential investment strategies (Slagsvold et al. 1984).

Collias (1984, 1993) has shown that individual Village Weavers in captivity (where environmental conditions can be expected to vary minimally) laid eggs of a consistent size and shape from one year to the next. In *oriantha,* however, significant interannual variation in egg volumes were found in three of six females whose eggs were measured over a span of four to seven consecutive years (Table 7.5).

Effect of clutch size

An inverse relationship commonly occurs between egg size and clutch size, suggesting that a trade-off exists between quality or size of young and their numbers (Blackburn 1991). This relationship was not found in *oriantha,* however (Table 7.6). Egg size did not vary significantly with clutch size (ANOVA $F_{5, 2024}$ = 2.26, P = 0.060).

TABLE 7.5.   INTERANNUAL VARIATIONS IN EGG VOLUME (%) IN SIX *Oriantha* FEMALES

Band number	Years of data	Number of clutches	Percent variation	ANOVA F	P
127169348	7	7	11.5	2.395	0.066
138116546	4	4	16.3	6.192	0.009
138116752	5	5	4.8	1.175	0.367
138116782	5	7	8.3	0.946	0.458
138116935	4	6	7.7	4.502	0.015
138116942	4	5	11.1	4.321	0.024

TABLE 7.6. Egg Volume According to Clutch Size in *Oriantha* at Tioga Pass

Egg volume (cm³)	Clutch size				
	2	3	4	5	6
Mean	2.98	2.98	2.98	2.39	3.12
SD	0.28	0.27	0.26	0.29	0.18
No. of eggs	18	228	1,592	180	12

Effect of season

Egg volumes did vary with season, however. When plotted according to laying date, a distinctive pattern emerged (Fig. 7.6). Volumes were lowest in May and June and highest in July and August, and the difference was highly significant (Table 7.7). This seasonal difference could be related to the nesting history of females because, as one might suspect from examining Fig. 7.6, eggs in first nests of the season were not as large as those in subsequent nests (Table 7.7). Linear dimensions also varied significantly when segregated seasonally by laying date or nest type (Table 7.7).

Egg size decreased significantly in late June then increased (Fig. 7.6). Inspection of the data revealed that this effect could be attributed to four years of light snowpack (1987, 1988, 1990, and 1992) when nesting began early. In those four years, eggs had a mean volume of 3.00 cm³ (SD = 0.23 cm³, N = 219) when laid before 20 June and 2.87 cm³ (SD = 0.22 cm³, N = 75) when laid between 21 and 30 June, a highly significant difference (t = 4.33, P < 0.001).

Effect of female age

Egg size was essentially invariant with female age in Great Tits and Pied Fly-catchers (*Ficedula hypoleuca*; Ojanen et al. 1979, Järvinen and Pryl 1989), but it seemed to increase in Tree Swallows (*Tachycineta bicolor*), at least for the first two years of life (Wiggins 1990). In *oriantha*, a regression of 1,729 egg volumes on the ages of the females that laid them indicated that there was no significant relationship between the two (r² = 0.032, P = 0.090), nor did clutch volume

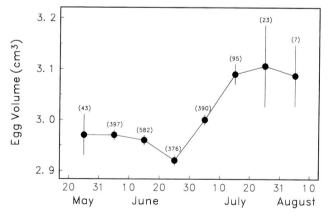

FIGURE 7.6. Seasonal changes in egg volume (mean ± 1 SE) in *oriantha* at Tioga Pass in relation to laying date. Number of eggs in parentheses.

TABLE 7.7. VARIATION IN SIZE OF *Oriantha* EGGS IN RELATION TO LAYING DATE AND TO TYPE OF NEST

Egg dimension	Laying Date								Type of nest							
	May–June			July–August					First nest			Renest				
	Mean	SD	N	Mean	SD	N	t	P	Mean	SD	N	Mean	SD	N	t	P
Volume (cm^3)	2.96	0.26	1,398	3.02	0.27	515	4.88	<0.001	2.95	0.26	1,005	3.01	0.26	502	4.62	<0.001
Width (cm)	16.25	0.49	1,398	16.42	0.87	515	4.09	<0.001	16.23	0.51	1,005	16.42	0.83	502	4.81	<0.001
Length (cm)	21.91	1.02	1,398	22.11	1.25	515	3.20	0.001	21.90	1.02	1,005	22.03	1.13	502	2.18	0.029

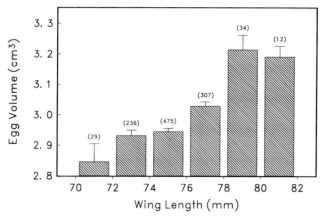

FIGURE 7.7.   Relationship of mean egg volume (+ SE) to female body size, as measured by wing length, in *oriantha*. Number of eggs in parentheses.

differ with female age ($r^2 = 0.060$, $P = 0.213$, $N = 438$). The influence of nest type (first nest or renest) observed in Table 7.7 persisted with age; eggs in renests (which included replacement clutches and double broods) were significantly larger than those in first clutches at all ages.

Effect of female size

A positive relationship between egg size and female size has been demonstrated in a large number of avian species (Ojanen et al. 1979, Otto 1979, Byrkjedal and Kålås 1985, Järvinen and Ylimaunu 1986, Rohwer 1988, Järvinen and Pryl 1989, Järvinen 1991), and *oriantha* were no different, although the relationship was weak ($r^2 = 0.048$, $P < 0.001$, $N = 1,093$; Fig. 7.7). King and Hubbard (1981) suggested that most variation in egg mass in fringillids can be accounted for by female mass and that any remaining variation will be small and of questionable ecological significance. They make an interesting point, but they may have underestimated the difficulties involved in evaluating female mass. Murphy (1986), for example, found that egg mass and female mass were not correlated in Eastern Kingbirds (*Tyrannus tyrannus*). Egg mass was correlated, however, with a measure of body condition, the flight muscle weight.

Effect of nutrition

In wild, unmanipulated birds it is difficult to tie egg size to female condition because the latter can change so rapidly in the time immediately preceding egg synthesis. In general, the summed contributions from stored nutrients and concurrent foraging are usually sufficient for females to lay high-quality eggs. At Tioga Pass, however, there were years when the snow cover persisted for many weeks into the potential breeding season. Females (and males) were present on the study area, but nesting sites were covered with snow and unavailable. In these situations, food appeared to be scarce and individuals were known to move periodically to lower elevations, probably to obtain better foraging opportunities (Hahn and Morton 1995).

Were egg sizes affected in females exposed to these kinds of environmental conditions? To address this question, egg volumes obtained from the 10 earliest

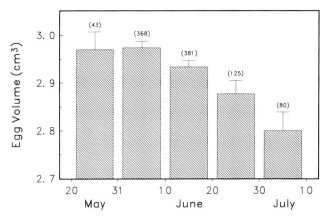

FIGURE 7.8.   Mean volume (+ SE) of eggs laid in the first 10 nests of the season by *oriantha* at Tioga Pass Meadow. Number of eggs in parentheses.

clutches produced in each season were separated out and plotted by laying date. These data show that females laid smaller eggs in the first week of the nesting season in years when onset of nesting was delayed until 20 June or later (Fig. 7.8, ANOVA $F_{4, 996} = 9.14$, $P < 0.001$). This could be evidence for a nutritional effect on egg size because delayed nesting was associated with deep snow, undeveloped vegetation, and trips to lower altitude, all indicators of suboptimal foraging conditions.

Effect of laying order

Egg volumes did not vary significantly with laying order, except in 5-egg clutches. The difference in volume between first- and last-laid eggs in a clutch was less than 2% for clutch sizes of 2, 3, and 4, although it did increase by more than 8% in 5-egg clutches (Table 7.8). Egg size was found to increase with laying order in 4-egg clutches, however, when sizes were standardized to account for intra-clutch variation (Mead and Morton 1985).

There is considerable interest in the way reserves are apportioned during the laying sequence because the most prevalent patterns may reflect differential in-

TABLE 7.8.   EGG VOLUME (CM^3) WITH EGG NUMBER (= LAYING ORDER) IN *Oriantha*, ACCORDING TO CLUTCH SIZE

	Clutch size											
	2			3			4			5		
Egg number	Mean	SD	N	Mean	SD	N	Mean	SD	N	Mean	SD	N
1	2.97	0.27	8	2.93	0.28	41	2.95	0.27	198	2.78	0.21	19
2	2.98	0.33	8	3.00	0.28	41	2.97	0.24	198	2.86	0.21	19
3				2.99	0.29	41	2.97	0.25	198	2.87	0.24	19
4							3.00	0.28	198	2.98	0.22	19
5										3.01	0.36	19
Percent change[a]		0.34			1.82			1.62			8.27	
ANOVA F		0.01			0.64			1.44			2.76	
P		0.948			0.529			0.229			0.032	

[a] Comparison of first and last eggs in the clutch.

TABLE 7.9. Frequencies at Which Eggs of Known Laying Order in 4-egg Clutches Were Smallest or Largest Within Their Respective Clutches (N = 198 Clutches)

	Laying order			
	1	2	3	4
Smallest (% of cases)	38.4	19.7	22.7	19.2
Largest (% of cases)	26.8	18.2	17.7	37.4

vestment strategies by females (Howe 1976, 1978). It is common among open-nesting passerines, for example, for the last-laid egg to be the largest in the clutch, and Slagsvold et al. (1984), in a highly influential paper, have argued that this is adaptive. [Larger eggs usually produce heavier but not dimensionally larger chicks; chicks are heavier because they have more nutrient (yolk) reserves (Williams 1994)].

Because passerines usually begin incubating before clutch completion, hatching asynchrony occurs and late-hatched young are competitively disadvantaged because they are behind their older siblings on the growth curve. Since egg size and hatching size of the chick are tightly coupled, and since increased body size confers competitive advantage, it is reasoned that last-laid eggs should be large to maximize survival of all members of the brood. This is the brood-survival strategy (Slagsvold et al. 1984). Alternatively, some species exhibit decreased egg size with laying order and the last egg or eggs are smallest. These species, many of which have large clutches, are said to be following a brood-reduction strategy (Slagsvold and Lifjeld 1989).

Is there evidence in our data, other than that already presented on small increases in volume with laying order, that *oriantha* might be following either one of these strategies? When we examined egg-size hierarchies in the modal clutch, 4-eggs, a surprising result emerged: egg 1 was indeed most often the smallest (38.4% of clutches) and egg 4 the largest (37.4% of clutches), but after egg 4, egg 1 was also most frequently the *largest* (26.8% of clutches, Table 7.9). Among the 198 4-egg clutches where all eggs were numbered on the day of laying and subsequently measured, two patterns prevailed in 91 (46.0%) of the clutches: in one, eggs 1 and 4 were both larger than eggs 2 and 3 (53 clutches), and in the other, egg 1 was the smallest in the clutch and egg 4 the largest (38 clutches). A close check of the data shows that the frequency of large first eggs decreased with season whereas the frequency of small first eggs increased. Since egg 4 remained fairly stable in hierarchical status throughout, a seasonal change in egg size pattern occurred (Fig. 7.9). Essentially, females laid eggs in decreasing size from 1 to 3 followed by a large number 4 during the first half of the summer. They then switched to a pattern of increasing size with laying order during the second half. Note that in both patterns the last egg tended to be large, as predicted by a brood-survival strategy. The seasonal switch in pattern of egg size with laying order supports Perrins' (1996) proposal that environmental cues, such as food supply, influence egg size. Perhaps both ecological (food availability) and evolutionary (brood survival) factors interact in laying *oriantha* to give these seasonal effects.

There are no consistent hierarchical patterns in egg size with laying sequence for passerines as a whole, although consistency can sometimes be found within

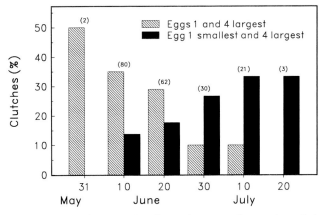

FIGURE 7.9. Seasonal changes in hierarchy of egg size, according to date of clutch start, within 198 4-egg clutches laid by *oriantha* at Tioga Pass. Number of clutches in parentheses.

species. For example, egg size increased steadily with laying order in Goldcrests (*Regulus regulus*; Haftorn 1986), Least Flycatchers (*Empidonax minimus*; Briskie and Sealy 1990), Tree Swallows (Wiggins 1990), captive Bengalese Finches (*Lonchura striata*; Coleman and Whittall 1990), Eurasian Blackbirds (*Turdus merula*; Rydén 1978), and Common Grackles (*Quiscalus quiscula*; Howe 1976). On the other hand, the opposite pattern was observed in Hooded Crows (Rofstad and Sandvik 1985), no difference was detected in Black-eared Wheatears (*Oenanthe hispanica*; Suarez 1991) and, in the present study, *oriantha* switched patterns seasonally. Still the majority of passerines appear to increase provisioning in their last-laid eggs, thereby following a brood-survival strategy.

At this time there is no agreement, however, that intra-clutch variations in egg mass are adaptive. Several investigators are convinced that such variations are unselected and simply the result of prevailing energetic conditions. For example, four species of hole-nesting passerines in subarctic Finland showed egg volume variations that were unrelated to laying order, laying date, clutch size, or female age. Instead, female mass or condition, and thus egg size, was correlated with ambient temperatures, presumably because of the energy costs of thermoregulation. Eggs were smaller when cold weather occurred prior to laying times, and larger when there was warm weather. The authors concluded that these environmental effects were sufficient to explain intra-clutch variations in egg size (Ojanen et al. 1981, Järvinen and Väisänen 1983, Järvinen and Ylimaunu 1986; Järvinen 1991, 1994).

Bancroft (1984) found that Boat-tailed Grackle (*Quiscalus major*) eggs were smaller early in the season because females were in relatively poor body condition. Egg size has also been linked to food availability or female body condition in various other species such as Eastern Kingbirds (Murphy 1986), Fieldfares (*Turdus pilaris*; Otto 1979), and European Starlings (Greig-Smith et al. 1988). Magrath (1992) found that egg mass in Eurasian Blackbirds correlated directly with air temperatures that occurred during the period of rapid follicular growth. Thus, seasonal increases in egg mass appear to be related to ambient conditions and associated thermoregulatory costs to laying females.

Magrath (1992) also pointed out that the variation in size of last-laid eggs is probably too small to have much effect on sibling competition in nestlings. Rather than endorse the ideas proposed about brood-survival strategies by Slagsvold et al. (1984), he suggests that last-laid eggs appear to be more vulnerable to environmental fluctuations, and since egg viability is tied to egg size, a tendency to lay larger eggs late in the clutch might be selected for to counter the increased risk. He calls this the environmental variance hypothesis. There are two corollaries: smaller species will be less-well buffered against environmental variance than larger ones and should, therefore, lay relatively larger last eggs, and open-nesting species should lay relatively larger last eggs than hole nesters because the latter have more sheltered nest sites. Both of these relationships have been documented by Slagsvold et al. (1984).

How can the *oriantha* data be interpreted in light of these hypotheses? The mid-summer decline in egg size (Fig. 7.6), which occurred in years of light snowpack, might have been related to deteriorating environmental conditions (a lowering of insect availability as the habitat dried up, for example), whereas the larger eggs in July and August (Table 7.7) might have been the result of decreased thermoregulatory costs to laying females because of warmer weather. The same could be said about the difference in egg size between first nests and renests. The decrease in egg size observed in the first eggs of the season in heavy snowpack years is evidence for an environmental effect on egg volume (Fig. 7.8); the later in the season females began laying, the smaller their eggs. We know that *oriantha* can subsist on a wide variety of foods, and that they readily move to lower altitude when exposed to storms or a persistent snow cover. This high degree of omnivory and mobility makes quantification of food availability an impossible task, but this might not be necessary if body mass of females is a reliable indicator of overall condition and readiness to lay.

This idea was evaluated by comparing body masses during the 21 days preceding the appearance of the first eggs on TPM in 1988 and 1995. Recall that, ecologically speaking, these were very different years, with commencement of first clutches being more than a month apart due to snow conditions (Fig. 5.4). Body mass during this 21-d interval was not different in females (1988: mean = 26.15 g, SD = 1.67 g, N = 60; 1995: mean = 25.80 g, SD = 1.72 g, N = 51; t = 1.08, P = 0.280), or in males (1988: mean = 27.96 g, SD = 1.60 g, N = 112; 1995: mean = 27.99 g, SD = 1.26 g, N = 88; t = 0.15, P = 0.880). This indicates that omnivory and altitudinal movements were effective strategies for maintaining energy balance under a wide range of environmental conditions. It is not known if the precise nutritional needs of these first 10 laying females were being met in late years, however, nor are there enough body mass data to see just how effectively they accumulated reserves during those few days when ovulations were occurring. Functionally speaking, that brief three- or four-day period could be the crucial window of time when body condition is translated to egg mass. Variable environmental conditions encountered by females during nesting attempts could also be the reason why some females exhibited significant differences in egg volumes among years and some did not (Table 7.5). Taken together, intra-clutch variations in egg size in *oriantha* provide support for both the environmental variance hypothesis and the brood-survival hypothesis.

Effect of sex

We discovered several years ago that the volume of male eggs in *oriantha* was slightly larger than that of female eggs. This difference was significant if one controlled for inter-clutch variation in egg size, but not if all male eggs were simply compared to all female eggs, regardless of their relative sizes within a particular clutch. In addition, males were larger at hatching than their female siblings (Mead et al. 1987). Since reproductive success of adult males is probably more variable than that of females, these results were interpreted as being an example of facultative manipulation of offspring sex according to parental investment abilities (Trivers and Willard 1973). At the time our paper was written the sample size was 102 male eggs and 86 female eggs. The data set now contains 283 males and 288 females but there is still no significant difference when the volumes are compared directly (female eggs: mean = 2.99 cm^3, SD = 0.26 cm^3; male eggs: mean = 3.02 cm^3, SD = 0.25 cm^3; t = 1.39, P = 0.166).

WEIGHT LOSS OF EGGS DURING INCUBATION

Bird eggs typically lose about 18% of their initial mass during incubation. Since the mass exchanged by O_2 and CO_2 through pores in the egg shell are equal during this time, all of this loss is due to the diffusion of water vapor from the egg's interior. The total amount of water transferred is a function of pore geometry and area, and of the water vapor gradient, the latter being about 35 torr (Rahn and Ar 1974). Since the diffusion coefficient for gases is inversely related to barometric pressure, water loss of eggs should increase when birds nest at high altitude. Carey et al. (1983) showed, however, that rates of daily water loss during incubation, and final water content of hatching embryos, were independent of altitude in both Red-winged Blackbirds and American Robins nesting at elevations ranging from sea level to above 3,000 m. They found that modifications in water vapor conductance in eggshells were responsible for this effect; it decreased as altitude increased. This relationship was also observed in Cliff Swallows (*Petrochelidon pyrrhonota*; Sotherland et al. 1980).

The daily rate of water loss of eggs can change markedly from time of laying onward, especially once incubation begins, because the eggs are then warmed regularly by the incubating parent. Changes in shell structure can also occur due to wearing away or fissuring of the egg's cuticle and/or to erosion of the inner shell as minerals are extracted for ossification of the embryonic skeleton. The erosion process can lead to an increase in the functional cross-sectional area of pores and an increase in shell permeability (Booth and Seymour 1987, Kern et al. 1992).

Between *nuttalli*, the coastal-dwelling subspecies, and *oriantha*, White-crowned Sparrows nest over substantial altitudinal gradients, but their eggshell properties have not been determined. Egg masses were obtained for nine 4-egg *oriantha* clutches, however, from laying until hatching. They indicate that mass loss occurred from first day to last throughout the incubation period in all eggs. Mean mass of these 36 eggs on the day of laying was 3.12 g and at pipping time it was 2.60 g, a 16.7% decrease.

Plots of individual eggs indicate that the rate of mass loss tended to increase slightly as incubation proceeded (Fig. 7.10, Table 7.10). Loss was slowest at the

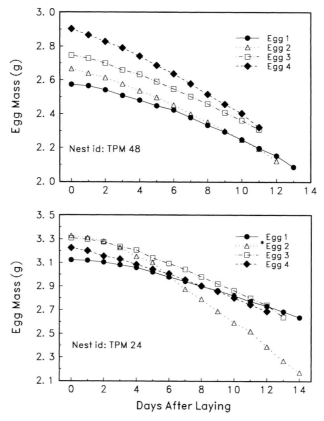

FIGURE 7.10.   Changes in egg mass for two *oriantha* clutches from day of laying onward. Note that egg no. 2 in nest TPM 24 (lower panel) was infertile.

TABLE 7.10.   PERCENT OF DAILY MASS LOSS IN *Oriantha* EGGS FROM DAY OF LAYING (DAY 0) ONWARD (VIABLE EGGS ONLY)

Age (days)	Mass loss from previous day (%)		
	Mean	SD	N
1	0.37	0.11	9
2	0.65	0.36	11
3	1.06	0.41	12
4	1.16	0.35	12
5	1.26	0.21	12
6	1.27	0.40	14
7	1.36	0.36	16
8	1.51	0.42	16
9	1.30	0.42	16
10	1.62	0.37	17
11	1.72	0.43	19
12	1.82	0.35	19
13	1.75	0.77	17
14	2.57	1.40	14

beginning, probably because females neglected their nests early in the laying period and first-laid eggs commonly became quite cold during the night (Zerba and Morton 1983b). The second egg in nest TPM 24 (bottom panel of Fig. 7.10) was infertile and it lost more mass than any of the other eggs. In contrast, a fertile egg in another nest (not shown) that suffered embryo death lost mass at a slower rate than other eggs in the clutch. The daily percentage of mass losses shown in Table 7.10 were obtained exclusively from eggs that hatched out live chicks.

CLUTCH SIZE

Clutch size is probably the most frequently assessed life history trait in studies of avian reproduction, and its variations have been correlated with a wide range of environmental and populational parameters as well as female condition. For example, it tends to decrease in passerines over the breeding season (Lack 1954, Klomp 1970, Middleton 1979, Bijlsma 1982, Ewald and Rohwer 1982, Daan et al. 1988, Perrins and McCleery 1989, Rowe et al. 1994, Brown and Brown 1999b), although this decline may be preceded by an early-season increase (Haukioja 1970, Smith and Andersen 1985, Askenmo and Unger 1986). It may also decrease when females are stressed energetically, as shown in handicapping experiments (Slagsvold and Lifjeld 1988, Winkler and Allen 1995). Clutch size has been observed to increase with population density (Slagsvold 1981), with age (Klomp 1970), with latitude (Morton 1976, Kulesza 1990), and with food availability (Hussell and Quinney 1987). Its variation also has a significant genetic component (Perrins and Jones 1975, von Brömssen and Jansson 1980, Gwinner et al. 1995).

The phenotypic plasticity of this trait has led some authors to conclude that it is optimized by individuals in response to environmental heterogeneity (Högstedt 1980, Tinbergen and Daan 1990). But clutch size can also covary with female survival rate (Nur 1988, Saether 1988, Lindén and Møller 1989), so a trade-off probably exists here between current and future reproduction (Charnov and Krebs 1974, Daan et al. 1990, Tinbergen and Daan 1990, Vander Werf 1992).

Interannual changes

Clutch size in 1,154 *oriantha* nests, observed during 23 years, ranged from two to six eggs, with the mode being four (878 or 76.1% of all nests) and the mean being 3.86 (Table 7.11). All two-egg clutches were laid after 15 July, near the end of the nesting season, whereas all 5- and 6-egg clutches were started before 15 July. Both of the 6-egg clutches that occurred in our study were deemed legitimate, and not the result of egg dumping, because eggs appeared in the nest at the rate of one per day, and because all the eggs in each clutch looked alike with regard to their background color and to the size and distribution of spots. Mean clutch size fluctuated among years by as much as 16.3% (1988 vs. 1992, Table 7.11), and this variation was significant (ANOVA $F_{22, 1153}$ = 3.36, P < 0.001).

Seasonal changes

There was also a significant seasonal change in clutch size. This was expressed as a monotonic decrease that became noticeable about midway through the time period used for nesting (Table 7.12). The data in Table 7.11 represent a 23-yr

TABLE 7.11.   Clutch Sizes in *Oriantha* at Tioga Pass During 23 Yr

Years	Clutch size					N	Mean	SD
	2	3	4	5	6			
1968	0	9	30	1	0	40	3.80	0.46
1969	0	5	41	1	0	47	3.92	0.35
1970	0	5	44	7	0	56	4.04	0.47
1973	0	3	23	0	0	26	3.88	0.33
1976	0	7	48	1	0	56	3.89	0.37
1978	0	16	36	0	0	52	3.69	0.47
1979	0	8	48	2	0	58	3.90	0.41
1980	1	14	50	4	0	69	3.83	0.54
1981	1	11	58	1	0	71	3.83	0.45
1982	0	14	58	9	0	81	3.94	0.54
1983	1	5	44	6	1	57	3.98	0.52
1984	0	13	40	5	0	58	3.86	0.54
1985	1	7	32	5	0	45	3.91	0.60
1986	0	3	46	3	0	52	4.00	0.34
1987	1	5	28	0	0	34	3.79	0.48
1988	0	0	16	2	1	19	4.21	0.53
1989	0	3	26	5	0	34	4.06	0.55
1990	0	6	37	3	0	46	3.93	0.44
1991	3	24	52	3	0	82	3.68	0.61
1992	4	23	52	1	0	80	3.64	0.62
1993	1	8	39	2	0	50	3.84	0.55
1994	1	5	23	1	0	30	3.80	0.55
1995	0	2	7	2	0	11	4.00	0.51
All	14	196	878	64	2	1,154	3.86	0.51

summary, but be reminded that in many years nesting did not begin until mid-June or later. This means that in early-nesting years many of the birds could be renesting during the same calendar period that those in late-nesting years were laying their first clutches. The question arises then, did clutch size vary seasonally in the same fashion in first nests as in renests? The answer is, yes. The seasonal pattern was, in fact, almost perfectly matched for the two types of nests, and means were not different in any of the five 10-day intervals wherein their schedules overlapped (Fig. 7.11).

Females gained considerable mass when preparing to lay and the brood patch was only partially defeathered when the season's first clutches were begun. Thereafter, until nesting was terminated, brood patches remained completely defeathered. From behavioral observations, body mass, and patch condition of known (banded) individuals, therefore, first nests could be distinguished from renests.

TABLE 7.12.   Seasonal Changes in Clutch Size in *Oriantha* According to First-egg Date (= Date of Clutch Initiation)

Date	Mean	SD	N
21–31 May	3.88	0.45	24
1–10 June	3.99	0.36	207
11–20 June	3.95	0.49	287
21–30 June	3.89	0.46	197
1–10 July	3.73	0.61	197
11–20 July	3.56	0.61	68
21–31 July	3.21	0.56	29
1–10 August	3.33	0.58	3

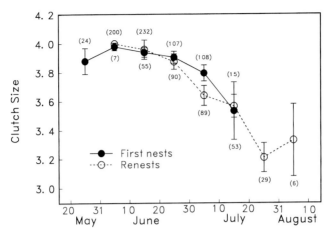

FIGURE 7.11. Seasonal changes in clutch size in first nests and renests (replacement clutches and double broods) in *oriantha* at Tioga Pass. Symbols indicate means ± 1 SE. Sample sizes (in parentheses) are shown above the symbols for first nests and below the symbols for renests.

Note that interannual variation in ecological conditions could be quite large at the time when initial clutches and replacement clutches were laid. Many of the initial clutches in heavy snow years were started in July in small islands of vegetation that had only recently thawed out from under the covering snow. Willows were unleafed and low and herbaceous vegetation, such as grasses and forbs, were also undeveloped; full growth of the vegetation did not occur in these years until the nesting season was nearly completed. In contrast, in light or moderate snow years nesting began in late May or early June. By early July the vegetation was completely regrown and all new nests were replacements.

Although clutch sizes of first nests and renests were evenly matched in size at all calendar intervals where they co-occurred, first nests tended to occur in higher numbers earlier in the season. Therefore, given the seasonal trend shown in Table 7.12, it is no surprise that clutch size of first nests was greater than that of renests: 3.92 ± 0.48 (N = 770) vs. 3.74 ± 0.57 (N = 342), respectively (t = 5.40, P < 0.001).

Clutch size did not vary with the age of either parent (females: r^2 = 0.004, P = 0.073, N = 783; males: r^2 = 0.003, P = 0.189, N = 652), nor did it vary with age of paired birds. A contingency table of pair ages arranged from 1 to 4+ yr of age for both sexes gave the following: Chi-square = 21.88, df = 15, P = 0.111. Clutch size also did not vary with body size, as expressed in wing length (females: r^2 = 0.003, P = 0.344, N = 284; males: r^2 = 0.001, P = 0.704, N = 234).

Compared to some passerine groups, such as hole-nesting parids, clutch size did not vary appreciably in *oriantha*; 76.1% of all clutches had four eggs and together three- and four-egg clutches comprised 93.1% of the 1,154 clutches reported in Table 7.11. Still there was a significant seasonal decrease in clutch size of about 0.8 eggs. When this decrease was partitioned into first nests or replacement nests, the seasonal change was the same in both nest types; within-season reproductive history did not affect clutch size but calendar date did (Fig. 7.11). The tendency for clutch size to decline with season has been linked to a presumed decrease in the quantity of food available to feed dependent young (Lack 1954, 1966), and with a decrease in offspring value (Rowe et al. 1994).

Laying dates are usually distributed on the upward slope of food supply, but fledging may occur before, during, or after the seasonal food peak (Daan et al. 1988). In *oriantha,* nesting often occurred under greatly different ecological conditions from year to year because of variation in the residual snowpack and in the frequency of early summer storms. As Lack (1947) pointed out long ago, confusion about the evolution of clutch size can occur because we fail to distinguish between the ultimate factors affecting survival value and the proximate factors affecting physiological control.

Because egg production is presumed to be energetically and nutritionally demanding for laying females, the development of theory about proximate control of clutch size has centered mostly on food availability in relation to energy requirements. But food supplementation studies of passerines in the wild have shown that while extra food tends to advance laying dates, clutch size usually remains unaffected (Ewald and Rohwer 1982, Davies and Lundberg 1985; Slagsvold and Lifjeld 1988, 1990). In other words, clutch size is largely independent of food supply (Daan et al. 1988, Rowe et al. 1994). The identical clutch sizes of *oriantha* in the same calendar period, despite greatly different environmental conditions wrought by snowpack variation, is consistent with this generalization. It has been hypothesized that a seasonal decrease in clutch size probably evolved because it is a strategic response to seasonally unfavorable conditions that might affect offspring survival (Rowe et al. 1994, Winkler and Allen 1996).

If not by food supply and its effects on female condition, how then might inhibition of ovarian function increase as the reproductive season progresses? It may be helpful, at this point, to take a more mechanistic or physiological view of clutch size regulation. Egg production is controlled through an axis of endocrine tissues contained in the hypothalamus, anterior pituitary, and ovary. Among many temperate zone passerines, this axis is widely understood to be stimulated by the vernal increase in photoperiod. Less appreciated, however, is that the endocrine pathway is inactivated toward summer's end by the inception of a photorefractory condition. Reproduction is terminated, while days are still long, through a shift to a new functional state. Gonadal involution is a key component of this altered physiological condition, and because the change in gonad size occurs rather quickly, onset of photorefractoriness was assumed to be abrupt. It is now evident, however, that refractoriness actually develops slowly, over weeks or months, possibly through a gradual depletion of hypothalamic gonadotropin releasing hormone (Nicholls et al. 1988).

The seasonal decrease in clutch size observed in *oriantha* began about when daylengths started to shorten (see Fig. 7.11 and Table 7.12). The stimulatory effects of daylength are directly related to their duration, but for present purposes this should not enter into consideration because the inception of refractoriness occurs spontaneously, as shown in captive *Zonotrichia,* males and females alike, held on long days (Harris and Turek 1982, Moore et al. 1983, Morton et al. 1985).

Meijer et al. (1992) have made a convincing argument, based on data from captive Eurasian Kestrels (*Falco tinnunculus*) breeding under controlled photoperiods, that seasonal decreases in clutch size are likely due to the development of photorefractoriness by a slow, spontaneous turning off of ovarian function, and

TABLE 7.13.   SUCCESS OF *Oriantha* NESTS IN RELATION TO CLUTCH SIZE

	Clutch Size			
	2	3	4	5
Number of nests	7	105	638	54
Nests fledging at least one chick (%)	28.6	42.9	50.6	46.3
Mean chicks produced per successful nest	1.50	2.67	3.31	4.08
Fledglings produced per nesting effort	0.43	1.15	1.67	1.89

that this inhibition of gonadal function might be related to prolactin secretion. Interestingly, prolactin both inhibits gonadal function and stimulates brooding behavior, and since several species, including Eurasian Kestrels, tend to incubate their first-laid eggs more attentively toward the end of the season, Meijer et al. (1992) suggest that the seasonal progression toward smaller clutch sizes could be a function of prolactin secretion rates. The data on *oriantha* are consistent with the hypothesis that a photoperiodically-controlled down-regulation of ovarian function is responsible for a seasonal decline in clutch size. In a thorough review of clutch size dynamics in nidicolous birds, including influences of abiotic factors, Murphy and Haukioja (1986) pointed out that because calendar date often seems to be the best predictor of seasonal changes in clutch size, photoperiod is probably the cue for these adjustments. Presumably such a response has evolved because ecological conditions at laying time do not predict trophic conditions weeks hence, when dependent young are present, as reliably as daylength.

Reproductive success in relation to clutch size

One oft-used measure of reproductive success is the frequency at which nests fledge at least one chick. In relation to clutch size, this varied from a low of 28.6% in 2-egg clutches to a high of 50.6% in 4-egg clutches (Table 7.13). Neither of the two 6-egg clutches produced fledglings and they have not been included in the table.

It is also instructive to compare the number of fledglings produced in relation to clutch size. As might be expected, these numbers increased steadily with clutch size, from 1.50 to 4.08 (Table 7.13). The product of two measures, the percentage of successful nests and the average number of chicks that fledge in those nests, yields the number of fledglings produced per nesting effort in cases wherein the clutch had been completed. This shows that 5-egg clutches were the most productive (Table 7.13).

The most productive clutch size is sometimes the modal one (Haukioja 1970, Dixon 1978, De Steven 1980, Boyce and Perrins 1987), but our results, like those of many other studies (Murphy 1978, Smith and Andersen 1982, Murphy and Haukioja 1986, Power et al. 1989, Møller 1991, Robinson and Rotenberry 1991), show that the modal clutch size (four) was smaller than the most productive one (five). Only 5.5% of all *oriantha* nests held five eggs, however, and their frequency per year ranged from none to as many as nine (see Table 7.11). Five-egg clutches could be either first nests or renests and although they could be preceded or succeeded by clutches of another size, usually one of four eggs, close inspection of nesting records revealed that within one season individual females sometimes laid two or even three 5-egg clutches in succession. These results suggest that favorable conditions on individual territories can generate short-term environmental feedback that affects clutch size, a type of input that can have adaptive value (Högstedt 1980). In the long run, however, *oriantha* appear to produce smaller clutches than they can raise. Like many other species, they are following a risk-averse strategy (Brown and Brown 1999a).

Lack's (1954, 1966) suggestions that clutch size must be limited by the capacity of the parents to rear their young and that the modal clutch size within a population should be the most productive remain as useful concepts, but they need to be expanded to include new data and new hypotheses. For example, clutch size might be affecting mortality in adults and lifetime reproductive success (Charnov and Krebs 1974, Högstedt 1981) as well as postfledging survival of offspring and recruitment (Pettifor 1993). An inclusive view of reproduction energetics should also come to include consideration of the operative energy threshold for clutch production. As pointed out by King and Murphy (1985), the true threshold for energetically costly functions are seldom expressed under field conditions and often lie well below that which is presumed by investigators. For example, egg size in the earliest *oriantha* nests of the season did not vary unless snow conditions delayed laying until after 20 June (Fig. 7.8). Apparently an energy threshold was finally crossed at that time and females did not have enough reserves to produce eggs of the usual size.

Relevant too, to regulation of clutch size in colder climates, are the difficulties faced by incubating females in maintaining sufficient brood patch contact in large clutches so that embryo viability is unaffected. This could have been a problem for *oriantha* females with 5- and 6-egg clutches (Chapter 9). Also, a brood size of four is the most efficient one in terms of heat conservation (Sullivan and Weathers 1992).

INCUBATION

During incubation the female applies heat to the eggs from the naked skin of her incubation patch to stimulate and maintain embryo development. With her body she can also shield offspring from direct exposure to weather conditions such as sun, wind, rain, hail, and snow and, perhaps, from predation. At the same time she must maintain her own health and condition by leaving the nest periodically to eat and drink. By recording egg temperatures, it is possible to deduce the tending female's on-off pattern while accomplishing this balance and also to obtain a description of the thermal environment experienced by embryos. Both of these are rich sources of information on the physiology and behavior of nesting birds, especially when examined over the wide range of diurnal fluctuations in ambient conditions that are typical of high altitudes. Relatively large oscillations in egg temperature can occur in these environments and they can define the limits of embryo tolerance, both to the frequency of such excursions themselves and to their extremes.

Incubation period

The incubation period is defined as the interval between the laying of the last egg in a clutch and the hatching of that egg. This was measured in 256 *oriantha* nests where eggs were numbered on the day of laying and where the time when chicks hatched from the various eggs was known. Nearly all clutches (93.0%)

TABLE 7.14.   INCUBATION PERIODS AND THEIR FREQUENCIES IN 256 *Oriantha* NESTS AT TIOGA PASS

Incubation period (d)	Number of nests	Percent of nests
11	9	3.5
12	161	62.9
13	77	30.1
14	7	2.7
15	2	0.8

had an incubation period of either 12 or 13 d, 12 being the mode (Table 7.14). The mean was 12.34 d (SD = 0.63 d) and the range was four d (11 to 15).

The incubation period tended to decrease as the season wore on (Fig. 7.12), and a regression of its duration on the day of year that incubation began yielded a negative slope ($r^2 = 0.04$, $P < 0.001$). Some years ago we pointed out that the incubation period of all eggs in the clutch became shorter as the season progressed and that the last-laid egg was least affected (Mead and Morton 1985). This decrease was probably related to a seasonal increase in temperature; in warmer air eggs tended to cool less when females were off the nest, thereby enhancing embryo development and decreasing the incubation time.

Surprisingly, there was an effect of female age on incubation period (ANOVA $F_{4, 188} = 3.15$, $P = 0.015$). It decreased after age two yr and was significantly shorter in the older females, age three yr or older, than in the young ones, age one or two yr ($t = 3.30$, $P < 0.001$; Table 7.15). This effect could not be related to season because nesting schedules did not vary with female age. Perhaps older females were somehow more attentive than younger ones. They might have spent more time incubating and less time on other activities, such as foraging, especially if they were more efficient foragers or occupied territories with better habitat. There are good indications that the latter does occur (Chapter 8). It seems remotely possible, too, that older females interfered with the nesting efforts of the younger ones.

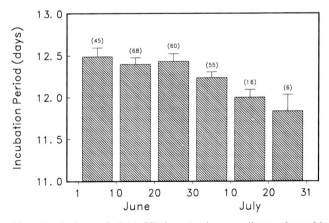

FIGURE 7.12.   Mean incubation period (+ SE) in *oriantha* according to date of incubation onset. Number of nests in parentheses.

Plate 1. The Tioga Pass area, as seen from Tioga Peak, looking south into Yosemite National Park. Tioga Lake is in the mid-foreground and directly above it, extending for 1 km, is Tioga Pass Meadow. The photos were taken in different years, but on the same day of year, July 4th, and they illustrate the large interannual variation in conditions encountered by *oriantha*.

Plate 2. Two views of Tioga Pass Meadow, the subalpine meadow that was an important part of the study area. The upper photo was taken in mid-June at a time when snow cover was about 10% and when *oriantha* nesting was in progress. The lower photo was taken in mid-September when nesting had ceased and when *oriantha* were fattening in preparation for migration.

Plate 3.   Upper: An adult *oriantha* being fitted with a radio transmitter at Tioga Pass Meadow. Lower: Tom Hahn tracking a transmitter-bearing individual that had descended from the snow-covered meadows to more open ground near Mono Lake.

Plate 4.   An *oriantha* nest built on the ground (upper) and another in a small lodgepole pine (lower). Eggs exposed directly to sun, such as those in the photos, were usually shielded by the incubating female.

Plate 5.   An *oriantha* nest in a lodgepole pine. The female is brooding chicks (upper) and one of the adults is bringing food (lower).

Plate 6. The major mammalian predator of *oriantha* nests at Tioga Pass, the Belding's ground squirrel (upper) and the major avian predator, the Clark's Nutcracker (lower).

Plate 7. Upper: An *oriantha* nest that was successfully defended by the tending female during a snowstorm. Lower: A nest that failed because it became buried in snow and inaccessible to the tending female (shown perched on a willow twig above the nest's location).

Plate 8. Upper: An adult *oriantha* with its wing spread to show an early stage of postnuptial molt, when the inner primaries are starting to be replaced. Lower: The author in 1978 (age 44).

TABLE 7.15.   INCUBATION PERIOD IN *Oriantha,* ACCORDING TO FEMALE AGE

Age (yr)	Incubation period (d)		N
	Mean	SD	
1	12.33	0.64	116
2	12.48	0.59	42
3	12.00	0.50	17
4+	12.00	0.57	18

Attentiveness patterns and egg temperatures

All parental care of eggs was performed by females and their activity or attentiveness patterns at the nest were obtained by direct observation and by changes in egg temperature measured from implanted thermocouples (Zerba and Morton 1983a,b). As can be seen from warming and cooling cycles in the eggs, females began to tend their eggs in daylight hours even from the first egg onward (Fig. 7.13). Most of their visits to the nest during the laying period were made at midday and they were observed standing over the eggs rather than sitting on them. Although there could be several functions for daytime attentiveness during laying, its primary purpose appeared to be protection from solar heating because the temperature of an egg left in an unshaded, untended nest soared quickly to lethal levels (Zerba and Morton 1983b). Untended nests can act as heat traps and, unless females intervene, eggs in unshaded nests would surely not survive the laying period, much less incubation. In fact, females clearly adjusted their daytime attentiveness throughout the incubation and nestling periods in response to solar heat loads, especially in poorly shaded nests. They were more attentive in nests fully exposed to the midday sun than in those that were shaded by a full or partial canopy of vegetation; females used their own bodies to shade the eggs and nestlings.

Daytime attentiveness varied in duration during the laying period, but tended to increase as eggs were added (Fig. 7.13). When clutch size was four, females

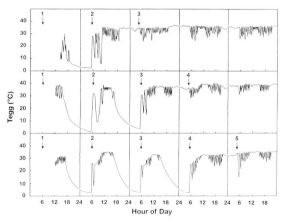

FIGURE 7.13.   Five-day recordings of egg temperatures from three *oriantha* nests. Clutch sizes were three, four, and five eggs (top, middle, and bottom sequence of panels, respectively). Arrows with numbers show when each egg in the clutch was laid. A thermocouple was installed in the first egg of each clutch about 6 hr after it was laid.

were on the nest in daylight hours about 8% of the time the day the first egg was laid, about 16% the day of the second egg, 30% the day of the third egg, and about 75% of the time on the day of the last egg (Zerba and Morton 1983b). The transition to nighttime attentiveness was much more abrupt because females rarely visited the nest during the night prior to laying the penultimate egg. In the daytime, following that event, they became fully attentive and then transited to continuous occupation of the nest at night, with full application of the brood patch promoting high egg temperature on all nights thereafter. This pattern for the onset of full-time incubation was consistent no matter the clutch size (Fig. 7.13). Because of nocturnal neglect, some of the earliest-laid eggs dropped to near-freezing temperatures. This did not result in retarded growth or extension of the incubation period, as found in some species when prolonged periods of neglect occurred (Baerends 1959, Kashkin 1961, Hoyt et al. 1978, Boersma and Wheelwright 1979, Lill 1979, Prinzinger et al. 1979, Wheelwright and Boersma 1979, Vleck and Kenagy 1980, Vleck 1981b, Morton and Pereyra 1985). Still, there are indications that hypothermia caused mortality in *oriantha* embryos (Chapter 8).

Published around-the-clock records of attentiveness during the laying period in birds are scarce, but hole nesters commonly roost in their nest cavity at that time and so do some open-cup nesters, such as American Tree Sparrows (*Spizella arborea*; Weeden 1966). We have recorded egg temperatures from the first egg onward in several additional species of open-cup nesters at Tioga Pass, including Dusky Flycatchers, Hermit Thrushes, American Robins, and Song Sparrows. All roosted in their nests at night except Dusky Flycatchers; they neglected their eggs during laying, much like *oriantha* (Morton and Pereyra 1985). So some species appear to protect their eggs (and embryos) from excessive cooling at night during the laying period and some do not. Haftorn (1988) has suggested that low egg temperatures are associated with adaptive incubation rhythms. It would be interesting to know if parental behavior in these cases is related to abilities of incipient embryos to tolerate chilling. If so, it may mean that the nocturnal egg defenders at Tioga Pass, such as Hermit Thrushes, have cold-intolerant embryos because they are more recent and, therefore, less well adapted occupants of high altitude areas than the egg neglectors, such as Dusky Flycatchers and *oriantha*. Another possibility is that nocturnal egg temperatures reflect interspecific variation in antipredator behavior by laying females. It may be, for example, that small mammals could be deterred from eating eggs by the presence of the female in the nest.

During the laying period females undergo major adjustments in endocrine function as ovulatory cycling is first stimulated, then inhibited completely, once final clutch size is attained. Behavioral changes parallel those in physiology because females must make the transition from regular maintenance behaviors to those of full-time incubation. This transition occurs gradually in passerines (Kendeigh 1952, Davis 1955, El-Wailly 1966, Jehl and Hussell 1966, Weeden 1966; Haftorn 1978a, b, 1981; Morton and Pereyra 1985), and it, along with the subsequent maintenance of regular incubation behavior, has often been associated with elevated prolactin levels (Dawson and Goldsmith 1982, Goldsmith 1982, Hall and Goldsmith 1983, Silverin and Goldsmith 1984).

During incubation, *oriantha* embryos experienced brief excursions to low temperature (17 to 30 C) when females left the nest to forage (Zerba and Morton 1983a). It is doubtful that this retarded embryo growth or extension of the in-

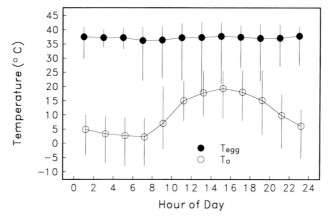

FIGURE 7.14. Mean egg temperatures recorded from eight *oriantha* nests at 3-min intervals, along with mean air temperatures measured near the nests, also recorded at 3-min intervals, between 13 June and 11 August 1980 at Tioga Pass. Vertical lines show ranges of temperatures that occurred above and below the means. Adapted from Zerba and Morton (1983a).

cubation period because their incubation period, about 12 days, was the same as that of conspecifics breeding at low altitude (Blanchard 1941, Morton 1976), where embryos are probably not exposed to such low temperatures.

Once laying had ceased and full-time incubation was underway, *oriantha* females managed to maintain mean egg temperatures, both day and night, between 36 and 38 C. This was accomplished even though there were frequent trips off the nest in daytime in order to forage, and in the face of air temperatures that were sometimes below freezing at night and in the early morning hours (Fig. 7.14). Egg temperature was between 36 and 40 C for more than 65% of the time during the female's active day and for more than 84% of the time during her period of night rest (Table 7.16). Mean egg temperature was 37.3 C (SD = 2.3 C) when taken at 3-min intervals in eight nests throughout the incubation period. This is quite similar to the average temperature of incubation reported for other

TABLE 7.16. Occurrence of Egg Temperatures as Percent of Time During Active Day and Night Rest Periods of Incubating Female *Oriantha* (Zerba and Morton 1983a)

Temperature interval (C)	Percent occurrence	
	Active day	Night rest
16–18	0.01	0.00
18–20	0.02	0.00
20–22	0.03	0.00
22–24	0.10	0.00
24–26	0.19	0.00
26–28	0.26	0.01
28–30	0.72	0.04
30–32	2.27	0.04
32–34	6.59	1.06
34–36	16.13	8.63
36–38	32.50	46.11
38–40	33.11	38.83
40–42	7.90	5.28
42–44	0.09	0.00

passerines (Huggins 1941, Irving and Krog 1956, Kendeigh 1963, El-Wailly 1966; Drent 1972, 1975; Haftorn 1978a,b, 1979; Morton and Pereyra 1985, Weathers and Sullivan 1989).

Mean egg temperature was significantly higher in ground nests than in elevated nests (37.5 C vs. 36.8 C, P < 0.001). The absolute difference here was not great and hatchability was unaffected; in 140 ground nests (540 eggs) that were not manipulated by investigative techniques other than direct observations, hatchability was 92% and in 109 elevated nests (421 eggs) it was 91% (Zerba and Morton 1983a).

Mean egg temperature increased by 2–3 C during the first four days after clutch completion, then remained virtually steady thereafter (Zerba and Morton 1983a). This initial rise early in incubation has been noted in a variety of species and may be due to an increase in heat-transfer abilities of the developing brood patch (Bailey 1952, Farner 1958b, Jones 1971, Drent 1975, Afton 1979, Barrett 1980). Along these lines, Bailey (1952) showed that vascularization of the brood patch in White-crowned Sparrows began approximately two days before the first egg of the season was laid and reached completion on the third or fourth day of incubation. By that time the dermal tissue had become thickened and edematous, a condition that persisted throughout the remainder of incubation and during brooding of the young.

Mean brood patch temperature, obtained by application of a thermocouple to hand-held females, was 41.84 ± 0.81 C (N = 37). Mean core (cloacal) temperature of these same females was 42.48 ± 0.77 C, so patches were less than one degree cooler, on average, than core body temperature.

Despite evidence for energy costs associated with incubation alluded to earlier in this chapter, particularly at night and in elevated nests, females were able to maintain modest fat stores throughout incubation (Fig. 6.3B), a condition of positive energy balance that is likely facilitated by their spending so much time in the favorable microclimate of the nest (Walsberg and King 1978). In Zebra Finches (*Poephila guttata*), ameliorating effects of the nest microclimate approximately compensates for the energy cost of incubation (Vleck 1981a), and in European Starlings, heat from normal metabolism is sufficient to maintain egg homeostasis even in sub-freezing conditions (Biebach 1979).

The rhythm of incubation in *oriantha* was characterized by constant attentiveness or sitting at night followed by a regular pattern of alternating periods on and off the nest during the daylight hours. Periods on (incubation bouts) during the active day averaged 19.6 min (SD = 2.7 min). Periods off (foraging bouts) averaged 7.8 min (SD = 0.5 min). The proportion of time spent on the nest by females during the active day, the mean daytime attentiveness, was 74.5% (SD = 1.3%). Females did not depart on foraging trips until their eggs had reached a consistent temperature, or set-point value, of about 38 C (Zerba and Morton 1983b). This observation is in agreement with White and Kinney's (1974) suggestion that attentiveness ceases when eggs reach a "release" temperature. Likewise, Calder (1971) found that Calliope Hummingbird (*Stellula calliope*) females did not depart to forage until nest temperatures were restored to within a consistent range (34–37 C).

White and Kinney (1974) made the generalization that passerines tend to decrease their attentiveness as air temperature comes near to the optimum incubation

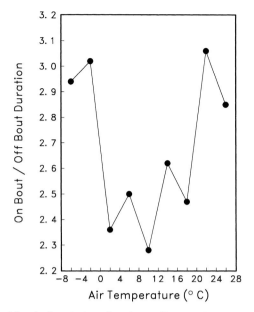

FIGURE 7.15. Ratio of incubating (on) to foraging (off) bouts in incubating female *oriantha*, in relation to air temperature. Adapted from Zerba and Morton (1983b).

temperature. Essentially, egg and ambient temperatures approach an equilibrium condition and little input is required of the tending bird. This model does not incorporate actual operative temperature, however, so it does not extend smoothly to high elevation conditions. For example, total daytime attentiveness by *oriantha* females tended to *increase* slightly as ambient temperature began to exceed 20 C (Zerba and Morton 1983b). This pattern of increased attentiveness with increasing temperature was even more pronounced in Dusky Flycatchers nesting at Tioga Pass (Morton and Pereyra 1985). Neither incubation nor foraging bout durations were constant throughout, however, so it is instructive to evaluate daytime attentiveness during incubation by the ratio of on to off bout durations.

This ratio had a U-shaped pattern during the active day, being highest when ambient temperatures were either at their lowest or at their highest (Fig. 7.15). That females would sit longer at low temperatures, relative to the time taken off for foraging, is understandable in that eggs cool more quickly when the air is cold and it takes longer to rewarm them. The high ratio of on to off bouts when ambient values were at maximum is not to be expected from the White and Kinney model, however. This behavior does not make sense unless one returns to the theme recounted earlier, that open-nesting birds in high altitude environments must cope with potentially lethal overheating of eggs from solar radiation. Females protect their offspring from these conditions by spending relatively longer periods on the nest during the hotter portions of the day.

In contrast, at low altitude, particularly at the higher latitudes, exposure to solar heating appears to generate a more moderate microenvironment in nests. Lapland Longspurs in the Northwest Territories, for example, may actually benefit from solar warming of the nest because it allows incubating females to extend the duration of their foraging bouts (Lyon and Montgomerie 1987).

CHAPTER 8: Nestlings and Fledglings

HATCHING

If all has gone well during incubation, the day arrives when chicks begin to cut through the eggshell. Eventually they hatch and, in the case of *oriantha,* begin a nine-day period as nestlings that is terminated when they fledge. The proportion that succeed in hatching out provides a measure of egg viability or hatchability. Because eggs are laid at 24-hour intervals, each one in the succession is a day younger than its predecessor. If the eggs remain cold and below the threshold for development until the end of clutch completion, conceivably they might hatch in unison with perhaps only a few minutes or hours separating them. This does not happen because females sit in the nest during the laying period for varying amounts of time, and this causes asymmetries in development and hatching schedules (Chapter 7). This female-promoted hatching spread can cause substantial differences in nestling age (a day or more) and competitive abilities—a condition that appears to facilitate mortality, especially in the last-hatched, when food shortages occur. Reduction of the brood in this way is a widespread phenomenon that has spawned a plethora of hypotheses to explain its reason for being. Seasonal changes in the relative contributions of male and female parents to rearing the young make this aspect of passerine biology even more difficult to understand.

Hatching mechanics

Pipping of eggs by incipient hatchlings usually began on the day before hatching, but sometimes on the same day if started in the early morning. Eventually, the shell was cut completely around about mid-way of the egg and the chick emerged. At six nests we watched from nearby blinds while chicks were hatching out. During that time the females turned the eggs with their feet or beaks and made shaking and settling movements with their bodies. One female assisted the hatching process by removing a half-shell that was still adhering to the chick. Shell fragments, large and small, were always consumed by females at the nest. Chicks that died during hatching, or at any other time, were carried from the nest and discarded some distance away.

Hatching times

The temporal distribution of hatching times in alpine and subalpine populations of *oriantha* has been described as being primarily an early-morning phenomenon (Morton et al. 1972b, King and Hubbard 1981). But those data were gathered more-or-less during regular daytime working hours. During two breeding seasons, Mead (1983) checked *oriantha* nests at Tioga Pass around-the-clock. He found that hatching peaked at dawn and that 110 of 198 hatching times (55.6%) occurred between 04:00 and 12:00. Another 68 hatchings (34.3%) occurred between noon and 20:00, and the final 20 (10.1%) during the following eight hr of darkness. Skutch (1976) pointed out that hatching may occur at any hour of the day or night, but that it tends to be a rhythmic process wherein most of the hatching effort by chicks occurs toward the end of the night and in the early morning, coincident with maximum warmth derived from brooding. Mead's data are in agreement with this generalization.

TABLE 8.1. HATCHABILITY OF *Oriantha* EGGS IN RELATION TO LAYING DATE

Interval	Hatchability (%)	N^a
20–31 May	62.7	67
1–10 June	70.0	470
11–20 June	67.7	668
21–30 June	76.9	532
1–10 July	75.4	532
11–20 July	74.0	231
21–31 July	83.3	66
1–10 August	100.0	3

[a] Total number of eggs in each time interval.

Hatchability

Hatchability, the percentage of eggs surviving to the time of hatching that produce a chick, increases with latitude, but not with altitude (Koenig 1982). It is generally greater than 90% in passerines, although it has been found to be as low as 70 to 80% in some species (Ricklefs 1969, Koenig 1982).

In *oriantha,* hatchability for the whole study was 72.6% (1,962 of 2,701 eggs). This is low, and was unexpected since an earlier sample of unmanipulated eggs had shown viability to be 91.6% (Zerba and Morton 1983a). It seems probable that the examination, marking, and measuring of eggs caused damage and subsequent mortality in some of them. Our field notes are inadequate for quantifying the amount that each egg was handled, but those that were measured with calipers can be compared to those that were not. Of 1,390 measured eggs, 970 (69.8%) hatched, whereas 992 of 1,311 unmeasured eggs (75.7%) hatched. This difference was significant (Chi-square = 11.75, df = 1, P < 0.001), so handling of this type reduced hatchability by at least 5.9%, and it follows that other procedures such as numbering eggs and checking them for hatching pips could also have contributed to mortality. Beyond these manipulations, however, could environmental factors have also impacted hatchability?

Several lines of evidence can be explored. For example, there was a nest in 1985 and another in 1988 wherein sub-freezing weather conditions prevailed while the females were laying. In both nests the first two eggs froze and cracked slightly whereas the second two eggs survived and later hatched, probably because they were protected by the onset of nocturnal attentiveness by the females. Usually females abandoned the nest when part or all of the clutch was frozen, or at least they removed eggs that were cracked or broken, but in these two nests this did not happen.

A seasonal variation in hatchability provided additional evidence for a temperature effect. Eggs laid early in the season (before 21 June), when sub-freezing temperatures were most prevalent, were less likely to hatch than those laid later on (Chi-square = 21.85, df = 6, P < 0.001; Table 8.1). Eggs were particularly vulnerable during the laying period because they were not tended during the first few nights. Harmeson (1974) also observed a seasonal increase in hatchability in Dickcissels (*Spiza americana*), from 72% to 88%, but attributed it to an increase in food availability (which allowed females to spend less time foraging and more time tending their eggs). Hendricks and Norment (1994) found that hatchability decreased in American Pipits (*Anthus rubescens*) nesting in the alpine when laying

TABLE 8.2. HATCHABILITY OF *Oriantha* EGGS IN RELATION TO CLUTCH SIZE

Clutch size	Hatchability (%)	N[a]
2	78.6	14
3	77.3	132
4	73.0	529
5	58.1	31
6	00.0	1

[a] Number of nests.

was delayed because of a late spring. They hypothesized that the lower egg viability could have been due to poor nutrition in females or to increased exposure of eggs to cold; they could not distinguish.

Nesting experience did not affect hatchability because it was the same in one-year-old females as in older females (Chi-square = 2.68, df = 1, P = 0.102). On the other hand, there was an effect related to clutch size, primarily because hatchability decreased substantially in 5-egg clutches (Chi-square = 21.50, df = 3, P < 0.001; Table 8.2). It may be that females could not adequately protect and incubate clutches of that size or larger from freezing temperatures because the area occupied by the eggs exceeded the boundaries of the incubation patch. Thus, high altitude conditions could be selecting against 5-egg clutches even though, compared to other clutch sizes, they tended to fledge the most chicks (Chapter 7). Snow (1958) obtained results in Eurasian Blackbirds that were the opposite of these. Hatchability was lower in one-year-olds than in older females (92.2% of hatching failure being due to infertility), and hatchability was unaffected by clutch size. Of course, a low-temperature effect on embryo survival was unlikely in Snow's study, the climate undoubtedly being milder in the Botanic Garden at Oxford than at Tioga Pass!

Eggs fail to hatch because they are infertile or the embryo dies. In order to see if the number of hatching failures due to embryo death was unusually high, and possibly induced by environmental conditions such as chilling, it is useful to compare the *oriantha* data to those gathered by Rothstein (1973) on Cedar Waxwings (*Bombycilla cedrorum*). He found that 58 of 73 unhatched eggs (79.5%) were infertile and that 15 were fertile but contained dead embryos (20.5%). In a sample of 78 unhatched, unmanipulated *oriantha* eggs 42 were infertile (53.8%) and 36 had dead embryos (46.2%). These ratios are different from Rothstein's (Chi-square = 11.05, df = 1, P < 0.001), suggesting that embryo deaths were disproportionately high in *oriantha,* a result that is consistent with the hypothesis that egg survival at Tioga Pass was reduced by low temperatures. Finally, although hatchability did vary substantially among years (for example, 64.9% in 1984 and 87.1% in 1970), this variation was not significant (Chi-square = 25.22, df = 21, P = 0.241).

Hatching sequence

In general, *oriantha* eggs hatched in the order laid (Chi-square = 69.05, df = 3, P < 0.001; Table 8.3), but there were some interesting exceptions. For example, there were three 4-egg clutches wherein the last-laid egg was the first to hatch. In two of these cases storms with sub-freezing temperatures occurred during lay-

TABLE 8.3.   Hatching Order in 45 4-egg *Oriantha* Clutches Wherein Both Laying Order and Hatching Order Were Known for Every Egg in the Clutch

Hatching order	Laying order			
	1	2	3	4
1	35	6	2	3
2	6	31	8	0
3	3	6	32	3
4	1	2	3	39

ing, but ended about the time the last egg was laid. It appears that cold-shock caused development to be delayed in untended eggs and that this phenomenon explains much of the out-of-sequence hatching events shown in Table 8.3.

When hatching times of all eggs in the clutch were plotted in relation to hatching time of the first-laid egg, considerable asynchrony was apparent (Fig. 8.1). No matter the clutch size, the last-laid egg tended to hatch considerably later than the first one. This pattern was undoubtedly due to the schedule early in incubation (see Fig. 7.13), specifically the tendency of females to begin full-time incubation when the penultimate egg was laid.

Hatching asynchrony increased between early June and mid-July. Presumably, this was a warm-weather effect. Eggs did not cool down as much when females were inattentive during the laying period and some additional development of embryos occurred (Mead and Morton 1985).

BROOD REDUCTION

Because of hatching asynchrony, siblings were often of different ages and at very different places on their growth curves. This caused hierarchies in both body size and competitiveness to be established in the nest. Such hierarchies occur in many avian species and Lack (1954) suggested that they are adaptive because when food shortages occur the smallest and least competitive nestlings would be fed the least, and if mortality occurred they would die first. This orderly reduction

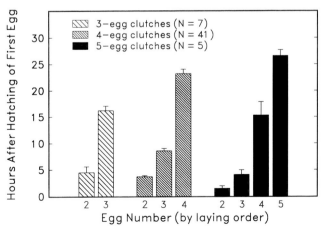

FIGURE 8.1.   Hatching times of *oriantha* eggs with laying order, in relation to hatching of the first-laid egg. Lines show 1 SE. Adapted from Mead and Morton (1985).

TABLE 8.4.   AGES OF *Oriantha* NESTLINGS WHEN THEY DISAPPEARED FROM BROODS

Nestling Age (d)	Percent of All Brood Reductions	N
0	5.2	4
1	13.0	10
2	18.2	14
3	20.8	16
4	22.1	17
5	7.8	6
6	9.1	7
7	2.6	2
8	1.3	1
9	0.0	0

of the brood might allow some of the older, larger nestlings to be spared long enough to survive periods of food deprivation, such as might occur during a storm. In other words, hatching asynchrony has been selected for because, under certain conditions, it can enhance reproductive success.

A partial loss of nestlings occurred in 14% of otherwise successful *oriantha* nests. Since the smallest chicks received the fewest feeding offers, even during moderate weather, it was assumed that these losses were due to starvation. And, true to Lackian expectations, two-thirds of the mortality could be traced to the smallest nestling. Aside from these instances of naturally-occurring brood reduction, it was also induced experimentally by trapping and holding the male parent. Without his contribution toward feeding of nestlings the whole brood sometimes died, but, again, the smallest and youngest died first (Mead and Morton 1985). In subsequent experiments it was discovered that brood reduction occurred when both parents were trapped and held for only two hours, even in good weather. Once rewarmed by the female, these briefly-deprived nestlings appeared to be ravenous and the oldest and largest aggressively competed for feedings. The smallest nestling(s) obtained little or no food and died within a few hours. These experiments mimicked events that sometimes unfolded after one of the brief-but-violent summer storms that occurred on the study area, and they suggest that brood reduction can be avoided if the parents bring food as soon as the storm is over, but they must provide it to *every* nestling (nestlings can survive for several days at reduced growth rates if given only relatively small amounts of food). These observations, and others, have often caused us to question the general applicability of hypotheses which suggest that brood reduction is adaptive.

There were 77 cases of naturally occurring brood reduction so it was possible to examine when it occurred with regard to both nestling age and time of season. First, it increased with nestling age through Day 4 then decreased sharply (Table 8.4). This result shifts attention to nestling growth and thermoregulatory abilities. Clearly, the period of exponential growth in nestlings (Fig. 8.5) and that of maximum brood reduction tended to occur together. At that time (Day 4 of age and earlier) disparities in body size, and probably competitive abilities, were largest and energy was being heavily partitioned into biomass rather than into thermoregulation. Once nestlings became more equal in body size and began to develop thermogenic capacities (about Day 5), to shiver and defend their own body temperature without dependence upon maternal brooding, their vulnerability to epi-

TABLE 8.5. SEASONAL CHANGES IN PROPENSITY FOR BROOD REDUCTION TO OCCUR IN *Oriantha*

Interval	Number of nests with nestlings	Percent of nests showing brood reduction
10–20 June	153	5.2
21–30 June	193	6.7
1–10 July	153	12.4
11–20 July	158	5.1
21–31 July	67	31.3
1 August +	26	30.8

sodes of bad weather decreased. Very little brood reduction occurred from Day 7 on, when they were fully functional endotherms (Table 8.4). Second, brood reduction had a strong seasonal component. It was about 5–12% in nests with young through mid-July, but rose sharply in the following weeks to around 30% (Table 8.5).

Brood reduction at Tioga Pass was often associated with foul weather. During storms, nestlings were sometimes directly exposed to rain, hail, snow, and thermolytic winds while the tending female was away gathering food. Once the young and the nest became cold and wet, mortality sometimes ensued. But why the seasonality? More rainstorms occurred in July and August than in other summer months, but there were also fewer snowstorms (Table 9.1). The most important factor here may have been a decrease in provisioning by males. In many late-season breeding attempts nestlings were fed only by females.

The consequences of this shift in parental behavior can be seen in data on body mass obtained from six broods that hatched relatively late in the season, in the last week of July (Fig. 8.2). Growth curves shown in nests A and B were for broods of four and three, respectively, and they were representative of normal weight-change trajectories. Also shown is an example of brood reduction, even though both parents were bringing food (nest C). In that nest the youngest nestling was not competitive, it grew slowly and died at four days of age. It should be noted that runt nestlings gave every indication of being hungry because they begged incessantly. In three other nests (D, E, and F) the female was the sole provider. In nest D all three chicks fledged, although at reduced weight, whereas in E and F the youngest and smallest nestling died. In nest F the nestling died at seven days of age. Excluding predation, this was the latest that nestling death was observed except for the unusual situation, mentioned earlier, when lone nestlings were neglected because females were engaged in excessive brooding of inviable eggs (for specific examples see below).

HATCHING ASYNCHRONY

There have now been at least 17 hypotheses advanced in explanation of hatching asynchrony (Clark and Wilson 1981, Slagsvold and Lifjeld 1989, Magrath 1990, Amundsen and Slagsvold 1991, Ricklefs 1993, Murray 1994, Stoleson and Beissinger 1995). Most of these, including the brood-reduction hypothesis, have proposed that the hierarchy in nestling size generated by asynchrony is adaptive. But numerous field studies, many of which involved manipulations of brood and nestling size differences, have not provided convincing evidence that this hierarchy either increases offspring survival after hatching or reduces parental in-

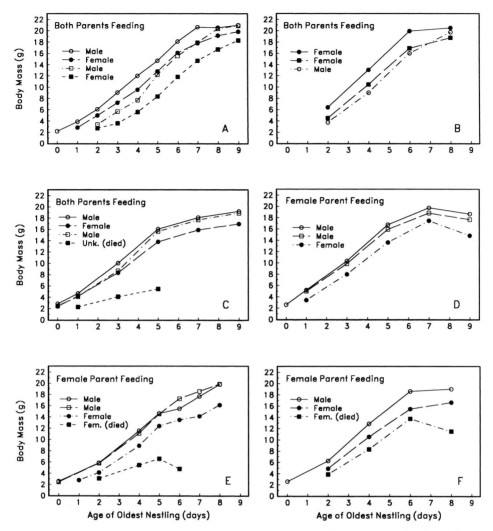

FIGURE 8.2.   Body mass changes of *oriantha* nestlings in six different nests during late July. In nests A, B, and C both parents were known to be bringing food. In nests D, E, and F only the female was observed feeding the nestlings. The sex of each nestling is given in the legend.

vestment (Stoleson and Beissinger 1995). As Stoleson and Beissinger point out, studies that address hatching patterns have uniformly ignored the physiological, environmental, and social constraints that affect the onset of incubation and, other than the resultant effects on nestling size differentials, the possible adaptive significance of beginning incubation prior to clutch completion.

There are a few hypotheses which propose that early incubation is itself adaptive: it could maintain viability of first-laid eggs (Arnold et al. 1987), protect eggs from predators (Dunlop 1910), protect the clutch from brood parasites (Wiley and Wiley 1980), or protect the eggs during the day from potentially lethal solar heating and at night from freezing (Zerba and Morton 1983b). There are also two hypotheses which propose that hatching asynchrony is simply an epiphenomenon. One states that hatching patterns may reflect energy constraints experienced by laying females (Stoleson and Beissinger 1995); the female's attentiveness pattern might vary indirectly with food availability, for example. The other, the hormonal hypothesis, suggests that hatching asynchrony is the by-product of a physiological mechanism that evolved originally for the dual purpose of stimulating incubation and terminating laying (Mead and Morton 1985). Next, I will elaborate on this hypothesis and provide a graphical model for consideration.

The hormonal hypothesis

To begin with, follicles do not mature synchronously in the avian ovary—there is a hierarchy in their size. At regular intervals, usually one day in laying passerines, the currently largest follicle is ovulated. This event is preceded six to eight hr by a surge in luteotropic hormone. The ovum or egg then spends about 24 hr in the oviduct before being laid. There is a close relationship between ovulation and oviposition (laying) in that ovulation of the next ovum in the hierarchy occurs 15 to 75 min after oviposition (Follett 1984, Birkhead 1996). Oviposition of the final egg in the clutch is not succeeded by an ovulation, of course. This means that at some point in the preceding 24 hr the sequence of ovulations was halted, presumably soon after the final ovum entered the oviduct. Although interest abounds in the regulation of clutch size, this key determining step in the mechanism responsible for termination of ovulation has not been thoroughly investigated, probably because most of the information about ovarian physiology has been derived from domestic fowl (Sharp 1980), and these particular birds have been artificially selected for continuous laying.

Stimulation of gonadal activity is controlled via the hypothalamus-anterior pituitary-gonadal axis, and we assume that the same regulatory pathway is also involved in gonadal inhibition, either through a decrease in gonadotropin secretion and/or the activation of some other inhibitory mechanism such as down-regulation of receptors. In any event, it appears in *oriantha,* and probably many other birds as well, that ovarian inhibition must be occurring at nearly the same moment as onset of full-time incubation behavior. This temporal coincidence, noticed first by Paul Mead, led to a conservative model (Mead and Morton 1985), which suggests that the early onset of incubation evolved because it was the result of an adaptive outcome, one wherein one mechanism, executed perhaps through the action of a single hormone, was selected both to turn off a physiological phase of reproduction (ovulation) and to turn on a behavioral phase (incubation). Hatching asynchrony resulted from this adaptation, but it was an unselected by-product. This idea can be visualized in a simple diagram (Fig. 8.3) in which the thresholds for these two functions are displayed amidst a changing hormonal milieu. The threshold for ovarian inhibition should be crossed shortly after the final ovum is ovulated, in other words, at about the time the penultimate egg is laid. As illustrated in Fig. 8.3, this would be the third egg in a 4-egg clutch. The inhibition threshold is characterized as being fixed because it should not vary appreciably among species of determinate layers. They must all shut down the ovulatory sequence at the proper time in order to exert control over clutch size. The threshold for incubation onset, however, is depicted as being adjustable (arrows). In *oriantha* it must be very close to where it has been drawn in Fig. 8.3 because both thresholds are crossed at about the same time.

An upward adjustment of the threshold for incubation onset would serve to

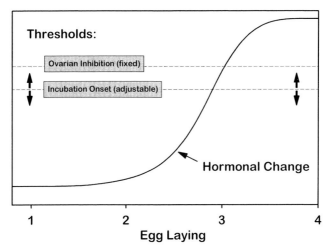

FIGURE 8.3.   The hormonal hypothesis: model proposing the control of ovarian inhibition and onset of full-time incubation behavior by hormonal changes in relation to the time of egg laying in a 4-egg clutch.

decrease hatching asynchrony because incubation would begin closer to the time of clutch completion, and setting it lower would increase hatching asynchrony because incubation would begin closer to the time of clutch initiation. A change in the slope of hormone titer (secretion rate) might also be an effective regulation tactic. Realize here that ovarian inhibition sufficient to halt the ovulatory sequence is an all-or-nothing response whereas onset of incubation behavior often is not. There is abundant evidence that attentiveness in laying females can develop gradually and at different times during the egg-laying period (Lehrman 1961; Haftorn 1978a,b, 1979, 1981; Richter 1984, Morton and Pereyra 1985, Hebert and Sealy 1992, Hillstrom and Olsson 1994). We contend that the hormonal hypothesis describes the primitive condition, and the reason why hatching asynchrony evolved in the first place. Furthermore, the hatching-pattern dynamic that stems from it should prove to be the most commonly observed one, otherwise hatching asynchrony would likely increase with environmental instability and unpredictability, as with latitude or altitude (which it does not). This is not to deny that natural selection could still be acting on the hatching spread in some species. For example, and in concordance with hypotheses suggesting that brood reduction is adaptive, asynchrony might increase in localized regions where episodes of bad weather occur randomly during the nesting season. This could be the explanation for the highly asynchronous patterns observed in Yellow-headed Blackbirds (*Xanthocephalus xanthocephalus*) nesting in Iowa (Richter 1984). Our model allows for such perturbations and even suggests, in a mechanistic sense, which element of the system could be most easily modified to obtain individual patterns (in this case, by lowering the threshold for onset of incubation behavior).

What might be the hormone or hormones involved in this regulatory pattern? As pointed out earlier (Mead and Morton 1985), prolactin is a strong candidate because it is well known to have antigonadal effects. It has also been implicated in both the induction and maintenance of parental care (Ball 1991, Wingfield and Farner 1993), and its levels increase at the onset of incubation, much as we have shown for a hypothetical hormone in our model. For examples, see studies by Goldsmith (1982) on the Common Canary (*Serinus canaria*) and Sockman et al. (2000) on the American Kestrel (*Falco sparverius*).

Progesterone is another hormone known to have potent effects on the female tract (Sturkie and Mueller 1976), and both increased (Lehrman and Wortis 1960, Lehrman 1961) and decreased levels (Sockman and Schwabl 1999) have been observed in relation to incubation onset. In 1987 progesterone was implanted subdermally in five laying *oriantha* (8 mm Silastic capsules) in the mid-morning. Although these females all had incomplete clutches when implanted (one or two eggs), and must have ovulated only a few hours earlier, none laid again. Three tended their nests for a few days, at least intermittently, and two abandoned immediately. It appears that the smooth muscle of their reproductive tracts was completely inhibited. One female was recovered in 1988 with an empty capsule still in place, the other four were never trapped again. Two other females provided with empty implants (controls) completed their clutches and incubated normally. Progesterone, therefore, is an unlikely candidate for stimulation of incubation in *oriantha* although it might be useful for control of clutch size.

Despite uncertainties surrounding the control mechanism (a recent study by Sockman et al. 2000, for example, has yielded equivocal results), this model provides a starting place for explaining a commonly observed hatching pattern and shows that in species wherein a different pattern might be selected for, all that would need to be modified would be the threshold for induction of incubation behavior. This might be as simple as altering the structure or activity of a gene coding for hormone receptors in the membranes or cytoplasm of neurons that control incubation behavior. Whatever the physiological signals turn out to be, or even the usefulness of the hormonal hypothesis itself, we agree with Stoleson and Beissinger (1995) that studies of hatching asynchrony should be shifted from the search for adaptive hatching patterns to the events that occur during egg laying because this may be where adaptation truly lies.

SEX RATIO

The sex ratio in *oriantha* nestlings was determined from 214 clutches wherein every egg hatched out and every individual in the brood was then sexed by laparotomy. There were 681 nestlings in the sample, 342 males and 339 females, a ratio that was not different from 1:1 (Chi-square = 7.14, df = 1, P = 0.712).

COWBIRD PARASITISM

Brown-headed Cowbirds (*Molothrus ater*) rarely parasitize White-crowned Sparrows (Lavers 1974, King et al. 1976). At Hart Mountain, Oregon, however, 6 of 42 *oriantha* nests (14.3%) contained cowbird eggs or nestlings (King et al. 1976). Within the last two decades Brown-headed Cowbirds have become increasingly abundant in and around campgrounds located in the lower end of Lee Vining Canyon, about 10–15 km from the Tioga Pass study area. They have probably propagated there from nearby pack stations and cattle ranches, and do well in the campgrounds because of numerous bird feeders put out by campers. Cowbirds were observed frequently on the lower parts of the study area, especially around Ellery Lake and along Lee Vining Creek, but they were known to have

TABLE 8.6. FOOD DELIVERY TRIPS PER HOUR, INCLUDING PERCENT OF TRIPS BY EACH PARENT, TO BROODS OF THREE OR FOUR *Oriantha* NESTLINGS, IN RELATION TO NESTLING AGE

Nestling age (d)	Number of broods	Feeding trips by adults		Percent of feeding trips	
		Mean trips per hour	SD	By males	By females
0	3	3.5	0.7	13.3	86.7
1	6	5.3	3.4	24.0	76.0
2	5	5.2	2.1	30.6	69.4
3	8	8.2	2.8	33.2	66.8
4	6	11.4	4.4	35.5	64.5
5	7	13.0	3.8	45.5	54.5
6	8	14.7	4.3	38.8	61.2
7	7	16.7	3.4	37.4	62.6
8	4	15.5	4.0	33.5	66.5
9	3	16.5	3.9	22.0	78.0

Notes: Data derived from 57 broods. Nestling age 0 refers to day that first hatchling appeared (a full brood may not have been present until the next day).

laid in only a few Dusky Flycatcher nests (Pereyra 1998) and in one *oriantha* nest, an attempt that was unsuccessful.

PROVISIONING RATES

Nestlings could make gaping movements within a few minutes of release from the egg and were sometimes fed by the female almost immediately thereafter. One chick even obtained food while lying on its back, still struggling to become free of the half-shell adhering to its dorsal surface. The very first feedings were always provided by females. In some cases a male approached with food while hatching was in progress but the female would not let him feed new hatchlings. She took the food from him and swallowed it or sometimes stood up and fed it to the hatchlings lying beneath her. This type of behavior by females ceased within the first day or two and males began to feed nestlings directly.

During 77 observation periods (mean = 2.9 hr, SD = 2.3 hr) made on 61 nests during nine different years at all times of the season, 1,799 deliveries of food to the nest occurred. Of these, 699 (38.9%) were made by males and 1,100 (61.1%) were made by females (Chi-square = 89.38, df = 1, P < 0.001). Although males usually brought food to the nest, females consistently made more trips throughout the nine-d nestling period (Table 8.6). It should be warned that males were sometimes less inclined than females to ignore an observer's presence. They took longer to settle down and resume normal activities when observation blinds were entered, and some inhibition of their intent to feed nestlings could have occurred despite our precautions. Still the downward trend in body mass observed in males, while not as pronounced as that of females (Fig. 6.4), indicates that care of nestlings was energetically stressful for both parents.

Close-up observations plus collections made from collared nestlings indicate that arthropods, adult insects and their larvae in particular, were the primary type of food being delivered to nestlings. On occasion a few bits of plants, including leaves, buds, and flowers, were also delivered.

A distinctive diurnal pattern of feedings per hour was observed at one nest containing three Day 7 nestlings that was observed from first light to last (Fig. 8.4). The parents began feeding about 45 min before sunrise and stopped feeding

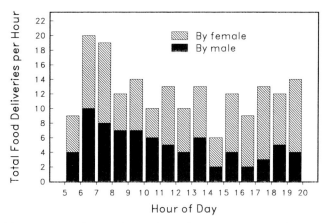

FIGURE 8.4. Diurnal pattern of parental provisioning in an *oriantha* nest with three Day 7 nestlings.

about 45 min after sunset. There were 186 food deliveries made during this one entire day, 77 (41.4%) by the male and 109 (58.6%) by the female. Two things stand out in this pattern. First, nestlings were fed most frequently in the early morning, the time when they were probably hungriest and begging most vociferously from the overnight fast. Second, parental care was shared about equally in the hours before noon but thereafter the male's contribution decreased substantially. Males were known to devote more time to territorial behavior in afternoon hours, especially to singing (Morton et al. 1972b).

As nestlings aged and grew, the rate at which food was delivered to the nest increased. Day 0 broods (those wherein at least one hatchling was present) were fed about three times per hr whereas those that were Day 7 and older were fed about 16 times per hr (Table 8.6). Note that these data were for deliveries to the whole brood, not to individual nestlings. Earlier, it was calculated that each nestling was fed about twice per hr on Day 0, and that this increased to about seven times per hr by Day 5 (Morton et al. 1972b). Also, as thermoregulatory abilities of nestlings improved, females spent less time brooding and more time feeding them. Eventually, feeding time was extended by about three hr, mostly in the early morning, the coldest time of day (Morton 1979).

NEST SANITATION

Nests were maintained in sanitary condition because the adults usually ingested the fecal sacs of nestlings, either at the nest or after carrying them away to a perch. Each nestling produced about 0.5 to 1 fecal sacs per hour from Day 0 through Day 9, with each sac weighing consistently about 2.5% of the nestling's total body mass throughout this time. A brood of four, therefore, produced more than 20 g of fecal sacs per day from Day 4 onward. Digestive efficiency of nestlings, especially of fats and proteins, improved substantially in the first two days after hatching, but because of the large volume of sacs involved, approximately 5 to 10% of the daily energy expenditure of the adults could be met from their consumption and recycling of nestling fecal material (Morton 1979).

PATTERNS OF PARENTAL CARE

As indicated above, males tended to show decreased parental effort toward the end of the season, as well as the end of the day. Delivery of food by male parents was highest in the earliest nests, remained fairly constant through July, then dropped precipitously in nests that were present in August. In 34 nests active in August that were observed from a distance with binoculars, the male was not delivering food at seven of them (20.6%). These seasonal effects, along with the extra demands imposed when double brooding occurred, caused considerable variation in patterns of parental care. Four seemed to be most common: 1) Both parents fed nestlings and fledglings. 2) Both parents fed nestlings and males took over care of fledglings when the female began a second nesting cycle (double brooding). 3) Both parents fed nestlings but only the female fed fledglings. 4) All parental care was provided by the female.

The necessity for biparental care is often described as an agent selecting for monogamy (Wittenberger 1976, 1982). Widowed females raise fewer offspring of lower quality, although the need for male assistance varies seasonally and/or interannually, depending upon food availability (Bart and Tornes 1989). Monogamy, therefore, could be a bet-hedging strategy, especially in unpredictable and fluctuating environments, such as those occupied by *oriantha* and Snow Buntings (Lyon et al. 1987). When food is dependably in surplus, females may provide all the parental care, as in Aquatic Warblers (*Acrocephalus paludicola*; Heise 1970), a species with a quasi-promiscuous mating system and high levels of multiple paternity (Schulze-Hagen et al. 1995).

When parental care is less demanding, as during times of exceptional food abundance, it has been suggested that males in monogamous mating systems should decrease their parental efforts to allow themselves more time and energy for extra-pair matings (Westneat 1988, Carey 1990, Westneat and Sherman 1993). Paternity exclusion data show that *oriantha* males engaged in extra-pair matings (Sherman and Morton 1988) and since they usually provided fewer than half of the feedings to nestlings (Table 8.6), there may have been time for extra-pair sexual activity during most of the reproductive season, especially in the afternoon hours (see Fig. 8.4). But the reduction, even total cessation, of parental care by males in the last nests of the season (patterns 3 and 4, above) suggests that other forces may be at work here.

Theoretically, males should not provide care to non-related young (Trivers 1972), but there is no reason to suspect that cuckoldry rates escalated at the end of the season. Furthermore, male birds apparently do not discriminate against non-related offspring (Kempenaers and Sheldon 1996, MacDougall-Shackleton and Robertson 1998). Why then would *oriantha* males withdraw parental care, particularly if it could be contributing toward mortality in their own offspring? It may be that their behavior is the solution to a conflict between their own long-term survival and the immediate survival of their young: current versus lifetime reproductive success. Mated males captured at season's end that were not feeding at the nest were invariably well into the postnuptial molt (Chapter 11). Once this molt was fully developed it may not have been feasible energetically for them to then begin caring for nestlings. It should be acknowledged, however, that females were sometimes known to be feeding fledglings while in the midst of heavy molt.

The outcome of opposing selective forces, parental care and self-maintenance, seems to be different, therefore, for adult males and females during this one period in the reproductive season. And this has a number of ramifications. For example, the seasonal reduction in clutch size and, thereby, the number of offspring that would eventually have to be cared for might have evolved as a hedge by females against decreasing parental efforts of males. This could be costly to females, however, because their survival rates decrease when males desert (Hemborg 1999b).

Sexual differences in pattern of reproductive investment occur in a variety of avian taxa and mating systems and it has been argued that these differences are primarily the result of sexual selection (Parish and Coulson 1998). It should be mentioned too that parental care by males might not be very important. For example, Freeman-Gallant (1998) discovered that the contribution of male Savannah Sparrows during the nestling stage was only weakly correlated with offspring quality and survival. Compensatory feeding by females may have been largely responsible for this result.

GROWTH AND THERMOREGULATION IN NESTLINGS

During their relatively brief time in the nest the altricial young of passerines typically undergo rapid changes in their morphology and physiology. Body mass increases by about an order of magnitude, a nearly complete plumage is grown, and transition from ectothermy to endothermy is accomplished. It is a period when differential abilities in parental care are likely to be exposed, as are the potential vulnerabilities of nest structure and nest site (the nest microenvironment) to effects of weather. In terms of survival, it is probably the most perilous time in a bird's life.

Earlier, basic information was presented on developmental changes in *oriantha,* including growth rates and thermoregulatory capacities of nestlings (Morton and Carey 1971). Here those data are bolstered with others and extended conceptually for their comparative value and for fresh insight on how variation in nestling growth and thermal responses may reflect both parental behavior and competitive interactions among nestlings.

Nestling development

The appearance and behavior of *oriantha* nestlings were very similar to those of *pugetensis* and *nuttalli,* as described in detail by Blanchard (1941) and Banks (1959), respectively. Supplementary observations are provided below for *oriantha.*

Day 0. Bodily movements were feeble and poorly coordinated except for the gaping response associated with begging. Nestlings could gape soon after hatching and were usually fed within the hour. In one case we observed a successful feeding 14 min after hatching. Gaping occurred when the female left the nest, sometimes while she was gone, and again when she or the male returned and hopped onto the nest rim.

Day 1. Wings and legs were flexed vigorously when nestlings were handled. Gaping occurred when the female left the nest and intermittently thereafter until her return; vibration of the nest was a strong stimulus for the begging response.

Day 2. Motor coordination was improved. Some nestlings had enough strength and coordination to right themselves when placed on their backs. Gaping occurred as on Day 1, and a rudimentary alarm vocalization (a *cheep*) sometimes occurred during handling. The primaries had erupted by midday.

Day 3. Nestlings could locomote slightly through scrambling efforts when removed from the nest. Gaping occurred as before except that it sometimes now took place well before the adult hopped onto the nest, indicating that the ears were becoming functional. The eyes were still closed. Feather sheaths protruded slightly from the ventral and spinal tracts. The first noticeable increase in metabolic rate occurred (Morton and Carey 1971).

Day 4. Righting was now easily accomplished by most nestlings. Gaping tended to occur only when adults approached the nest. The eyes were starting to open. Feathers in all major tracts except the caudal tract had erupted. Nestlings made alarm calls and defecated when handled.

Day 5. Some nestlings gaped when handled and some crouched in an apparent fear reaction. The eyes were open in almost all individuals. The mean age at which eyes opened in 87 nestlings was 4.6 d. Rectrices were now erupted and barbs had broken through at sheath tips in the major body tracts. In terms of feather development, *oriantha* were about a day ahead of *nuttalli,* as described by Banks (1959).

Day 6. Nestlings were alert and their movements were fairly well coordinated. They could sit erect and balance on their feet with wings held to the sides. When placed on a perch they maintained themselves, but awkwardly. Barbs had erupted from tips of sheaths in both flight and contour feathers. All nestlings exhibited a well-developed shivering response when exposed to cold air. They cued visually on the parents and sometimes gaped when an adult was still a meter or so away in its approach to the nest.

Day 7. Nestlings sometimes lifted up in the nest and exercised their wings. Many now defecated, gave an open-mouth threat display, or a loud frightnote when handled. This note caused siblings in the nest to hop out immediately and hide in nearby vegetation. They could survive overnight out of the nest at this age. Perching abilities were good and the insulative feather layer and control of metabolism were sufficient for maintaining a high body temperature. Oakeson (1954) noted one case wherein a disturbed *gambelii* chick left the nest on Day 7.

Day 8. The responses to handling were the same as on Day 7. When placed on the ground, nestlings were capable of running.

Day 9. Nestlings were very alert. When approached, they sometimes fledged by jumping out and running into cover. If tossed gently into the air, they flapped but usually did not make much horizontal progress. However, one chick flew about 10 m in a low ground-skimming flight when frightened from the nest. Most nestlings fledged on this day even when undisturbed. The last-hatched chick, although it was often age Day 8, generally fledged along with its older siblings.

TABLE 8.7. BODY MASS (G) OF NESTLING *Oriantha*

Age (d)	Mean	SD	N
0[a]	2.65	0.36	173
1	4.16	0.71	229
2	6.33	1.04	194
3	9.08	1.45	175
4	12.02	1.71	203
5	15.21	1.61	134
6	17.60	1.88	123
7	18.64	1.81	96
8	19.71	1.80	94
9	20.70	2.09	30

[a] Day of hatching.

Day 10+. A few nestlings remained in the nest beyond Day 9, usually because they were underweight and retarded otherwise in their development. Such retardation could usually be traced to exposure to bad weather, to being a lone hatchling, or, rarely, to disease or injury.

For the next three weeks of life, up to about one month of age, fledglings were dependent upon their parents for food. They gradually developed flying and foraging abilities (they could survive on their own in captivity beyond Day 19), and tended to disperse away from natal territories (Morton et al. 1972b). The role of the male parent was more variable than that of the female during this time. The newly fledged brood was usually split between the parents, but some males fed fledglings little, if at all, and the parent most likely to be seen caring for fledglings at the very end of their period of dependency was the female.

Growth rates

The mean body mass of *oriantha* nestlings taken in the morning, beginning with the day of hatching (Day 0), was 2.65 g, and at the time of fledging nine days later it was 20.70 g (Table 8.7). Converted to a logarithmic scale, mass changes appeared to follow a near-linear increase for the first few days of life, then declined in rate during the remaining two-thirds of the nestling period (Fig. 8.5). During these early days growth exceeded 40% per day, as is usual in various sparrows and buntings (Dawson and Hudson 1970).

Because nestlings grew in approximately log-linear fashion up to Day 4, logarithmic growth rate constants per day (K) were calculated for nestlings weighed at least twice during that time period. The K values, which are simply slopes, can then be used to inform us about the trajectory of growth and how it might vary with biological and environmental factors. For example, growth rate in young nestlings did not vary with sex (males: mean K = 0.158, SD = 0.023, N = 103; females: mean K = 0.155, SD = 0.026, N = 104; t = 0.853, P = 0.190), or with parent's age (male parent: ANOVA $F_{6,256}$ = 0.74, P = 0.622, N = 263; female parent: ANOVA $F_{4,347}$ = 0.32, P = 0.861, N = 352).

Nestling growth rates during these first few days of life did change with season, however. They were highest in June, then declined steadily thereafter (ANOVA $F_{5,387}$ = 5.16, P < 0.001; Fig. 8.6). They also varied with hatching order; the first chick that hatched grew slowest and the last chick the fastest (ANOVA $F_{4,329}$ =

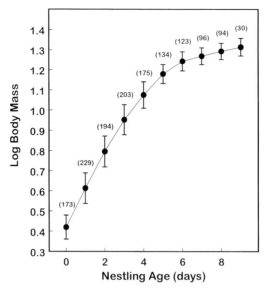

FIGURE 8.5.   Semi-logarithmic plot of body mass in nestling *oriantha*. Means ($\pm$ 1 SE); sample sizes in parentheses.

5.61, P < 0.001). This relationship was almost completely consistent through the hatching sequence, no matter the brood size (Fig. 8.7).

As can be deduced from Fig. 8.7, nestling growth rates tended to increase with brood size (ANOVA $F_{4, 387}$ = 6.50, P < 0.001; Table 8.8). Note that brood size refers to the number of nestlings alive at the time body masses were measured; it could be lower than clutch size if all of the eggs did not hatch. To summarize: as chicks were added to the nest due to hatching, growth rate in each newcomer was higher than that of its predecessor, and the larger the brood the higher the collective growth rate tended to be for members of that brood (Table 8.6, Fig. 8.7). There was also variation in growth rates obtained in different years. For example, in five years when substantial numbers of nestlings were weighed in the

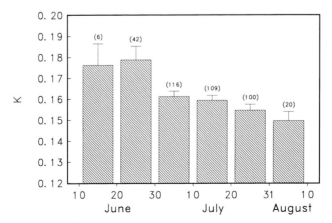

FIGURE 8.6.   Growth rates (K) of *oriantha* nestlings during the first four days of life in relation to hatching date. Bars show mean (+ 1 SE); number of nestlings in parentheses.

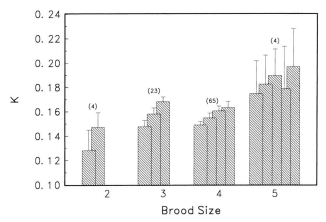

FIGURE 8.7. Growth rates (K) of *oriantha* nestlings during the first four days of life in various-sized broods, arranged first-to-last (left-to-right) in hatching order. Bars show mean (+1 SE); number of broods in parentheses.

first days after hatching, the mean value of K varied from 0.154 to 0.175 (ANOVA $F_{4, 388} = 9.99$, $P < 0.001$; Table 8.9).

King and Hubbard (1981) compiled growth rate data in *gambelii* and *oriantha* from six populations and found that the growth curves for the whole of the nestling period were congruent and independent of brood size and locality. They took this constancy to mean that growth rates in White-crowned Sparrows are physiologically maximized. This might only be expected, however, when optimum ecological conditions prevail (Ricklefs 1968, 1973). As the data presented above show, growth in the period right after hatching does vary in *oriantha,* sometimes subtly, but one needs more than the limited data set applied by King and Hubbard to detect it. They were comparing mean body masses at various days of age and had inadequate information on interannual variation and none at all on growth rates according to parent age, hatching date, or hatching order.

What could be contributing to the growth rate variations observed in *oriantha?* One logical place to focus is on the energy budgets of nestlings. Their total metabolizeable energy (TME) is equal to resting metabolic rate plus growth (energy put into tissue) plus the costs of activity and thermoregulation (Williams and Prints 1986, Weathers and Sullivan 1991). The scope of variation in these parameters will depend upon interactions among them and on how effectively the parents supply food. The growth rate of a nestling might vary, therefore, according to how much it is fed and to how it partitions TME. It appears that experience

TABLE 8.8. LOGARITHMIC GROWTH RATE CONSTANTS (K) DURING THE FIRST FOUR DAYS OF LIFE IN *Oriantha* NESTLINGS, IN RELATION TO BROOD SIZE

Brood size	Mean	SD	N[a]
1	0.143	0.016	3
2	0.148	0.027	31
3	0.160	0.025	136
4	0.161	0.030	197
5	0.197	0.042	15

[a] Number of nestlings weighed.

TABLE 8.9. LOGARITHMIC GROWTH RATE CONSTANTS (K) OF *Oriantha* NESTLINGS ACCORDING TO YEAR

Yr	Mean	SD	N[a]
1982	0.153	0.025	125
1991	0.154	0.028	47
1992	0.154	0.037	69
1993	0.175	0.023	84
1994	0.167	0.030	68

[a] Number of nestlings weighed.

in food gathering for dependent offspring was not a factor in *oriantha* because nestling growth rates did not change with parent age.

The increase in growth rate with hatching order introduces additional variables to be considered: sibling competition and the female's brooding propensities. Sibling competition has been invoked as a dominant force in the evolution of avian growth rates (Werschkul and Jackson 1979), and although evidence for this hypothesis is not always robust, intense competition for food has often been observed among passerine siblings (Ricklefs 1982). Generally the larger, first-born young are the ones that obtain the most food, either because they are stronger or because they are fed preferentially by the adults (Lack 1956, Hussell 1972, Howe 1976). This leads one to expect that growth rates should decline with hatching order—exactly the opposite of what was observed (Fig. 8.7). How can this be explained?

As noted earlier, females sat tightly on the nest during the time of hatching, even though their body mass was declining, and fed first-hatched nestlings sparingly until all eggs in the clutch had hatched. When bad weather caused partial mortality so that only one or two eggs or hatchlings survived, or when its effects caused hatching asynchrony to be greatly exaggerated, prolongation of attentiveness typical of incubation occurred. For example, in a nest wherein only one egg out of four was viable the female brooded the hatchling and the three eggs almost continuously for at least five days. The lone nestling was fed irregularly and weighed 3.2 g on Day 5, about 20% of the mass expected at that age (see Table 8.7). It eventually reached 13.7 g on Day 11, two days beyond the usual fledging time, but was dead in the nest on the next day. In another nest with five eggs, three of the chicks hatched out three days before the other two. Again, the female was reluctant to leave the nest and growth of the early chicks was greatly retarded until the others hatched. At that time growth in all five began to proceed at the normal rate. The propensity to starve hatchlings in order to remain on the nest and supply heat to unhatched eggs has not, to my knowledge, been previously reported.

The maintenance of nest attentiveness typical of incubation during the hatching period, even though it puts females into negative energy balance and slows growth in hatchlings, suggests that it is important for females to minimize the hatching spread induced by the early onset of incubation behavior. I hypothesize that a trade-off is occurring here because, in the long run, hatching asynchrony probably increases nestling mortality.

More rapid growth with brood size is a response that calls for more investigation. Several factors, some of them clearly interdependent, may have contributed to this surprising pattern. For example, the presence of more nestlings could have stimulated a disproportionate increase in parental feedings. Also, defense of broods against cooling is known to improve as the number of chicks increases (within normal brood size ranges) because of the increased effectiveness of huddling (see below). This would spare more energy for incorporation into biomass and it could also increase the female's ability to provision because the chicks would require less brooding.

Although the ANOVA indicated that inter-brood growth rates varied, inspection of the data (Table 8.8) reveals that brood sizes of three and four, which comprised 87% of all broods measured, had similar K values. Most of the variation was due to differential rates in the smallest and largest broods. Chicks in broods of one and two grew the slowest and, as pointed out above, were sometimes neglected. In addition, because clutch size decreased seasonally, these broods tended to occur at the end of summer when insect food was diminishing (see below) and when care by male parents was unreliable. The high growth rates observed in broods of five could also have been related to food abundance. Recall that short-term environmental feedback operating during favorable trophic conditions seemed to favor the laying of 5-egg clutches (Chapter 7), so territories containing broods of five may have been optimal for parental provisioning and, consequently, for hatchling growth.

It should be re-emphasized that growth rates were only measured during the first few days of nestling life, the most propitious time to detect differences that might occur because of variations in brooding and provisioning. It is unclear if these differences carried through to fledging or beyond, but perhaps they did not (see Fig. 8.2, A, B, C). A comparison of growth rates taken in the present study with those derived by other methods, such as the logistic conversion of asymptotic mass (Ricklefs 1967), would be instructive, especially if concurrent data were obtained on parental behavior and the type and volume of food being brought to nestlings.

The fact that growth rates declined with season (Fig. 8.6) should not be attributed to an increase in thermoregulatory demands because ambient temperatures ameliorate through the summer. Also, at the ages when growth rates were measured, nestlings were still ectothermic (see below), and their thermoregulatory costs must have been low. Aside from shifts in parental care, discussed above, it may be that appropriate food for nestlings also wanes in availability with season at Tioga Pass. Biomass of flying insects (adults) tended to increase until late July, or even into August in some years at Tioga Pass (Pereyra 1998, Fig. 24). Interannual variation was quite large, being on the order of a 20-fold difference. These data do not address abundance of insect larvae, which should decline well before that of adults, but they do indicate that variation in food supply could be influencing interannual and seasonal differences in growth rates of *oriantha* nestlings.

Ontogeny of thermoregulation

As nestlings added biomass, their surface-to-volume ratio decreased, insulation was added as feathers grew in and brushed out, and their thermogenic abilities increased. In a period of three or four days, midway the nestling period, they made the transition from ectothermy to endothermy. At the time they fledged, usually Day 9, they were homeothermic and could thermoregulate effectively

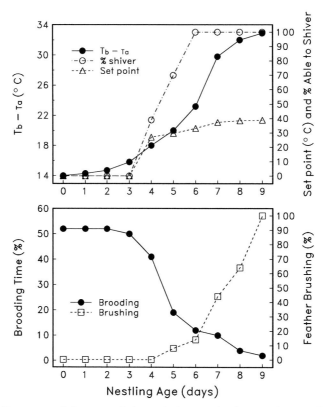

FIGURE 8.8.   Parameters of thermoregulation and plumage development in *oriantha* nestlings, and of daytime brooding by tending females. Means are shown for each day of age. Chicks were cold stressed by exposing them individually to 5 C air temperature for 10 min. Sample sizes were 15–50. Adapted from Morton and Carey (1971).

enough to survive even sub-freezing temperatures on their own (Morton and Carey 1971). The first expression of incipient endothermy occurred about Day 4, the time when some of the chilled nestlings began to shiver, to open their eyes, and to grow less rapidly. If they were taken out of the nest in the early morning on Day 4 when ambient temperature (T_a) was about 5 C, their body temperature (T_b) decreased such that they were only 18 degrees warmer than T_a after 10 min (Fig. 8.8, upper). The T_b-T_a gradient in cold-stressed nestlings increased to about 30 degrees over the next three days and on Day 7 they were already capable of resisting the cold and surviving premature fledging, should it occur.

On Day 4 about 40% of the nestlings tested were able to shiver and two days later all of them were doing it (Fig. 8.8, upper). This schedule was nearly two days ahead of that found in a close relative, the Song Sparrow, living at low elevations (Sogge et al. 1991). The T_b at which shivering began in *oriantha,* the manifestation of a hypothalamic set point, also showed some maturational changes within this time frame, increasing by 10 degrees from about 29 C to 39 C (Fig. 8.8, upper). In parallel with increasing thermogenic capacities, nestlings also became better insulated due to their new feathers becoming brushed out at the tips and covering the bare skin of their apteria (Fig. 8.8, lower).

These field experiments were performed to discover nestling thermoregulatory

TABLE 8.10. Mean Decrease in Body Temperature of *Oriantha* Nestlings Measured in the Nest, After Exposure to Ambient Temperature of 10 C for 15 Min

Nestling Age (d)	One Nestling			Four Nestlings		
	Mean	SD	N	Mean	SD	N
2	10.8	1.8	7	5.4	1.9	7
4	6.8	1.2	7	2.3	1.2	7
6	1.3	1.3	7	0.2	0.4	7
8	0.5	1.0	7	0.1	0.1	7

capacities, particularly their ability to avoid heat loss. Normally, of course, chicks benefit by being in the nest where they are surrounded by its walls and by siblings, and from being brooded by their mother (the duration of which she modified as they gained thermal independence; Fig. 8.8, lower). As a result, mean T_b of nestlings was actually quite stable. Measured *in situ,* with as little disturbance as possible, it varied only about five degrees, averaging 34 C in the youngest (Day 0) and 39 C in the oldest nestlings (Day 9).

Huddling

Huddling of neonates reduces the collective surface area exposed to the elements and the heat they produce also warms the immediate microenvironment, further affecting energy exchange rates (Hayes et al. 1992). When the air was cold, *oriantha* nestlings invariably packed themselves tightly against one another. To evaluate the effect of huddling, T_b was measured in intact broods of four and in lone nestlings when the female was kept away by our presence near the nest. It was found that Day 2 broods cooled by a mean of 5.4 degrees when subjected to early morning cold for 15 min whereas singleton nestlings decreased by 10.8 degrees, a significant difference (t = 5.01, P < 0.001; Table 8.10). Although this difference decreased as nestlings grew older (Table 8.10), the effectiveness of huddling by full broods helps to explain why brooding time of females in daylight hours decreased rapidly after Day 3 (Fig. 8.8, lower). The acquisition of functional endothermy by broods well ahead of individuals has often been noted in altricial birds (Dunn 1975, 1976, 1979; Sullivan and Weathers 1992, Pereyra and Morton 2001), and the ability of broods to function as thermoregulatory units that can buffer T_b decrease while the nest is untended probably contributes to their own health and to the time available for females to engage in self maintenance and food gathering (Verbeek 1995).

In recent years it has become possible to measure metabolic rates of nestlings with the doubly-labeled water (DLW) technique. One immediate revelation was that, because of thermoregulatory costs, energy budgets of nestlings were substantially higher in the field than in the lab. Even resting or basal metabolic rates of the field-tested nestlings were unexpectedly high (Williams and Hansell 1981, Williams and Nagy 1984, Williams and Prints 1986).

Sullivan and Weathers (1992) used DLW to measure nestling energy requirements in Yellow-eyed Juncos in relation to brood size and found that the modal clutch size (4) was also the most efficient brood size. Reducing the brood size increased the metabolic cost per nestling because benefits from huddling were lower. Augmenting the brood was also costly because the chicks no longer fitted properly within the nest walls. Ambient temperature accounted for the greatest amount of the variation in field metabolic rates, 21.0%, but brood size was also a large factor, accounting for 17.5% of the variation. In the future it would seem important that data from the DLW studies of nestling thermoregulatory costs be taken into consideration when conclusions are being drawn about optimal clutch sizes and "benefits" of brood reduction.

Implications from the foregoing are that loss of heat subtracts from growth and survival, and that this might be of great concern in high altitude environments where cold is imposed nocturnally and summer storms are frequent. This is true, but it is also true that the thinned-out layer of water vapor in the atmosphere exacerbates the problem of overheating from solar radiation. Intra-nest temperatures can soar when exposure to direct sun occurs, causing mortality in eggs and nestlings within 20–30 min (Morton and Carey 1971, Zerba and Morton 1983b). Solar heating can also cause older nestlings to leave the nest temporarily to lower their discomfort and may even stimulate fledging itself if they are at the appropriate age.

If a nest is exposed to direct sun its contents can be protected in several ways. One is that females can stay on the nest and shade it, and attentiveness does increase as solar heating increases (Zerba and Morton 1983b). Another, at least for nestlings, is that some protection can be afforded by evaporative cooling from the respiratory tract. Active heat defense is well known in altricial birds and thermostatic controls can be observed at an early age (Dawson and Hudson 1970). For example, less than an hour after hatching, *oriantha* nestlings will pant when exposed to heat loads. The efficacy of this behavior has not been adequately examined, but the T_b set point for panting was found to be about 41 C and, most impressively, did not vary significantly from the day of hatching onward (Morton and Carey 1971). It should not be overlooked that the plumage of nestlings, including the downy feathers, may serve to deflect or exclude solar radiation (Verbeek 1988).

NATAL DISPERSAL

From the moment they leave the nest, young passerines begin a journey that will take them from their place of birth to where they will eventually settle and breed. In sedentary species, the total distance involved in this natal dispersal is ordinarily a few kilometers or less, and it is usually covered within the first few months of life, before the arrival of winter weather (Tompa 1962, Nilsson 1989). Because of the migration to and from wintering areas that intervenes, natal dispersal in migratory species is a temporally discontinuous process, and its distances and biology are poorly understood.

Oriantha fledglings remained hidden in vegetation close to the nest for the first few days after leaving it. If both adults were feeding them, each one tended to focus on part of the brood, repeatedly feeding the same one or two fledglings, for example, rather than all of them. Thus, the family became divided into subunits that after about a week, and coincident with the development of flying and foraging abilities in the fledglings, began drifting away from the area of the nest (Fig. 8.9). At about one month of age, some three weeks after fledging, the family subunits dissolved. By then the young were of adult body size, able to survive independently, usually living well away from their natal site (Fig. 8.9), and en-

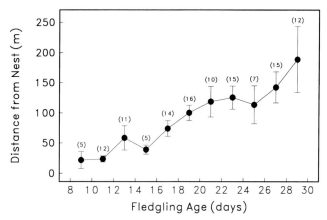

FIGURE 8.9.   Mean distance moved (+ SE) with age by *oriantha* fledglings in relation to their nest. Sample sizes in parentheses.

tering the postjuvenal molt. Although no longer interacting with their parents, some siblings probably continued to travel together for several additional weeks because they were often trapped simultaneously at the same location.

Most of the observations on post-fledging movements were made on TPM and some of the juveniles that were born there stayed on that meadow until departing on migration. Most moved away or died, however, because they were no longer observed nor did they show up in traps. Another measure of mobility in juveniles was obtained from individuals banded as nestlings at locations 2–5 km from TPM that were subsequently captured on TPM. These nonlocal juveniles ranged in age from 32 to 78 d upon first arriving at TPM (mean = 52.8 d, N = 17 males and 15 females).

As summer progressed first captures of juveniles born on TPM (locals) declined, but members of the other cohort (nonlocals) began to increase. The frequency distribution for first captures of these two groups was about one month out of phase, and every year the nonlocals outnumbered the locals by about two to one (Fig. 8.10). The postjuvenal molt occupied the second month of life in juveniles and about 90% of the nonlocals were either in its final stages or had fresh plumage. Thus, most of the nonlocals were two months old or older when they arrived on TPM. It seemed likely that many had traveled more than 5 km to get there and may have moved in from watersheds outside the Lee Vining Creek drainage (Morton et al. 1991, Morton 1997).

Natal dispersal is a permanent movement from birth site to first breeding site, but, as pointed out above, it is discontinuous in migrants being separated into two stages, one between fledging and migration departure in the fall, the post-fledging period, and the other between arrival and settlement the next spring, the pre-breeding period (Morton 1992b, 1997).

Dispersing juveniles must locate suitable breeding habitat and then be able to settle there. Obviously, the first of these processes could take place during the post-fledging period whereas the second must wait until the pre-breeding period. It has been suggested, in fact, that the critical time for habitat imprinting in various species of passerine migrants is when they are only about 30 to 50 days of age, the very first few weeks after they have become independent and can travel alone

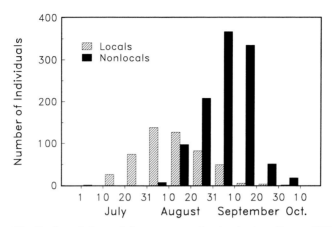

FIGURE 8.10.   Distribution of dates of first captures of *oriantha* juveniles on TPM. Locals were born on TPM, nonlocals elsewhere. Samples were derived from 10 yr of data (1978–1987), N = 506 locals and 1,083 nonlocals.

(Löhrl 1959, Haukioja 1971, Van Balen 1979, Morton et al. 1991, Sokolov 1991). During post-fledging dispersal, juveniles could also be learning landmarks that would be useful to them the next spring when they return after an absence of eight months, and at a time when the habitat looks very different (Löhrl 1959, Wiltschko and Wiltschko 1978, Able and Bingman 1987). Furthermore, post-fledging meanderings may help young birds find enough food for growth, maintenance, and premigratory fattening (Morton 1997). In Green-tailed Towhees (*Pipilo chlororus*), for example, such movements were longest during drought years (Morton 1991).

The trapping data reveal some additional subtleties about habitat imprinting in *oriantha.* For example, the return rate of birds to the study area as adults that had been banded there as juveniles was different for the sexes. In males it was 13.9% (124 of 894) and in females it was 10.0% (70 of 700), a significant difference (Chi-square = 5.50, df = 1, P = 0.019). This effect could be traced to differences in return rates that were related to the amount of time spent on TPM as juveniles. If males were in residency on TPM as juveniles for more than four weeks their return rate increased significantly, from 11.1% to 28.5% (Chi-square = 30.64, df = 1, P < 0.001; Fig. 8.11), but return rate did not change between these periods of residency in females, 10.3% vs. 8.4% (Chi-square = 0.35, df = 1, P = 0.552). The return rate of 28.5% for males that were sedentary as juveniles was extremely high in comparison to rates observed in other migratory species (Weatherhead and Forbes 1994), and nearly all of these particular individuals that survived the winter must have returned to TPM. Apparently the selection of breeding habitat was entirely completed by this group during the post-fledging period. The return rate of sedentary female juveniles (8.4%) was significantly lower than that of males (Chi-square = 15.49, df = 1, P < 0.001).

The lower return rates observed in females and in non-sedentary males (as compared to sedentary males) may simply be a function of some birds, females especially, traveling over greater distances than others during their post-fledging dispersal period. Thus, they were more scattered when returning the next spring as adults and not as many showed up on the study area.

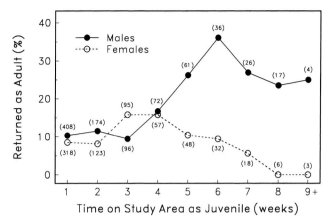

FIGURE 8.11.   Return rates of *oriantha* adults to the study area in accordance with their duration of residency as juveniles in the previous year. Sample sizes in parentheses.

Despite limitations imposed by study area size (which invariably causes dispersal distances for a population to be underestimated) there were indications that *oriantha* females followed the pattern observed in most avian species in that they tended to disperse greater distances than males (Gauthreaux 1978, Greenwood 1980, Pusey 1987, Plissner and Gowaty 1996). Mean natal dispersal distance (distance from nest of birth to first nest as a one-year-old adult) was 1.7 km (SD = 1.1 km) in females (N = 15) and 1.2 km (SD = 1.0 km) in males (N = 25). Median dispersal distance was 1.7 km in females and 0.8 km in males. Although these differences were large, they did not reach statistical significance (Morton 1992b).

Did experiences gained during the post-fledging period subsequently affect reproductive success? This cannot be answered with certainty, but it can be pointed out that such exposure may have influenced recruitment or philopatric tendencies in the sexes. Of 188 one-year-old males known to have nests on TPM, 68 (36.2%) had been captured there the previous year as juveniles; in females it was 45 of 256 (17.6%), a significant difference (Chi-square = 19.75, df = 1, P < 0.001). Males were more philopatric than females.

CHAPTER 9: Nest Failure

The causes of nest failure and the responses to them are at the heart of repro-ductive success. Of 1,331 *oriantha* nests found and monitored during 22 summers, 626 managed to fledge at least one chick, a success rate of 47.0%. But what were the modifying factors that caused the other 53.0% to fail? The primary reason for interruption of the nesting cycle proved to be predation. It accounted for 57.0% of all nest failures. Beyond that, desertion of nests (22.3%), bad weather (16.2%), and other factors (4.5%) impacted nesting attempts. The latter, the other factors, included nests falling apart due to poor construction (N = 2), death of the tending female (N = 8), flooding caused by rising streams (N = 10), and additional cases that were unfathomable to us (N = 12). The top three causes of nesting failure, and ramifications thereof, will now be considered in more detail.

PREDATION

During the years that comprehensive data were obtained on nest fates, predation rates were remarkably constant (Fig. 9.1). The mean annual rate was 30.5% of all nests (SD = 4.7%). This constancy was attributed to the presence of a large and stable population of Belding's ground squirrels (*Spermophilus beldingi*) on the study area (Morton et al. 1993). These rodents are thought to be the principal predator on *oriantha* nests and they have been observed eating both eggs and

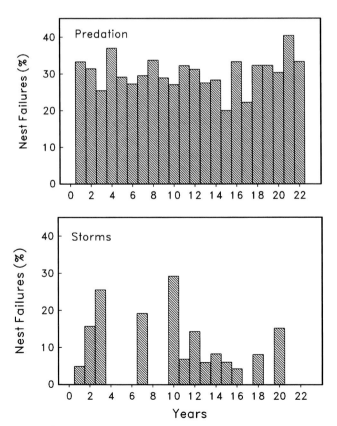

FIGURE 9.1.   Percent of *oriantha* nests lost from predation (upper panel) and storms (lower panel) at Tioga Pass during 22 breeding seasons.

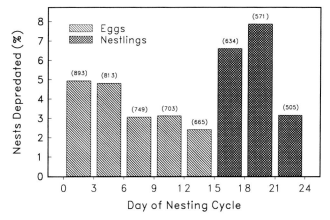

FIGURE 9.2.   Percent of *oriantha* nests depredated per 3-d interval throughout the nesting cycle. The cycle begins with the laying of the first egg (day 0) and ends at fledging (day 24). Number of nests in parentheses.

nestlings. Other mammalian predators of import, across the study area as a whole, were long-tailed weasels (*Mustela frenata*) and coyotes (*Canis latrans*). Coyote predation was not observed directly but tracks in the snow showed that they sometimes followed our circuit of nests or traps, and their presence at nests was known from both tracks and tufts of hair snagged on bushes. And nests built off the ground were sometimes tipped down and indented as though by a coyote reaching up and pulling the nest down with its muzzle. Early in the season, patches of habitat that had recently emerged from beneath the snow were often used by *oriantha* as nesting areas. Coyotes habitually hunted through these patches, probably in pursuit of small mammals such as voles or ground squirrels, but they undoubtedly chanced upon nests at such times.

Among avian predators, Clark's Nutcrackers (*Nucifraga columbiana*) were probably the most important. They were observed eating eggs, nestlings, and fledglings of several species, including *oriantha* (Mulder et al. 1978), and Common Ravens (*Corvus corax*) did the same. Ravens were not observed on the area until 1979 but they had become regular residents by the end of the study. They can be expected to have an increasingly greater impact on the nesting birds of Tioga Pass in the years ahead.

Predation rate varied as nests passed through various stages of the cycle from laying to fledging, a process that lasted about 24 days (Fig. 9.2). About 5% of all nests were depredated per three-day period when eggs first appeared in the nest (laying and early incubation), and the rate then tailed off somewhat. This was probably because the most easily located nests were depredated early on. As the first hatchlings began to appear, at about day 15 in the nesting cycle, predation rates more than doubled. Doubtless, the added activity, noise, and odors at the nest provided cues that attracted predators at that time. This kind of effect has been verified experimentally in nestling passerines by Leech and Leonard (1997).

Because the number of viable nests decreased at about 2% per day, the total number of nests lost per three-day interval was not as variable as one might expect from Fig. 9.2. For example, 19.1% of all nest losses occurred during laying, days 0–3, and 18.2% when nestlings first appeared, days 15–18. Predation rates did not vary with nest location (on the ground vs. above ground), nor with the age of either parent (Morton et al. 1993).

Both members of pairs tried to distract or drive away predators in the vicinity of the nest. Females on nests would sit tightly if one looked directly at them at close range. If the gaze was then averted, however, they would immediately slip quietly away. They sometimes displayed a distracting tail-wag maneuver when running from ground nests. If disturbed early in the nesting cycle by a real or perceived (human) predator, females sometimes deserted even though the eggs had not been touched.

DESERTION

Other than exposure to bad weather (treated separately below), the reasons why females deserted nests varied widely. For example, a clutch was sometimes reduced in size with the female alive but no longer in attendance. Hill and Sealy (1994) also found that clutch reduction caused desertion in Clay-colored Sparrows (*Spizella pallida*). Such episodes could have been due to partial predation (observed once when a juvenile Clark's Nutcracker removed one of four eggs from a nest then flew off to join siblings), to interference by nesting heterospecifics (in one case we thought the culprit was a Lincoln's Sparrow, *Melospiza lincolnii*), or to conspecifics; usually we could not tell. About one-third of all desertions could be attributed to these types of natural causes and the other two-thirds to investigator activities (Morton et al. 1993).

Once an adult *oriantha* (sex unknown) was observed at close range from a blind to kill and remove two hatchlings from a nest. Of 10 probable cases of infanticide, where chicks were pecked about the head and neck and left dead inside the nest or immediately outside it, this was the only time we actually saw it happen. Interestingly, five of these 10 cases occurred on the day after male songs were broadcasted on territories where there were nestlings. The males at those locations were unresponsive and seemed reluctant to counter-sing, thus allowing their dialects to be identified (the purpose of the experiment). As a result, the playback experiments were conducted for an hour or more at each location. Although males with dependent young usually have low levels of circulating testosterone, it can increase if they are exposed repeatedly to simulated intrusions (Wingfield and Wada 1989), thereby increasing the likelihood of aggression (Wingfield et al. 1987, 1990). It may be that prolonged periods of song playback induce high testosterone levels in either the parent or a neighbor thereby facilitating infanticidal behavior.

Investigator activities that involved spending considerable time at the nest, such as measuring eggs or implanting thermocouples, especially during laying or the first few days of incubation, were the ones most likely to cause desertion. Females flushed at close range while engaged in nest building or laying were also known to desert. As implied above, females were most prone to desert early in the nesting cycle. Once nestlings were present they did not desert even though we sometimes spent prolonged periods at the nest conducting procedures such as banding, weighing, laparotomies, feather measurements, or thermoregulation experiments. On the other hand, these activities undoubtedly caused increased predation rates on nestlings (Mead and Morton 1985). Desertion of offspring appears to be a part of normal reproductive behavior in many avian species, and it may be advantageous

TABLE 9.1. Types of Storms and Their Mean Frequency of Occurrence from May to October at Tioga Pass, as Extracted from Logbooks of F. Castillo (N = 15 yr)

Month	Type of Storm			Total storms
	Snow	Hail	Rain	
May	4.6	1.1	2.6	8.3
June	2.2	1.9	4.5	8.6
July	0.1	1.9	6.3	8.3
August	0.8	2.3	6.1	9.2
September	1.1	1.3	3.2	5.6
October	6.2	1.2	3.3	10.7

if it provides the opportunity to abort a flawed breeding attempt and to renest (Székely et al. 1996).

STORMS

As is typical of montane climates (Ehrlich et al. 1972, Hendricks and Norment 1992), summer storms were a frequent occurrence at Tioga Pass. Usually these swept through in the afternoon or evening and seldom lasted for more than an hour or two. Often only trace amounts of moisture were deposited, but readable quantities of precipitation were sometimes left in our rain gauges. Mean depth recorded from 39 storms was 0.97 cm (SD = 0.90 cm) with the minimum measured being 0.19 cm and the maximum 3.94 cm. Nest mortality from these storms sometimes occurred and their effects varied immensely from year to year; during 22 seasons with complete data, mean annual rate of mortality from storms was 7.3% of all nests (SD = 8.8%).

A valuable source of information on weather at Tioga Pass was compiled by F. Castillo, a National Park Service employee who was in summer residence for many years at the southern end, and highest elevation, of the study area. Castillo recorded daily weather observations in logbooks from which we extracted 15 years of data (1968–1982). These show that storms occurred at their lowest frequency in September, when *oriantha* were completing molt, fattening, and leaving on migration (Table 9.1). During the key nesting season months of June and July there were 8+ storms per month. As one might expect from seasonal temperature changes, snowstorms and rainstorms tended to vary inversely in frequency, with the former being most common at the beginning and end of the summer season, and the latter during the middle. Hailstorm frequency also tended to peak during the middle months (Table 9.1).

How many of these storms caused mortality in nests and how lasting was their effect? In nine of 22 years none of the storms induced mortality; in the other 13 years a total of 22 storms occurred that caused death in *oriantha* offspring. If it is assumed that eggs and nestlings were present over about a two-month period between May and August in any particular breeding season, then in 22 years, according to the Castillo data, they must have been exposed to about 374 storms (17 × 22). Thus, about one storm in every 17 (6%) was a selective event.

As can be seen from Fig. 9.1 (bottom panel), nest failure due to storms varied from zero to nearly 30% of all nests in any one year. In eight of the 13 years during which mortality occurred there was one killer storm, in three years there were two, and in two years (1984 and 1992) four such storms occurred. These

TABLE 9.2. EFFECTS OF 22 STORMS ON EGGS AND NESTLINGS OF *Oriantha* AT TIOGA PASS (DATA OBTAINED FROM 13 YR)

Storms		Eggs			Nestlings			All individuals		
Type	Date	N	Killed	Mortality (%)	N	Killed	Mortality (%)	N	Killed	Mortality (%)
Rain	7–8 July 68	—	—	—	31	7	22.6	31	7	22.6
Rain	13 July 69	44	10	22.7	48	8	16.7	92	18	19.6
Rain/Hail	21 July 69	16	0	0.0	14	8	57.1	30	8	26.7
Snow	8–14 June 70	31	23	74.2	—	—	—	31	23	74.2
Snow	26–27 June 78	16	6	37.5	—	—	—	16	6	37.5
Snow	17 June 79	92	47	51.1	—	—	—	92	47	51.1
Rain/Hail	19 July 79	7	1	14.3	18	2	11.1	25	3	12.0
Snow	28–30 June 82	120	78	65.0	5	5	100.0	125	83	66.4
Hail	26 July 82	20	2	10.0	85	19	22.4	105	21	20.0
Rain	9 Aug 83	4	0	0.0	7	2	28.6	11	2	18.2
Snow	4 June 84	6	6	100.0	—	—	—	6	6	100.0
Snow	6 June 84	10	7	70.0	—	—	—	10	7	70.0
Snow	13–14 June 84	24	8	33.3	—	—	—	24	8	33.3
Rain/Hail	18 July 84	7	7	100.0	17	17	100.0	24	24	100.0
Rain/Hail	23 July 86	15	0	0.0	22	18	81.8	37	18	48.6
Rain/Hail	28 June 87	22	0	0.0	20	2	10.0	42	2	4.8
Snow	6 June 88	6	3	50.0	—	—	—	6	3	50.0
Snow	14–15 June 90	114	21	18.4	—	—	—	114	21	18.4
Snow	13–15 June 92	69	42	60.9	36	19	52.8	105	61	58.1
Snow	29 June 92	62	4	5.5	15	8	5.3	77	12	15.6
Rain	12 July 92	43	0	0.0	37	15	40.5	80	15	18.8
Rain	14 July 92	48	0	0.0	17	7	41.2	65	7	10.8
	Totals	776	265	34.1	372	137	36.8	1,148	402	35.0

storms were evenly divided as to type; 11 involved snow and 11 rain and hail. All 11 of the snowstorms occurred in June and the other storms thereafter (Table 9.2). Together, the 22 killer storms affected 233 nests containing eggs and another 108 with nestlings.

The outcome of each of these storms is chronicled in Table 9.2. Of 776 eggs that were present during storms, 265 (34.1%) did not survive. Of 372 nestlings, 137 (36.8%) did not survive. These mortality rates were not different (Chi-square = 0.793, df = 1, P = 0.373). More than twice as many eggs as nestlings were exposed to storms, and looking within Table 9.2 it can be seen that eggs were present in 21 of 22 storms, but nestlings in only 14 of 22. In nine of the 22 storms total mortality was 20% or less. In two storms, however, mortality was 100%. One of these occurred at the very beginning of the season, 4 June 1984, and involved six eggs in five newly started nests. All were wiped out. The other occurred on 18 July in the same year and involved seven eggs in two nests and 17 nestlings in five nests. This was a particularly violent storm that included hail and torrential rains. It lasted for three hr in the late afternoon, and it was the only time that all eggs and nestlings under surveillance were lost. Despite these two storms, plus two others in 1984 (see Table 9.2), weather caused mortality in only 14.3% of all nests in 1984.

The most individuals killed at one time was 83, 78 of which were eggs, in a three-day snowstorm that began on 28 June 1982. At least 20 cm of snow accumulated in this storm, burying much of the low-lying vegetation and many nests. Some nests survived, however, because they were in naturally sheltered

TABLE 9.3. MORTALITY RATES AT TIOGA PASS OF *Oriantha* NESTS, AND INDIVIDUALS CONTAINED THEREIN, ACCORDING TO TYPE OF STORM

Storms			Nest mortality				Individual mortality		
Type	N	Nest status	None	Partial	Complete	% with mortality	Survived	Died	Mortality (%)
Snow	11	Eggs	82	9	73	50.0	305	245	44.5
	3	Nestlings	6	1	8	60.0	24	32	57.1
Rain/hail	10	Eggs	62	2	5	10.1	206	20	8.8
	11	Nestlings	55	11	27	40.9	211	105	33.2

locations and because some incubating females managed to defend their eggs even though their nests were covered by snow. They sat tightly and the falling snow completely covered them and the nest. Eventually they exited by tunneling out to the side leaving the covered nest in an igloo-like configuration. Nests were tended in this condition until the snow had melted away. By the morning of 2 July the storm had ended and females that had lost their nests were already building at new sites. Interestingly, Hendricks and Norment (1992) found that nestlings of the American Pipit that were old enough to thermoregulate could survive burial beneath the snow for at least 24 hr, even when unbrooded.

When a snowstorm causes many nests to fail simultaneously, the reproductive systems of the females involved are reset to the same physiological condition. Thus, when the storm ends they are synchronized and clutch starts of their renests tend to be clustered. Aside from *oriantha* at Tioga Pass (Morton and Allan 1990), this type of population-wide response has been documented in three species of thrushes (*Turdus*) in Finland (Pulliainen 1978).

Snowstorms usually occurred early in the nesting season and nestlings were present during only three of the 11 snowstorms that caused mortality. The total loss of nests containing nestlings and of individual nestlings was low, therefore, compared to that of eggs (Tables 9.2 and 9.3). Nestlings were more likely to be present later on when rainstorms occurred, and they proved to be more vulnerable than eggs to cold, drenching rains. One such storm occurred on 23 July 1986. Only 1.1 cm of rain fell, all in the first hour of the afternoon, but it was cold enough to include some hail and 18 of 22 nestlings died whereas all 15 eggs present survived (Table 9.2). In severe downpours females sometime had to leave the nest in self defense and could not prevent the nest-nestling unit from getting soaked. They would return immediately after the storm to brood, and even though the nestlings might already be dead they would stay on for several hours, apparently attempting to revive them. Eggs, of course, were only superficially wetted in such situations and often survived. Embryos appeared to be less susceptible to cooling than nestlings. Jehl and Hussell (1966) found much the same thing in young passerines exposed to chilling rains in Manitoba.

A summary of how the type of storm affected *oriantha* young shows that mortality was slightly higher in nestlings (57.1%) than in eggs (44.5%) during snowstorms, an insignificant difference (Chi-square = 3.25, df = 1, P = 0.072). Note, however, that only 56 nestlings from 15 nests were exposed to this type of storm as compared to 550 eggs from 164 nests. In rainstorms, overall mortality was again lower in eggs (Table 9.3), being only 8.8% (20 of 226) as compared to 33.2% in nestlings (105 of 316). So mortality from rain was nearly four times

TABLE 9.4. RATE OF STORM-INDUCED MORTALITY IN *Oriantha* NESTS ACCORDING TO DAY OF THE NESTING CYCLE (FIRST EGG BEING LAID ON DAY 0)

Day of nesting cycle	Type of offspring present	N[a]	Mortality (%)
0–3	Eggs	56	36.4
4–6	Eggs	129	31.5
7–9	Eggs	158	28.8
10–12	Eggs	92	32.4
13–15	Eggs	71	33.0
16–18	Nestlings	65	29.3
19–21	Nestlings	70	44.0
22–24	Nestlings	89	36.4

[a] Number of offspring (eggs and nestlings) that were present when killer storms occurred.

higher in nestlings than in eggs, a highly significant difference (Chi-square = 44.13, df = 1, P < 0.001).

The rate of weather-related mortality was fairly constant across the nesting cycle (Table 9.4). Among eggs it was highest during the laying period (days 0–3) but the effect was not significant (Chi-square = 1.52, df = 1, P = 0.218). The data on egg temperatures (Chapter 7) show that eggs were neglected for much of the time during laying, so one might expect storm damage to be high for that period. We have noticed, however, that females, even those with just a first egg, will come back onto the nest during storms even if it already contains snow or ice. This behavior seemed to be effective, although there were exceptions. In one case, for example, a nest with an incomplete clutch of two eggs became snow-filled during a storm. Over the course of the next two days the presiding female laid her third egg nearby on the ground and then instead of deserting as expected, laid her fourth egg in the still-frozen nest and began to incubate. None of these eggs hatched and the female continued in attendance for 22 days, 10 days beyond the normal period of incubation, before deserting.

Although unpredicted by the brood reduction data (Table 8.4), storm-induced mortality in nestlings was lowest in the recently hatched, days 16–18 of the cycle (Table 9.4); compared to older nestlings, the difference was significant (Chi-square = 4.77, df = 1, P = 0.029). Apparently, broods of young, ectothermic chicks tolerate chilling better than older ones whose members are endothermic or transiting to that condition. Younger nestlings may also suffer less during storms because they require less food overall than older nestlings (Hays 1969).

There are numerous published notes about storms impacting birds at various times throughout the year, sometimes catastrophically (Gessaman and Worthen 1982), but these reports invariably focus on one storm and its potential long-term effects usually are not addressed. For example, if a massive storm strikes a breeding population, what is the effect on productivity for that year? The same sort of question could be asked about variations in predation pressure. Information relevant to these questions can be derived from the Tioga Pass study because during eight years (1979–1985) the total number of independent juveniles on the study area was known (Chapter 8). A regression of those data on predation losses showed no significant relationship (r^2 = 0.053, P = 0.582), nor was there one for weather-related losses (r^2 = 0.177, P = 0.299).

Wingfield et al. (1983) found that *pugetensis* exposed to storms while caring for young were highly stressed, as assayed by depleted fat depots and high plasma concentrations of corticosterone. Despite the stress, however, circulating levels of gonadotropin and sex steroids remained normal, reproductive organs were maintained in a functional state, and renesting efforts proceeded immediately when environmental conditions improved (Wingfield 1984c). The fact that *oriantha* can respond in much the same manner and maintain productivity despite loss of nests shows high fitness for reproducing in an environment where stochastic events can interrupt or terminate reproductive efforts. Their ability to recover quickly from nesting losses would seem to hinge on energy availability, and on a mating system and reproductive physiology that are flexible enough to permit immediate renesting. As we will see next, they can renest and, if necessary, do it repetitively.

RENESTING

Predators regularly took about 30% of all *oriantha* nests, and weather effects, although unpredictable, could also cause substantial additional losses, to say nothing of investigator impacts. Reproductive success in the Tioga Pass population would seem to depend heavily, then, upon the birds' ability to recover quickly from disruption of the nesting phase (modifying information) and begin the nesting cycle anew. To accomplish this, pairs must re-initiate courtship and prepare physiologically. This is a larger task for females. Not only must they undergo reactivation of endocrine pathways involved in sexual behavior and ovarian development, they must also build a nest and re-acquire and mobilize nutrients sufficient for producing a new clutch. This same suite of responses can be used by pairs, environmental conditions permitting, to enhance their reproductive output by double brooding.

Renesting intervals

If a predator appeared near a nest with young, the parents would aggressively attempt to deter or distract it by close approaches, occasionally (in the case of ground squirrels) even by direct buffeting with their bodies and wings, and they always gave *chip* vocalizations. In one instance brood reduction occurred when a group of Clark Nutcracker's was near a nest for about three hr. The agitated *oriantha* adults did not bring food during this whole time and two of their four nestlings died from the neglect. If a predator removed all of the young and departed the parents continued *chipping* for several minutes. Eventually, they would cease and within one or two hr lose interest in the nest. Females then launched into sustained bouts of foraging and males appeared to increase their singing rates. Although these behaviors were not quantified, they are similar to Wasserman's (1980) observations, obtained under similar circumstances, on White-throated Sparrows.

Within the next few days the major elements of courtship reappeared in the *oriantha* pair, including mate guarding and copulations. If a nest was lost during egg laying, females sometime built a new nest as early as the third day after the depredation and laid the first egg of the replacement clutch on the next day. So the renesting interval, the time between the loss of a nest and clutch initiation in the next one, was as few as four d. As related in Chapter 7, nest building was speeded up in renests, building activity and vitellogensis were concurrent, and completed nests sat empty for less time.

TABLE 9.5. TIME USED FOR REPLACEMENT OF NESTS BY *Oriantha* FEMALES (= RENESTING INTERVAL)

Renesting interval (d)	N	Percent of nests
4	8	12.5
5	26	40.6
6	13	20.3
7	6	9.4
8	5	7.8
9	2	3.1
10	2	3.1
11	2	3.1

Accurate data on 64 renesting intervals were obtained when nests were lost from the usual variety of factors: predation, desertion, storms, etc. The mean of these intervals was 6.0 d (SD = 1.7 d) with five d being the mode (Table 9.5). Thirty-nine of 64 nests (60.9%) were replaced in five or six days. This schedule was followed when nests contained full clutches or nestlings when they were lost. The extension of the renesting interval to seven days or more was always coincident with bad weather. In those situations, females were forced to wait because of constraints on energy or nest site availability before they could nest-build and ovulate again.

The temporal realities of such nest losses are illustrated in the seasonal histories of nesting sequences that involved the loss of one or more nests by six different pairs (Fig. 9.3). In nesting sequence number one, for example, the first nest of the season was depredated during incubation. Five days later a replacement clutch was begun and nestlings eventually fledged from the second nest. Pair number two lost their nest to a predator during the laying period and started a nest five days later that was successful. Much the same occurred in nesting sequence three except that the renesting interval was extended to nine days because of a storm.

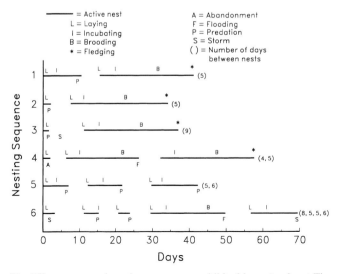

FIGURE 9.3.   Six different seasonal nesting sequences exhibited by *oriantha* at Tioga Pass.

Number four was unusual in that the female abandoned her first nest because it was located within a Song Sparrow territory and both members of that pair attacked her relentlessly. Her next nest proceeded without interspecific conflict but was lost to a flood. Fledglings were eventually produced from the third nest.

Sometimes a pair never managed to fledge young because every one of their nests was lost. Examples of this are shown in sequences five and six. Note that in number six, five different nests were built and laid in. Two nests were lost to storms, two to predators, and one to a flood. Despite the tenacity of this pair and their ability to renest repeatedly, they fledged no young that year. An important component of this temporal efficiency in renesting efforts was the durability of the pair bond. As pointed out in Chapter 3, pairs nearly always stayed together and on the same territory when nesting failures occurred.

Double brooding

When fledglings were produced relatively early in the season, from the first or second nesting effort, *oriantha* females sometimes attempted to produce a second brood. The time between occurrence of fledging in the first nest and laying of the first egg in the next nest, the mean inter-clutch interval, (Verhulst and Hut 1996), was 9.1 d (SD = 4.3 d, N = 28). The minimum interval was three d and the maximum 18 d. This 15-d range between efforts suggests that some females extended parental care to fledglings for a much longer time than others before renesting. Since males shared these responsibilities, and since females did not care for fledglings after they began a new nest, it seems possible that the inter-clutch interval varied with the number of fledglings (which ranged from two to five). In other words, the fewer the number of fledglings, the sooner the male might take over their complete care. A regression analysis shows, however, that the inter-clutch interval was not related to the number of fledglings (r^2 = 0.050, P = 0.251).

Fledglings achieved independence about three weeks after fledging so females with some of the longer inter-clutch intervals may have been caring for first-brood fledglings almost to the time when those young could survive without further parental assistance. Mortality among the dependent fledglings, as well as parental efforts by the male, could also have affected the inter-clutch interval.

The incidence of double brooding was highly irregular. Examples were found in only 11 of 22 years. In those 11 years it occurred once in six of them, twice in two of them, four times in two of them, and 10 times in one year, 1985. Except for 1985 then, double brooding was seldom seen. What was special about that year? Snowpack was 145.8 cm on 1 April, slightly below average, but 1985 was not a drought year. The key may have been that the weather in April and May was unusually mild and by the end of May about 90% of the study area was snow-free. Most *oriantha* began nesting in late May and early June and many pairs that brought off their first broods then went ahead with second ones. Clutch manipulation experiments on Great Tits indicate that double brooding was promoted by early breeding, as opposed to other factors such as pair quality (Verboven and Verhulst 1996).

Double brooding would seem to be a highly desirable tactic because it can enhance the number of fledglings produced, but it may have drawbacks. It can cause postnuptial molt to be delayed or to overlap with the period of parental

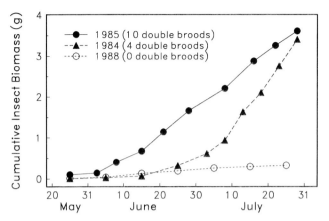

FIGURE 9.4. Cumulative insect biomass per collecting pan (dry mass), for three yr along with number of *oriantha* double broods that occurred in those years.

care, for example (Evans Ogden and Stutchbury 1996), and there may be an undesirable trade-off if it causes a reduction of the female's contribution to post-fledging care (Verhulst and Hut 1996).

The sporadic nature of double brooding at Tioga Pass tends to support the contention that this phenomenon may be inhibited in environments with relatively short breeding seasons because there is usually not enough time to raise two broods before a decline of invertebrate food occurs (Nilsson 1983). Another possibility is that a female's quality, determined by her fat stores or foraging skills, for example, could be limiting (Drent and Daan 1980, Rooneem and Robertson 1996). In view of the ability of *oriantha* females to readily produce replacement clutches in all years of the study, it seems unlikely that female quality was restrictive to double-brooding attempts. This leaves time available to produce two broods as a possible factor (but probably not a problem in many cases given the extension of renesting attempts into late summer), and another could be the quantity of food available for provisioning the young. The latter is difficult to measure, but during nine years (1984–1992) data were obtained on both the frequency of double brooding and on food availability (as indexed by the dry mass of insects collected in pan traps). All second nests were started by the end of July so the frequency of double brooding was compared to the cumulative insect biomass from 20 May to 31 July in these nine years. As it turns out, the two parameters were significantly related (Spearman's rho = 0.601, P = 0.043). To illustrate: in 1985 invertebrates were abundant from the beginning of the season onward and 10 cases of double brooding occurred (Fig. 9.4). In 1984 the bloom of insects was heavy, but delayed somewhat (Pereyra 1998), and there were four cases of double brooding. In 1988, as in many other years, cumulative insect biomass was relatively low and no cases of double brooding were detected. This suggests that the decision about going ahead with second nests depends upon food abundance.

Within-year breeding dispersal

If a female loses a nest and begins another or is multiply brooded, the distance between her successive nests is a measure of within-year breeding dispersal. This was obtained in 164 cases wherein the first nest was lost from either predation,

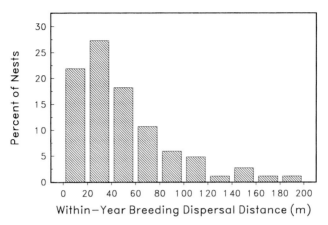

FIGURE 9.5.   Distances between successive nests in the same year in *oriantha* nesting on TPM, N = 186 nests.

bad weather, or desertion, plus 22 additional cases wherein young had been fledged and the female went ahead with a second brood. The distance between successive nests did not differ for these four categories (Morton 1997).

Areas defended by pairs, their territories, varied greatly in size and shape, depending upon the terrain, but TPM was large enough to contain many that were contiguous. In that setting, territories were estimated to be about one hectare in size or 112 m in diameter (Morton 1992b). Replacement nests or second nests were seldom placed beyond that distance (Fig. 9.5). The median distance of dispersal for within-year nests on TPM was 39.7 m. It should be noted, however, that T. Hahn (pers. comm.) has recently discovered through radio tracking that renesting females will travel greater distances than we have indicated, and even change mates. One radioed female, for example, had two failed nests on the south end of TPM then moved about 1 km to the upper East Slope (Fig. 1.3) for another attempt with a new mate—also a failure.

Among open-nesting passerines, within-year breeding dispersal distances are generally shorter than those observed between years (Bédard and LaPointe 1984). They can be quite lengthy in some species, however, such as the Gray Catbird (*Dumetella carolinensis*). If a breeding pair of catbirds experiences a nesting failure, they may shift to an entirely different area up to 450 m away (Darley et al. 1971). Nest failures in *nuttalli* often resulted in dissolution of the pair bond and movement of the female to a new (but nearby) territory (Blanchard 1941). In *oriantha,* however, nearly all pairs remained together and renested as soon as possible. They also tended to remain on their territory. This response to nest failure has ultimate consequences. Annual productivity in *oriantha* has been shown to be directly related to time available for nesting (Morton 1992b), and high altitude breeding areas, such as Tioga Pass, can have truncated summer seasons due to prolongation of winter conditions in the spring and to early onset of harsh weather in autumn. Natural selection, therefore, should favor immediate renesting. This can probably best be accomplished by retaining existing mates and territories, especially for birds like *oriantha* that inhabit ecological islands where suitable habitat is limited in area and availability.

Finally, it should be mentioned that after the nesting season, in August and

September, many adults were captured on TPM that had not been handled there previously that season. These newcomers were in the final stages of postnuptial molt or had recently completed it. They comprised 14.8% of the one-year-old females and 20.1% of the one-year-old males captured on TPM during the entire season. For birds two years old or older, these proportions were 8.6% for females and 4.7% for males. Usually the breeding areas that these individuals originated from was a mystery, although we assumed that they were nearby. One banded male was known to be a territory holder on the slope north of Ellery Lake, about 3 km away (see Fig. 1.3) and a female was known to have nested on Lee Vining Creek, about 4 km away. The purpose of this post-breeding dispersal onto a large meadow such as TPM is unknown. It could be that it was a highly suitable location for preparing metabolically and/or socially (by joining flocks) for migration. It might also have provided more protection from predators, a factor found to be important in postbreeding movements of Wood Thrushes, *Hylocichla mustelina* (Vega Rivera et al. 1999).

CHAPTER 10: Reproductive Success

Reproductive success, whether over the short term (cross-sectional), or the long term (longitudinal or lifetime), is the most essential of all measurements needed for evaluating individual fitness and for how extensively life history traits are bound together in various trade-offs, including those between the following: number, size, and sex of offspring; reproduction and survival; and current and future reproduction (Stearns 1992). Although the accurate determination of reproductive success is a central goal in studies of avian biology, it is a difficult one to accomplish. Ideally, the investigator would be dealing with a closed, tractable system, one that would favor the enumeration of offspring that not only survive to independence, but that eventually enter the population as breeders themselves. In practice this is often impossible, especially in passerine migrants, because dispersal by juveniles both before and after migration often causes them to settle as adults well beyond the boundaries of even the most ambitious study area. The pragmatic, and frequently employed, solution is simply to count the number of offspring reared to fledging, and a nesting effort is said to be successful if one or more of the young are known to have fledged.

ANNUAL REPRODUCTIVE SUCCESS OF NESTS

If only nests that had been laid in (one egg or more) were counted, the percentage of *oriantha* nests fledging young each year ranged from a low of 29.0% in 1992 to a high of 66.7% in 1989 (Table 10.1). The summer of 1992 was marked by bad weather and by considerable investigator impact. Four storms caused mortality and 18 nests were deserted, the most ever in one year. This happened because nests were visited frequently in the early morning hours to obtain data on laying times. As mentioned earlier, females flushed from the nest while building

TABLE 10.1. PERCENTAGE OF *Oriantha* NESTS THAT FLEDGED AT LEAST ONE CHICK

Yr	Number of nests	Percent fledging young
1968	42	50.0
1969	51	43.1
1970	63	41.3
1973	27	55.6
1976	55	56.4
1978	59	52.5
1979	78	43.6
1980	83	48.2
1981	76	57.9
1982	89	37.1
1983	59	38.2
1984	77	39.0
1985	51	56.9
1986	60	40.0
1987	50	54.0
1988	24	41.7
1989	36	66.7
1990	62	54.8
1991	96	52.1
1992	100	29.0
1993	57	40.2
1994	36	44.4

TABLE 10.2. NUMBER OF FLEDGLINGS PRODUCED PER NEST IN *Oriantha* NESTS THAT SURVIVED UNTIL FLEDGING OCCURRED

Chicks fledged per nest	Number of nests	Percent
1	14	3.4
2	70	16.8
3	135	32.5
4	181	43.5
5	16	3.8

or before clutch completion were prone to abandon. In contrast, there were no severe storms in 1989 and investigator interference at nests was low.

There was significant interannual variation in fledging success (Chi-square = 43.02, df = 1, P = 0.004), but in 17 of 22 years it was between 40 and 60%. Overall success was 47.0% (626 of 1,331 nests), and mean annual success was 47.3% (SD = 9.0%).

The mean number of chicks produced per nest, in those nests that survived until fledging occurred, was 3.28 (SD = 0.85, N = 416). Fewer than 4% of these nests fledged one (the fewest) or five (the most) chicks; in 76.0% of the cases, the number of fledglings was either three or four (Table 10.2).

ANNUAL REPRODUCTIVE SUCCESS OF INDIVIDUALS

The number of fledglings produced per season by an adult can be described as its annual reproductive success. This was 3.34 (SD = 1.69) for males and 3.16 (SD = 1.57) for females. Although polygyny sometimes occurred in the study population, these means were not different (t = 1.32, P = 0.188), nor were the medians (Mann Whitney U = 37,928, Z = −0.791, P = 0.429). The modal number of fledglings produced, per fledging event (Table 10.2) and per season, was four (Fig. 10.1). This was expected since four was the most common clutch size and most pairs were single-brooded. Recall, however, that, on average, more fledglings were produced when clutch size was five rather than four (Table 7.13).

About 10% of males and females had no success. This could be an over-

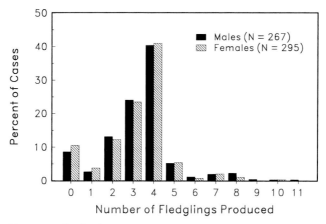

FIGURE 10.1. Frequency distribution of annual reproductive success of adult male and female *oriantha* at Tioga Pass.

statement because it is possible that a few birds counted in this category actually had successful nests very late in the season that eluded detection. Nonetheless, some birds did not bring off young. They were thwarted by predation, bad weather, and investigator activities. Reproductive failure was also known to occur in individuals that were in the crisis phase of infection by hematozoans (Richardson 1997).

Because of second nestings, a few birds were able to produce more than five fledglings in a season, with the maximum being 10 in a case wherein two successive broods of five were fledged. One male had 11 fledglings (Fig. 10.1). He was bigamous and one brood was fledged from one pairing and two broods from the other. Polygyny can greatly increase male reproductive success (Dhondt 1989a, Sternberg 1989), but it was uncommon at Tioga Pass (Chapter 3).

Effects of adult age

To determine if reproductive success varied with adult age, the following questions were asked: Did the number of young fledged per nest differ with age? Was success different among age classes if mortality of eggs during the laying period was excluded? Did the number of fledglings produced from successful nests differ with age? In all three analyses there was no difference with adult age for either sex. For example, data on the first question, which was aimed at finding out if parenting experience made a difference, showed that mean number of fledglings produced from successful nests did not vary significantly. It hovered between 3.0 and 3.3 for all ages (females: ANOVA $F_{6, 325}$ = 1.14, P = 0.339; males: ANOVA $F_{7, 285}$ = 0.76, P = 0.618).

In several studies of passerines the number of fledglings produced was slightly greater in older birds than in yearlings (Middleton 1979, Ross 1980, Yamagishi 1981), but in other cases no age effect was observed (Bédard and LaPointe 1985, Dhondt 1989b, Saether 1990). Obviously local environmental conditions, as well as social interactions, could be affecting populations in this regard (Crawford 1977). As pointed out by Clutton-Brock (1984), reproductive performance in birds and mammals, as opposed to other vertebrate classes, tends to remain constant with age although it may decline eventually. With some exceptions, birds do not show an increase in reproductive effort with age.

LIFETIME REPRODUCTIVE SUCCESS

At times it was possible to measure the total number of fledglings produced by an adult during every season that it was present on the study area, the lifetime reproductive success (LRS). LRS values are generally under-estimated because birds that leave the study area are assumed to be dead (Newton 1989a). *Oriantha* were site faithful and the analysis of their LRS was restricted to individuals known to be engaged in reproduction every year. Thus, floaters, which were usually yearling males that did not gain territories, were not included. Such males are known to have lower lifetime success (Smith and Arcese 1989). Another caveat is that the genetic LRS of males undoubtedly varied from the picture presented here due to the prevalence of extra-pair fertilizations in *oriantha* (Sherman and Morton 1988, MacDougall-Shackelton 2001).

Despite the restriction that an individual's complete reproductive history had to be known, LRS was determined for 95 males and 134 females (sample sizes

TABLE 10.3. PRODUCTION OF FLEDGLINGS BY *Oriantha* PARENTS OF VARIOUS LIFESPANS

Sex	Parents Lifespan (yr)	N	Number of fledglings produced Min	Max	Mean	SD
Male	1	38	0	8	3.39	1.64
	2	16	2	8	5.56	2.16
	3	18	4	14	9.89	2.81
	4	12	8	18	12.58	3.00
	5	3	13	18	16.00	2.65
	6	6	16	26	21.17	3.92
	7	2	25	26	25.50	0.71
	All	95	0	26	8.14	6.15
Female	1	63	0	5	3.06	1.31
	2	25	0	12	6.68	2.79
	3	19	4	15	10.05	2.80
	4	15	5	19	12.73	3.37
	5	7	8	22	15.86	5.11
	6	4	17	23	19.75	2.50
	7	1	19	19	19.00	—
	All	134	0	23	7.10	5.32

were larger for females because it was easier to associate them with a nest). Mean LRS was 8.14 (SD = 6.15) for males and 7.10 (SD = 5.32) for females. Males appeared to produce about one more fledgling per lifetime than females, but, as is true for most of the data on passerines, the coefficient of variation was high and the means were not different (t = 1.37, P = 0.296). Mean LRS increased steadily with lifespan in both sexes (Table 10.3), and a regression of LRS on age showed that the two were highly correlated. For females r^2 was 0.790 (P < 0.001) and for males it was 0.850 (P < 0.001). Visual inspection of a scatterplot revealed no evidence of senescence, in other words, no tendency for the rate of success to decline with age.

For purposes of comparison with other studies, the distribution of fledglings produced per lifetime was determined for both males and females (Fig. 10.2). These distributions were highly skewed, but did not differ for the sexes (Kolmogorov-Smirnov Z = 0.631, difference = 0.085, P = 0.820). The modal number of young was four for both sexes. This is anticipated because the mode for brood size was four and the mode for number of breeding seasons per lifetime was one. Total young produced ranged from 0 to 26 by males and 0 to 23 by females. Twenty-six offspring were produced by two different males, one of which lived for six years and the other for seven. The most successful female was one that lived for six years (Table 10.3).

The mean LRS of seven to eight found in *oriantha* is high in comparison to other short-lived open-nesting passerines. It was about six in Meadow Pipits (Hötker 1989), for example, and only three to four in Indigo Buntings (Payne 1989). As pointed out by Newton (1989b), enormous individual variations in LRS occur in natural populations and, typically, large numbers of offspring, far more than are needed for replacement, are produced by a relatively small fraction of the breeding population. For many avian populations, the LRS can provide gene frequency changes and a good approximation of fitness (Partridge 1989). Murray

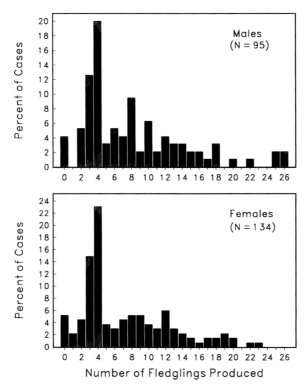

FIGURE 10.2.   Frequency distribution of lifetime reproduction in male and female *oriantha* at Tioga Pass.

(1992) agrees, but cautions that differences between individuals in this regard does not necessarily have evolutionary significance.

SNOW CONDITIONS

Snow has a key role in circumpolar and high-altitude ecosystems. It stores and releases energy, and acts as a radiation shield and as an insulator. It is a reservoir for water; a transport medium, moving as a vapor flux because of sublimation; and host for a food web that occurs both within the snow and at its upper and lower boundaries. These functions occur over time scales that are diurnal, seasonal, and decadal (Jones et al. 1994). In addition, snow can be an overburden on low-lying vegetation that is sometimes utilized by birds as nesting habitat. By controlling access to these nesting sites, it can greatly influence nesting phenology and breeding productivity. Furthermore, there is great interannual variation in snow depth and water content (see Table 1.2), and this, along with the vagaries of spring weather that affect melting rates, can generate large variations in the timing of habitat availability. Thus, in a long-term study natural experiments occur that offer unusual opportunities for learning about environmental adaptation in breeding birds.

In the beginning we thought that sub-freezing temperatures, or perhaps summer storms, might be the environmental factors that most strongly affected reproduction of migrants in the subalpine. Our attention was soon drawn to the snowpack,

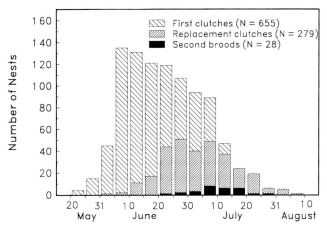

FIGURE 10.3. Distribution of clutch starts in *oriantha* during 20 nesting seasons at Tioga Pass according to nest status: first clutch, replacement clutch, or double brood.

however, because of the way it affected nesting schedules and nest locations (Morton et al. 1972a; Morton 1977, 1978, 1994a; Morton and Allan 1990). As pointed out previously, the attempts of *oriantha* pairs to settle and begin nesting could be delayed by a heavy snowpack (see Fig. 5.4). Next, interannual variations in reproductive schedules will be discussed in more detail, and how they, as well as productivity, were affected by snow conditions.

Effects on reproductive schedule

There were 20 seasons wherein an attempt was made to find every nest that was laid in and to determine, if possible, first egg dates. These were obtained by direct observation of the laying sequence and by back-dating from known hatching times in cases wherein the nest was found after clutch completion. In all, first egg dates or clutch starts were determined for 962 clutches. The earliest of these was on 23 May and the latest on 7 August, a span of 76 days. The greatest share of clutch initiations, 97.4%, were in June and July. Their frequency increased until early June, then decreased steadily thereafter (Fig. 10.3).

For much of the summer, if a nest was lost with either eggs or nestlings the female soon produced a replacement clutch. Some replacements were already present in early June and they were the last type of clutch produced during the nesting season. A few second broods were also produced, mostly in July. Eventually, in late July and early August, the birds became refractory and lost their ability to renest. Because the vegetation was so well developed, the last of these renests were difficult to find and their frequency toward the end of the nesting season must have been greater than that shown in Fig. 10.3. The 962 nests represented in Fig. 10.3 were restricted to those in which both starting date and status (first clutch, replacement clutch, or second brood) were known and they give a good view of the average seasonal pattern of clutch initiations by *oriantha* at Tioga Pass. Another representation of this pattern, one that was unrestricted as to nest status, can be found in Morton and Allan (1990). Note that Fig. 10.3 is a composite drawn from 20 different nesting seasons, and it does not inform us about among-year variation in clutch initiations.

TABLE 10.4.   INTERANNUAL VARIATION IN THE ONSET OF NESTING (MEAN OF FIRST 10 CLUTCH STARTS) BY *Oriantha* ON TIOGA PASS MEADOW

Date	Number of yr	Percent of yr
26–31 May	1	4.0
1–5 June	4	16.0
6–10 June	10	40.0
11–15 June	2	8.0
16–20 June	3	12.0
21–25 June	1	4.0
26–30 June	3	12.0
1–5 July	0	0.0
6–10 July	1	4.0

As it turns out, this variation, especially in nesting onset, was quite large. This can be shown from 25 years of data wherein the seasonal onset of laying by TPM-nesters was known, onset being defined as the mean date of the first 10 clutch starts of the season. The earliest of these mean dates was 27 May (in 1992) and the latest was 7 July (in 1995), a range of 41 days. In all of the remaining 23 years, nesting began in June and in 10 of these years within the interval of 5–10 June (Table 10.4). For all years combined, mean date for the seasonal onset of nesting was 12 June (SD = 9.5 d). In a study of *oriantha* in Colorado, Hubbard (1978) saw an interannual variation of about 14 days in nesting onset. He sampled for fewer years (4 vs. 25), however, so a smaller range in onset dates is not surprising. Also, on his study area at Niwot Ridge, *oriantha* were reliant upon thick, shrubby tree islands (krummholz) for nesting locations. Such sites are highly sheltered, and they were probably less affected by variations in environmental conditions, especially snowpack, than the krummholz-devoid subalpine vegetation at TPM.

Given the year-to-year variation in the beginning of egg laying, one might expect the complete schedules for first clutches of the season also to be quite different and for them to occur under largely differing ecological conditions. This, indeed, was the case. For example, in 1976, a drought year, nesting began on 29 May and all females had begun their first clutches by 16 June (Fig. 10.4). There was some renesting beyond that date, but the key point is that the meadows dried out very early in 1976 and nesting took place under snow-free conditions. In contrast, in 1983, because of an El Niño winter, snow did not completely disappear until August and all females started their first nests of the season while a considerable portion of the habitat was still covered (Fig. 10.4).

Clutches were initiated from one year to the next, therefore, under very different moisture and cover conditions (willows did not leaf out, for example, until they were snow-free), to say nothing of variation in other factors such as microclimate and food abundance. At times the temporal disparities were so great that the schedules of first clutches did not overlap at all when certain years, such as 1976 and 1983, were compared. This has important implications because this variation in the alignment of clutch start frequencies to photoperiod can have effects that extend both to clutch size (Chapter 7) and to fledgling survival (Chapter 11).

But did this wide range in snow conditions influence the nesting schedule in a regular, predictable pattern? The answer is, yes. Nesting onset dates were highly correlated with maximum snow depth ($r^2 = 0.70$, $P < 0.001$; Fig. 10.5). This

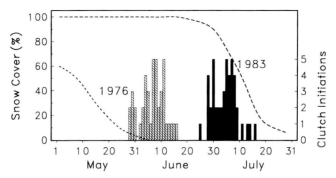

FIGURE 10.4. Temporal distribution of first clutches only in 1976 and 1983 on Tioga Pass Meadow.

happened because the birds had to wait until snow cover had decreased to 90% or less before there were adequate places for them to build and hide their nests; females would not build on the ground, or a site above it, unless that particular spot was snow-free.

A natural experiment in 1986, along with the deliberate manipulations recounted in Chapter 5, provides strong support for the hypothesis that nest site availability could operate as a proximate factor in the control of reproduction. In February of that year about 10 cm of rain fell within seven hr onto a previously accumulated snowpack. This added weight induced numerous avalanches in the central Sierra Nevada, including the Tioga Pass area. One major slide came off the west slope of TPM and several others from both north and south slopes above Lee Vining Creek. Lodgepole pines were snapped off by these moving masses of heavy, wet snow, incorporated into them, then deposited with the snow in run-out areas. In mid-May these pines, still fresh and green in appearance, lay scattered across the snow surface. Snow cover remained above 90% until early June at which time *oriantha* females began building nests in some of the avalanche pines. In fact, 14 of 35 first clutches and 3 of 25 replacement clutches were built in these pines during the 1986 season. The fallen trees were more than just places

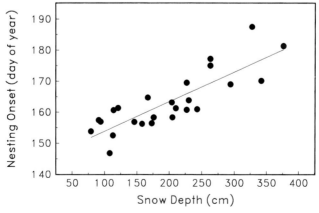

FIGURE 10.5. Onset of nesting (mean date of first 10 clutch starts) by *oriantha* on Tioga Pass Meadow in relation to 1 April snow depth (the date when snow was at or close to maximum depth). Data are for 25 yr.

to hide nests, they were the first places selected, and females using them tended to begin laying significantly earlier than their nearest neighbors which nested in more traditional sites (mean difference = 6.9 d; Wilcoxon Signed Rank Test, Wilcoxon statistic = 89.5, P = 0.002). One female that built in the base of a large unleafed willow laid four days before the neighboring avalanche-pine bird, another comparison pair started laying on the same day, and in all 12 of the other situations, neighbors started later (by as much as 15 days) than the avalanche-pine nesters. Interestingly, other species also utilized avalanche pines as nesting sites. These included American Robins, Hermit Thrushes (*Catharus guttatus*), Dark-eyed Juncos, and Dusky Flycatchers. Of these, only the junco habitually nests on or near the ground so the dense masses of branches and needles of these recumbent pines must have been, in general, a highly attractive location for building nests.

Effects on breeding productivity

During eight years of the study, 1979–1986, TPM was trapped three to five days per week from the time that fledglings first appeared until migration departures were completed. The goal was to band every *oriantha* on the study area. Aside from assuring an accurate population age structure, this extensive trapping effort provided an estimate of breeding productivity because it censused the independent juveniles.

A total of 1,467 juveniles was captured and banded in those eight seasons and their numbers varied between 88 (in 1982) and 290 (in 1985), a 3.3-fold difference. A regression of juvenile numbers on the date that nesting began gave a significant negative result (r^2 = 0.62, P = 0.020). An even stronger negative relationship existed between juvenile numbers, or productivity, and maximum snowpack (r^2 = 0.80, P < 0.001; Fig. 10.6). Compared to other years, 1983 had higher than expected productivity. This was the year with the deepest snowpack (376 cm) and 116 juveniles were captured. This was considerably more than in 1982, the year with the second-deepest snowpack (294 cm), when only 88 were captured. Productivity was relatively high in 1983 because the spring weather was unusually warm, and although the snow was deep on 1 April, it melted very quickly (see Fig. 10.4). This meant that nesting was not delayed as much as predicted. If 1983 is omitted from the data set, the regression of number of juveniles captured on maximum snowpack depth shows a very high negative correlation (r^2 = 0.98, P < 0.001).

As implied above, reproductive success was probably greater in light snow years because nesting began sooner. This allowed more opportunities for renesting and double brooding before refractoriness set in, the latter being a physiological condition that caused reproduction to be terminated at about the same date every year (Chapter 11). Deep snows decreased the time available for nesting by the population and, by delaying breeding, they also caused clutches to be started when the photoperiod was decreasing, a situation that may have caused smaller clutches to be produced (Chapter 7). Both of these effects, along with others that we did not detect, could have contributed to the variation in productivity displayed in Figure 10.6.

The snows of winter often endure into spring and summer in arctic and alpine regions. In so doing they influence both the timing and outcome of breeding

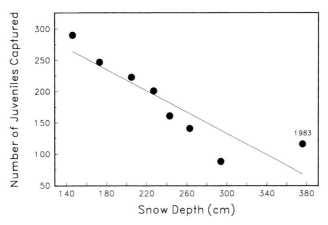

FIGURE 10.6.   Number of juvenile *oriantha* captured per season on Tioga Pass Meadow in relation to maximum snowpack depth (as measured on 1 April). N = 8 yr.

efforts of avian populations that occupy those regions. In alcids and shorebirds, for example, egg-laying schedules can be delayed by several weeks as the birds wait for snow to clear away from the tundra (Sealy 1975, Green et al. 1977). Furthermore, snow-free patches must be large, otherwise there is high vulnerability to predation (Byrkjedal 1980). Snow cover also affected egg-laying dates in arctic-nesting passerines such as Snow Buntings (Hussell 1972, Pattie 1977) and Lapland Longspurs (*Calcarius lapponicus*; Hussell 1972, Custer and Pitelka 1977, Fox et al. 1987). Like *oriantha,* breeding productivity was reduced in both of these species when there was a late thaw (Pattie 1977, Fox et al. 1987). As pointed out by Green et al. (1977), snow cover, not adaptations to seasonality of food supply, determines breeding dates in these wintery habitats.

Nesting success in White-tailed Ptarmigan (*Lagopus leucurus*) was negatively correlated with springtime snow depths (Clarke and Johnson 1992). Furthermore, Smith and Andersen (1985) found that Dark-eyed Juncos had longer breeding

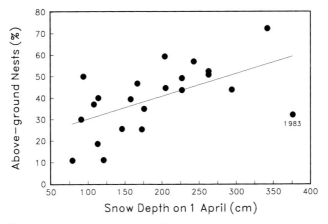

FIGURE 10.7.   Percentage of *oriantha* nests built in above-ground or elevated sites in relation to maximum snowpack depth (measured on 1 April, N = 22 yr, r^2 = 0.32, P = 0.010; if 1983 was excluded, a year when warm spring weather caused early melting of the snowpack, r^2 = 0.52, P < 0.001).

seasons when snowmelt was early; there was time for only one nesting attempt when it was late. What can birds do to ameliorate the negative effects of heavy snowpack on reproductive success? In Dark-eyed Juncos clutch size increased when nesting was delayed and Smith and Andersen (1985) suggested that females produced larger clutches because they were unstressed and had more time to accumulate energy reserves before the onset of laying. Clutch size did not increase in *oriantha* but they were able to adjust partially to the inhibitory effects of late-lying snow by altering nest-site preferences. This was untrue in other species. For example, no matter the ecological conditions at Tioga Pass, Hermit Thrushes always constructed their nests in elevated sites and Dark-eyed Juncos (a close relative of *oriantha*) built on the ground, but *oriantha* were more flexible. Although the junco pattern seemed to be preferred in most years, those propensities were modulated in response to snowpack persistence; the more snow there was in any given year, the higher the proportion of their nests built in elevated sites (Fig. 10.7). This plasticity in what is often a stereotyped response in avian species is a key adaptation of *oriantha* to the variation in snow conditions that occurs at high altitude.

CHAPTER 11: Late-season Events

GONADAL PHOTOREFRACTORINESS

Among migratory birds inhabiting the temperate zone, the nesting season must eventually come to a close so they can molt and prepare metabolically for migration before deteriorating environmental conditions reduce the chances of survival for young and adults alike (Immelmann 1973). In photoperiodic species, such as White-crowned Sparrows, breeding activity ceases because the system that controls the stimulation and maintenance of the reproductive organs becomes insensitive or refractory to the stimulatory effects of long days (Nicholls et al. 1988, Wilson and Donham 1988). The efficacy of this photorefractory response and its timing have presumably been acted on by natural selection such that seasonal reproductive efforts are terminated optimally (Farner and Lewis 1971, 1973; Farner et al. 1983, Farner 1986). Although terminating mechanisms are adaptive and comparable in significance to those that initiate and maintain periodic gonadal function, they have received little attention, particularly in field studies.

Gonadal regression

Logically, the onset of photorefractoriness should be followed closely by a decrease in gonadal size and functional ability. Spontaneous gonadal regression is, in fact, generally used by experimentalists as proof that refractoriness has set in (Wilson and Follett 1974). As can be seen from testis and cloacal protuberance lengths in *oriantha,* regression occurred in males between 10 July and 10 August (Fig. 5.1). This appears to be identical to the schedule followed by two migratory conspecifics, *gambelii* breeding in Alaska (King et al. 1966) and *pugetensis* breeding on the coast of Washington (Lewis 1975b). This is a surprise, given the latitudinal spreads involved and their respective photoperiods, because it is well known from studies of captives held under controlled conditions that the time of regression is an inverse function of daylength; the longer the days during photostimulation, the sooner involution occurs (Storey 1976, Moore et al. 1983). Furthermore, once the threshold daylength for the induction of photorefractoriness is exceeded, its rate of development becomes directly related to daylength (Nicholls et al. 1988). As Moore et al. (1983) pointed out, however, the onset time of regression is fixed relatively early in gonadal growth. Substantial gonadal development often occurs in migrants before they arrive at their summering areas, so if these three subspecies experience similar photoperiods at that time in the cycle, presumably while they are still on wintering areas or in transit to the breeding grounds, regression might very well be programmed to the same schedule in all of them. Implicit in this reasoning is that environmental feedback has not operated as yet to tailor optimally refractoriness onset for the separate breeding environments used by this subspecies cluster. The ovary is not as easy to evaluate *in situ* as the testis but, based on decreases in follicle diameter, loss of ovarian function occurred in *oriantha* within the same time frame as testicular regression (Fig. 5.1).

Although the refractory condition is usually assessed from data on gonadal condition, its functional advancement in wild birds can also be deduced from their renesting schedules. The rationale here is that if a mated pair is photosensitive, or at least the female is, and their nest is lost, she will replace it. If she has become photorefractory, she will not. The proportion of females failing to renest,

TABLE 11.1. PERCENT OF *Oriantha* FEMALES THAT RENESTED IN RELATION TO CALENDAR INTERVAL THAT LOSS OF EGGS OR NESTLINGS OCCURRED

Calendar interval	N	Percent that renested
20–25 June	32	100.0
26–30 June	52	100.0
1–5 July	37	100.0
6–10 July	21	100.0
11–15 July	24	91.7
16–20 July	20	90.0
21–25 July	11	36.4
26–31 July	7	14.3
1–5 August	8	12.5
6–10 August	8	0.0

therefore, should be directly related to the prevalence of refractoriness in the population. These assumptions seem correct because the data on renesting propensity yield the same temporal scale for refractoriness as those for ovarian collapse (Table 11.1). Before 10 July all females built replacement nests, but thereafter their tendency to do so decreased. There was no renesting if a nest was lost after 5 August and the tendency to renest toward season's end was not dependent upon a specific nesting stage. That is, renesting and its absence both occurred when nests were lost either with eggs or with nestlings.

Nesting termination

Another approach to identifying the termination of reproduction under field conditions is to examine the seasonal change in number of clutch starts or first-egg dates; their waning can be taken as a measure of refractoriness onset in the population (Fig 11.1). It is instructive also to look simply at the distribution of

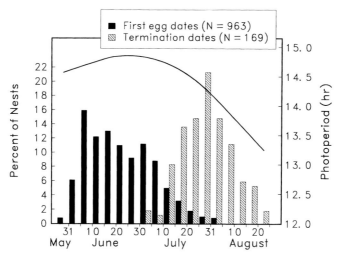

FIGURE 11.1. Seasonal schedule of clutch starts (first egg dates) and nesting termination dates (fledging or loss of nest without renest attempt) in *oriantha*. Line shows seasonal change in photoperiod at Tioga Pass.

all nesting terminations as they occurred, either from nest failures or from fledging events that were not followed by additional nestings (Fig. 11.1).

As would be expected from the data on ovarian stages (Fig. 5.1) and on re-nesting propensities (Table 11.1), egg laying ceased in early August. Previous to that time, of course, many females had already terminated reproduction (Fig. 11.1). These data raise several points for consideration. One is that photorefrac-toriness might productively be thought of as a trait that has considerable variation. It varied among female members of the population, for example, by at least a month (Table 11.1, Fig. 11.1). A second is that refractoriness may develop only gradually in the population. The seasonal decline in clutch size was previously pointed to as a possible symptom of this (Chapter 7). A third is that refractoriness is subject to modification by environmental or supplementary cues. For example, breeding tended to be prolonged in heavy snow years because the melt-off from large drifts kept the meadows wet and green until late in the summer (Morton et al. 1972b). Even in moderate snow years, late-season nestings sometimes occurred in a few territories that contained sumps, springs, or streamlets that helped to prolong green-vegetation conditions (Morton 1978). In *nuttalli,* nesting was ex-tended later in summers that had been preceded by winters of heavy rainfall, probably in response to increased food availability (DeSante and Baptista 1989). And using an experimental approach, Runfeldt and Wingfield (1985) found that estradiol implants caused sexual activity to be extended in female Song Sparrows. Interestingly, testicular regression in their mates was substantially delayed. These studies suggest that the onset and perhaps the progression of refractoriness can be modified by supplementary cues such as food quality and quantity and by social interactions. It would seem that females are particularly sensitive to the former and males to the latter.

Beyond this, photorefractoriness itself can be shown to have a considerable range in efficacy. In some species in captivity, such as White-crowned Sparrows and European Starlings, it has been found to be "absolute" because it induces gonadal regression even if daylengths remain long and without decrease. Other species, such as Japanese Quail (*Coturnix japonica*), are "relatively" refractory because regression can be halted or reversed if the birds remain on constant long days (Hahn and Ball 1995, Hahn et al. 1997). In earlier years, this interspecific variation in the terminating mechanism was often described as being an expression of separate evolutionary pathways (Immelmann 1973, Farner et al. 1983). Re-cently, with the benefit of new information gained from molecular and neurobi-ological studies, it has become clearer that this variation or flexibility may be due simply to differences in the expression of a common underlying control system. For example, gonadotropin releasing hormone synthesis is inhibited in cases of absolute refractoriness, whereas its release is inhibited in relative refractoriness (Ball and Hahn 1997, Hahn et al. 1997). As stated by these authors, it seems likely that small changes in information processing could greatly alter the re-sponses of this control system to supplementary information.

Understanding how breeding is terminated has been a mystifying problem that has been resistant to clarification. It has been difficult, for example, to separate experimentally the autumnal sequence of events that occur in migratory birds (gonadal regression, molting, and premigratory fattening) into individually regu-lated entities; physiologically, they seem to be very tightly coupled. Still, progress is occurring. There is evidence in some species, such as White-throated Sparrows (Harris and Turek 1982), House Sparrows (Dawson 1991), and Song Sparrows (Wingfield 1993), for example, that a decreasing photoperiod is an important source of information to the expression of photorefractoriness. In keeping with this, note that loss of reproductive ability did not occur in *oriantha* until after the summer solstice (Fig. 11.1). It seems possible, then, that their reproductive system shut-down is being cued by decreasing daylengths. If this is true, one would expect time measurement through the use of an endogenous program or clock to be a functional component of the photorefractoriness mechanism (Robinson and Follett 1982, Wingfield 1993). It should be mentioned that although refractoriness is commonly expressed when days are getting shorter, in some species this can happen even before the solstice (Hahn et al. 1997).

Another intriguing line of inquiry has to do with the role of thyroid hormones in organizing the expression of refractoriness: thyroidectomy causes the reproductive system to become unresponsive to photoperiod change (Dawson 1993), thyroxine must be present in order for gonadal growth to occur under long days (Dawson 1989), and an intact thyroid is essential for photorefractoriness to develop (Goldsmith and Nicholls 1984). Wilson and Reinert (1993, 1995, 1998) have suggested that thyroxine and long days interact during a critical period, early in the gonadal cycle, to program organizational effects on photoperiodic control circuits in the brain. This would be further support for the hypothesis that the onset of refractoriness is determined during the time that daylengths are increasing rather than decreasing. In a thorough review of endocrine mechanisms operating in wild species, Wingfield and Farner (1993) concluded that photorefractoriness lies at the hypothalamic level or higher in the central nervous system, with the exact location still awaiting discovery.

MOLT

Molting, the shedding and regrowing of feathers, is a lengthy and energetically expensive process, but a necessary one if the plumage is to be retained in a condition that is functionally optimal for insulation and flight. The integration of molt into the annual cycle, along with control of its timing and rate, is of considerable interest to avian and comparative physiology (Payne 1972). In many species of migratory passerines, adults undergo a postnuptial (prebasic) molt before they fatten and depart on migration. In *oriantha* this molt is complete; that is, the entire plumage is renewed. This does not cause a change in coloration or markings so adults do not change in appearance from one molt to the next; they look the same on both summering and wintering grounds. Juveniles also molt before migrating but their molt, the postjuvenal (first prebasic) molt, is incomplete or partial. It does not involve the flight or contour feathers of the wing and tail, the remiges and rectrices, only those of the body. Their flight feathers are still very new at that time and are not in need of replacement. Postjuvenal molt does cause an appearance change because the buff-colored feathers on the heads of fledglings are replaced by brown and tan stripes. Young birds carry these through the winter until they are replaced by the black and white ones, typical of adults, in their first prenuptial molt, prior to departure from the wintering area.

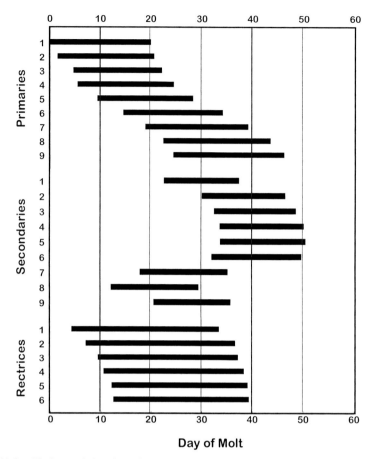

FIGURE 11.2.   Timing and duration of growth for individual flight feathers during the postnuptial molt in *oriantha.*

Postnuptial molt

Postnuptial molt began about when the first primary (P_1) was shed and this easily observed event was used to mark its onset. Molting proceeded centrifugally in the wing from P_1 through P_9 and soon the other flight feathers, the secondaries and rectrices (Fig. 11.2), along with the body feathers began to be replaced. During the first six weeks of molt we found that up to seven primaries could be growing simultaneously (Morton and Morton 1990, Morton 1992a), although the number was usually between two and five. Molt of body feathers peaked in intensity about midway through the molting period (Morton and Welton 1973).

While in molt, adults remained on their breeding territories, but they were quiet and unobtrusive and spent much of their time within and beneath vegetation, especially willows. At three to four weeks into molt, when the rectrices were about half-grown and many primaries and secondaries were in various stages of growth (see Fig. 11.2), they became reluctant to fly and when released from traps they would sometimes run to cover instead of flying. Still, all those tested could fly when released from the hand. Flight was labored, however, and those in heaviest molt also showed an inability to control their momentum when landing. Upon

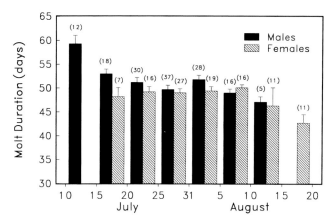

FIGURE 11.3.   Duration of postnuptial molt in *oriantha* in relation to day when molt began. Bars show mean (+1 SE); sample sizes in parentheses.

approaching a perch they descended in a downward arc rather than the usual upward one. Within a few weeks after starting molt many individuals had gained 10% or more in body mass because of an increase in blood volume needed for circulation to the growing plumage (Chilgren and DeGraw 1977, DeGraw and Kern 1985). This greater mass probably contributed to their flight control problems. An additional sign of reduced mobility during the time of heavy molt was a marked decrease in trapping rates of both males and females (Morton and Morton 1990). *Oriantha* in heavy molt probably seek sheltered microenvironments in order to reduce both thermoregulation costs (due to having blood-filled quills and a sparser plumage) and vulnerability to avian predators (due to impaired flying abilities).

As can be seen in Fig. 11.2, secondaries 4 and 5 were the last of the flight feathers to complete their growth, and they did so about 50 days after molt onset. Growth in body feathers was usually also completed at about that time.

When the whole population was compared, males were found to begin molt five d earlier than females, and in 105 mated pairs mean onset was 5.5 d earlier in the males. A few females did start molting before their mates, but usually they were later (Morton and Morton 1990). In one extreme case, a female began molting 23 d after her mate (Morton 1992a). Mean duration of molt was 50.9 d (SD = 5.3 d, N = 148) in males and 48.2 d (SD = 4.5 d, N = 107) in females. This difference of 2.7 d was highly significant (t = 4.28, P < 0.001).

Date of postnuptial molt onset varied in the population by more than a month, and there seemed to be an underlying seasonal component to its duration. For example, the longest mean duration, 59.2 d, occurred in males (N = 12), that started before 15 July (Fig. 11.3). Eight of these males were known to be one-year-old non-breeders or floaters. Floaters also molted earliest in *gambelii* (Wingfield and Farner 1979). The shortest mean duration of molt, 42.9 d, occurred late in the season in females (N = 11) that started molting after 15 August (Fig. 11.3). Although delayed in their molt, probably because of stimuli emanating from the young and/or interactions with mates, as well as high gonadal steroid levels, all of which can delay the onset of postnuptial molt almost indefinitely (Hahn et al. 1992, Nolan et al. 1992), when released from parental care, these females were

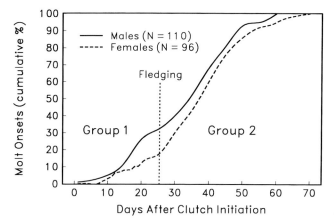

FIGURE 11.4.   Onset of postnuptial molt in *oriantha* in relation to reproductive schedule. All data were obtained from mated birds and their date of molt onset was standardized by setting it in relation to the date of the first egg in their last nest of the season. Note that Group 1 birds were ones that started molting at any time before fledging of their young had occurred and Group 2 birds began molting at any time after fledging had occurred.

able to accelerate their molt and to catch up with other members of the population. There is evidence that a trade-off could be in involved in this type of response, however. Dawson et al. (2000) have shown that accelerated molt in European Starlings (induced experimentally with shortened daylengths) results in the growth of poorer quality plumage. They suggest that this could diminish survival through decreased flight performance and increased thermoregulatory costs.

Overlap of molt and reproduction

Migrants have traditionally been characterized as proceeding step-wise through three major events on their summering grounds: reproduction, molt, and premigratory fattening. Because each of these involves major physiological and morphological changes and entails considerable time and energy expenditure, it has been usually assumed that there should be selection for their temporal separation (Farner 1983, 1986). Field studies have begun to show, however, that substantial overlap in reproductive and molting schedules sometimes occurs (Payne 1969, 1972; Verbeek 1970, Foster 1975a, Samson 1976a, Morton and Morton 1990, Hahn et al. 1992, Underhill et al. 1992, Hemborg 1999a). In *oriantha,* for example, about 20% of the females and 30% of the males began molting before their nestlings were fledged (Fig. 11.4). A few males even dropped P_1 while their mates were still ovulating. However, no females were known to start the molt until laying had been completed. Allowing for the period of post-fledging parental care (about three weeks), and assuming that both parents cared for fledglings, then molt and reproductive efforts actually overlapped in 71% of the females and 76% of the males. This was an unexpected result and it was motivation to look further into the data on molt timing and progression.

One approach was to compare molt parameters in adults known to be heavily engaged in reproduction while molting, designated as Group 1, with another that had less overlap between the two, Group 2 (Fig. 11.4). The time of fledging was established arbitrarily as the dividing point between the groups because beyond

TABLE 11.2. PARAMETERS OF POSTNUPTIAL MOLT IN GROUP 1[a] AND GROUP 2[b] *Oriantha* AT TIOGA PASS

	Group 1[a]			Group 2[b]			
	Mean	SD (d)	N	Mean	SD (d)	N	P
Males							
Molt onset date	28 July	6.9	36	31 July	7.6	74	ns
Molt completion date	17 Sept	8.0	36	19 Sept	7.6	74	ns
Molt duration (d)	51.1	4.6	25	50.4	5.8	51	ns
Females							
Molt onset date	1 Aug	8.6	18	4 Aug	9.6	77	ns
Molt completion date	20 Sept	9.2	18	20 Sept	9.3	78	ns
Molt duration (d)	49.9	4.9	18	47.1	4.8	47	0.048

[a] Molt began prior to fledging of their young.
[b] Molt began subsequent to fledging of their young.

that time parental effort decreased as the fledglings learned to feed themselves and because there was often uncertainty about the efforts of male parents during the postfledging period. Note that in Group 1 birds the temporal overlap between molt and reproductive activities could be on the order of 30–40 d, well over half of the molting period. In Group 2 birds, overlap could range from zero to a maximum of about 20 d.

In terms of molt timing (onset and termination) and duration, there were no differences between Group 1 and Group 2 males (Table 11.2). There were no differences in timing in females either, but molt was extended in duration by 2.8 d in Group 1 females, a significant difference (Table 11.2).

Molt characteristics of individuals also indicate that a few Group 1 males and females that were feeding fledglings were being stretched energetically. Although it began on time, their molt was greatly slowed or arrested, at least during the first 17 days. Some Group 1 individuals had only just shed P_3 at that juncture instead of being on the pace of those in Group 2, which were already growing in P_6 (Fig. 11.5). So there were signs that molt was sometimes slowed when *oriantha* were concurrently engaged in parental care. This is not surprising. The co-occurrence of increased self-maintenance costs (feather growth and thermo-regulation) and season-high foraging efforts, all the while in a condition of compromised flight efficiency, would seem certain to impose substantial energy balance problems.

One way to evaluate the energetic costs associated with life history events is to track changes in body mass associated with them. For example, female *oriantha* become extremely lean when feeding young, and are undoubtedly in or near negative energy balance during that time (Morton et al. 1973, Morton 1976). Males were also lean, but they began recovering mass about a month sooner than females. In addition, opposing patterns emerged when body mass changes in Group 1 birds were compared to those in Group 2. Group 1 females were lighter than those in Group 2 and since the former had much more overlap between molt and parental duties than the latter, this does not seem illogical; engagement in two energetically costly functions simultaneously might easily produce this result. Group 1 males, however, were consistently about 1 g heavier throughout the whole molting period than those in Group 2. This can be interpreted to mean that

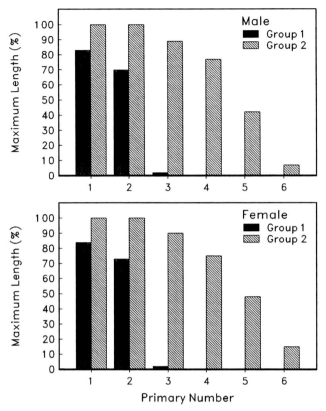

FIGURE 11.5. Percentage of maximum length attained in primaries 1–6 on 17th day of postnuptial molt in two males (one of Group 1 and one of Group 2, upper panel) and two females (one of Group 1 and one of Group 2, lower panel).

parental care declined or ceased altogether in males that began molting in the pre-fledging period. Lacking help from mates, females catabolized even more of their own tissues than usual in order to raise the young. If this construct is true (and it should be emphasized that parental feeding efforts by Group 1 and Group 2 individuals have not been well-quantified), then one might expect reproductive success to be lower for Group 1 birds. And it was. Males had significantly fewer nests that fledged young (Group 1 = 52.9%, Group 2 = 74.9%), and fewer chicks were fledged per nest (Group 1 = 1.29, Group 2 = 2.49). Similar effects were observed in females: 61.1% vs. 79.2% and 1.72 vs. 2.54 (Morton and Morton 1990). Group 1 birds, of course, were mostly individuals attempting to renest toward the end of the season because they had been unsuccessful in their earlier attempts. Apparently reduced success was better than none at all. Note that this lower success could have been influenced by seasonal tendencies for clutch size to be reduced and declining food supplies, as well as a molt-parental care conflict.

To summarize: If a pair was still attempting to bring off a brood in mid-summer or later, they were likely to have an overlap between their reproductive efforts and molting because the onset of molt was usually not delayed. This had fitness consequences because those birds that started molt in the pre-fledging period (Group 1) were less successful than those starting it in the post-fledging period

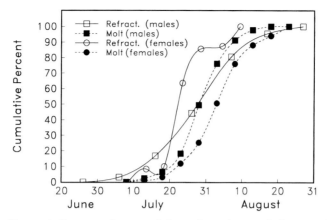

FIGURE 11.6.   Temporal alignment of onsets of photorefractoriness and of postnuptial molt in male and female *oriantha*.

(Group 2). It is suggested that this occurs, at least in part, because molting males reduced their parental care (Chapter 8) and females were then unable to provide adequately for the whole brood on their own.

Molt and photorefractoriness

The foregoing shows that no fixed phase relationship existed between reproduction and molt onset, and that molt could begin at any time once egg laying had occurred. On the other hand, no female in molt, even in its earliest stages, ever initiated a nesting cycle. This argues that molt begins after reproductive capability has ended, in other words, at the same time as, or after the onset of photorefractoriness, but never before it. This agrees with the generalization of Nicholls et al. (1988) that the onset of molt signals that the bird has already entered the refractory state.

The graphical representation of refractoriness onset, as shown by testicular involution for males and decline in clutch initiations for females, and of molt onset, with all functions shown as cumulative percentages of occurrence through time, indicates that the two occurred nearly simultaneously in males (Fig. 11.6). In females refractoriness clearly led molt, often by about 10 d. This is in general agreement with Wingfield and Farner's (1978a) observation that molt follows gonadal regression in *gambelii*. Dawson and Sharp (1998) have discovered that prolactin secretion is at its seasonal maximum in European Starlings when refractoriness and postnuptial molt occur. They suggest that prolactin does not itself cause refractoriness but it may accelerate gonadal regression and it is required for the induction of molt.

As noted above, the onset of photorefractoriness was independent of reproductive stage because it could occur at any time in the nesting cycle. Since postnuptial molt began with refractoriness, or followed closely on its heels, it too should show independence from reproductive activities. We found, in fact, that the majority of the adult population was simultaneously involved in rearing young to independence and in replacing their worn plumage. This is contrary to a long-standing paradigm which suggests that these energetically costly events should not have overlapping schedules (Kendeigh 1949; Farner 1958c, 1964). The supposition has been that breeding birds must struggle to maintain a positive energy balance. In fact, this may not be so. As King and Murphy (1985) have warned, the limits of tolerance of organisms to nutritional and energetic demands have often been underestimated, and it is best to evaluate them under natural conditions in order to reveal their true scope.

It is my perspective that the terminology traditionally used to discuss the re-production–molt overlap issue has been used a bit too vaguely for at least 50 years now. The contention that these two are usually separated temporally seems actually to mean that molt does not occur until reproductive *capabilities* have been lost. In other words, molt does not take place until gonadal regression or photorefractoriness has occurred, which seems to be true. The underpinnings of this logic are that it is more efficient to separate energetically expensive events than to have them co-occur, but its purveyors are ignoring the fact that birds can be heavily engaged in reproductive *activities* well beyond the time when they become refractory. I propose that if molt occurs at any time from nest building through feeding of fledglings, that it be described as overlapping with reproduction. Furthermore, I predict that many more cases of overlap will be found in temperate zone breeders as the data come in from other field studies (see Hahn et al. 1992).

Under what circumstances would this overlap be expected? As pointed out by Foster (1975b), if sufficient resources are present, then species may evolve a temporal pattern wherein costly events occur simultaneously, energy is simply allocated between them. This pattern should be highly adaptive in environments such as high altitude and high latitude where summer is relatively brief, providing that food is abundant. One promising line of inquiry has already been utilized, the examination of molting patterns in species with large latitudinal breeding ranges. For example, Mewaldt and King (1978) found that postnuptial molt duration decreased as latitude increased in *nuttalli* and *pugetensis* living along the Pacific coast. Molt took 83 d at 35.2°N and only 47 d at 48.9°N. This was a decrease in duration of 2.6 d per degree of latitude. Underhill et al. (1992) observed that onset of molt was delayed by 3.5 d per degree of northward progression in Willow Warblers in Europe. Furthermore, there was overlap between breeding and molt at the higher latitudes. Reproduction and molt can be lengthy affairs and if they overlap instead of occurring end-to-end, considerable time can be saved, time that is potentially available for reproduction attempts and, at the end of the season, for fattening and migration prior to arrival of winter conditions.

Postjuvenal molt

Soon after fledging, at about 12–14 d of age, the last traces of natal down disappeared and young *oriantha* assumed their juvenal plumage. This plumage was never present in a completely finished condition, however, because many of the flight feathers, especially the rectrices, were not fully grown in before replacement of the natal body feathers was initiated by the postjuvenal molt (Morton et al. 1972b). Apparently, this pattern is pervasive in fringillids, having been observed in all 11 species studied by Sutton (1935).

To evaluate accurately the progress of molt, one must examine repeatedly the plumage of the same individuals. After many years of trapping, good information was obtained on the parameters of postjuvenal molt in *oriantha* of known age.

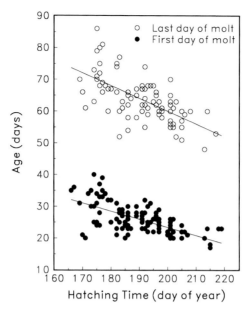

FIGURE 11.7.   Age (in days) at onset and termination of postjuvenal molt in *oriantha* in relation to day of birth (hatching time). Data are from 136 individuals. Regression lines were fitted by least squares.

We found, for example, that this molt had about the same seasonal schedule as the postnuptial molt (Morton 1992a), and that a regular relationship existed between days of age and the growth of brown feathers into the crown (Morton et al. 1991).

Mean age at molt onset for all birds examined was 26.0 d (SD = 4.8 d, N = 110), and mean age on the last day of molt was 63.8 d (SD = 7.1 d, N = 87). The difference between these two means, 37.8 d, can be taken as a measure of postjuvenal molt duration. Another measure, and probably the best one, was obtained when both the first and last days of molt were known in the same individuals. This was 37.2 d (SD = 5.3 d, N = 62). These durations were in close agreement and were both substantially longer than the one of 32.4 d found in seven captives (Morton et al. 1972b). This was not a major surprise because the caged birds were fed an *ad libitum* high-protein diet and they even fattened somewhat because of the energy surplus. One result from these investigations of free-living birds was surprising, however. It was discovered that the later in the season that a bird hatched, the younger it was when its molt began and ended (Fig. 11.7). Late-hatched young began molting about 13 d of age earlier and completed molt about 18 d of age earlier than those hatched at the beginning of the season. (The five-day difference between these two measures suggests that molt duration also decreased seasonally, but the difference was not statistically significant, P = 0.060).

The younger age of molt onset in juveniles with seasonal progression indicates that their response was not strictly developmental; in other words, it was not the result of a genetically-based program that was expressed at a certain age. Rather, the flexibility in onset suggests that environmental factors were serving to cue the beginning of molt. The obvious candidate in this case, because of the time period in question, would be decreasing daylength. Might young birds, only a few days old, be sensitive to this environmental signal? Evidence is accumulating which suggests that this could be the case. For example, Berthold et al. (1970) and Berthold (1988) showed that development, including molt, of hand-raised juvenile Blackcaps (*Sylvia atricapilla*) and Garden Warblers (*Sylvia borin*) could be speeded up by either an increasing or decreasing photoperiod. Additionally, Kroodsma and Pickert (1980) found that the song-learning period of Marsh Wrens (*Cistothorus palustris*) varied substantially with hatching date; those born late in the season delayed their learning until the next spring when the adults had resumed singing. And, directly relevant to the *oriantha* study, postjuvenal molt began at an earlier age (by 17.5 d) and took less time (by 6.5 d) in young Marsh Wrens held on a simulated August photoperiod than in those held on a June photoperiod. Previously, Haukioja (1969) had stated that postjuvenal molt occurred more rapidly in Reed Buntings (*Emberiza schoeniclus*) born late in the season, although no corroborating data were presented. In adult *gambelii*, postnuptial molt and autumnal fattening occurred more rapidly as days became shorter, helping late-starting individuals to be prepared on time (Moore et al. 1982). So the molt-accelerating effect of decreasing daylengths occurs in adults as well as juveniles. Lastly, a series of experiments designed to reveal the ontogeny of photorefractoriness in European Starlings showed that they could distinguish between long and short days early on, even before three weeks of age (Dawson and McNaughton 1992, McNaughton et al. 1992).

There is a long-standing hypothesis that autumnal events in migrants are cued indirectly by increasing photoperiods experienced in the spring (Farner 1964, Farner and Follett 1966). This paradigm cannot apply to juveniles, of course, because they are not even alive until later in the summer and they usually go through the first sequence in their life of molt, fattening, and migration while experiencing only decreasing photoperiods.

TIMING OF SEASONAL BREEDING

Cockrem (1995) has proposed a model to explain the timing of seasonal breeding in birds. It suggests that most or all of them are photoperiodic and possess an internal rhythm of reproduction that is synchronized with the environment by external factors. He suggests that avian breeding seasons begin with recovery from photorefractoriness in late autumn or early winter and are timed thereafter primarily by daylength increases following the winter solstice, with supplementary information being derived from social cues, food availability, ambient temperature, etc.

Given our current knowledge, this model is sensible and appealing, but it would have greater utility, and be more unifying, if it were expanded to account for the biology of hatching-year birds along with the major events in the annual cycle. Without this we are left to wonder if the young birds are supposed to have a unique control system that is used only once (to time their first schedule of molt, fattening, and migration) then discarded for something different when they become adults. This seems unlikely. The data on Blackcaps, Garden Warblers, Marsh Wrens, Reed Buntings, European Starlings, and Mountain White-crowned Sparrows all indicate that decreasing photoperiods have functional consequences in young birds such as repression of gonadal activity, rescheduling of the sensitive period for learning conspecific song, and stimulating the early onset and/or increased pace of molt (the latter so that late-born young can catch up and migrate at the appropriate time).

I suggest that Cockrem's model might be modified to give it broader applicability as follows: Birds have a genetically controlled circannual rhythm of sequentially arranged components that are cued both by increasing and decreasing photoperiods (Aschoff 1955; Gwinner 1977a, 1986, 1996). All the major events of the annual cycle are included in this rhythm and their expression is dependent upon neuroendocrine axes that are finely tuned in their activity by proximate, ecological conditions. Furthermore, this rhythm begins at a very young age, in the egg or at hatching. Young are born in the photorefractory condition (see Dawson and McNaughton 1992) and perceive daylength changes from the beginning. Their first molt, fattening response, and migration departure are all cued by the (usually decreasing) photoperiod. Eventually, upon sufficient exposure to the short days of late autumn, they become photosensitive and are now in phase with adults. The rhythm then continues, more-or-less in synchrony for all members of the population, regardless of age, through the remainder of life.

PREMIGRATORY FATTENING

Birds commonly fatten prior to their initial migratory movement from wintering or summering areas and during pauses or stopovers that occur along the way. The positive energy balance required for this response is achieved by an active, hypothalamically-regulated hyperphagia which leads to fat accumulations that can approach 50% of total body mass in some species (Kuenzel and Helms 1967, 1970). This impressively obese condition is highly adaptive because the fat is both fuel for flight and a buffer against bad weather and uncertain food supplies that are sometimes encountered (King and Farner 1965). The pattern of fattening in relation to migration itinerary is highly variable (King 1972) but, in general, increased lipid stores are associated with increased speed of migration and with greater flight and migration distances (Berthold 1975, Blem 1990, Kaiser 1992). Hyperphagia and lipogenesis are facilitated throughout the migration period by a hormonal milieu that involves elevated levels of corticosterone (Holberton et al. 1996).

Premigratory hyperphagia, as expressed by rapid weight gain, began near the end of the postnuptial molt in *oriantha* adults. The best way to detect this phenomenon was to examine and weigh repeatedly the same individuals at short time intervals, daily if possible. Data from one such frequently captured male illustrate this principle (Fig. 11.8). It can be seen that this male (band number 125135996) was present on the study area for six years (1980–1985). During that time, he began molting between 23 July and 1 August and finished between 11 and 28 September. Because of changes in blood volume, his body mass increased slightly then decreased during the molting period. Recapture intervals became lengthened at mid-molt, a time when *oriantha* were often relatively immobile and reclusive. Every season, as the molt waned, body mass of this male veered to an upward trajectory. Presumably this was the result of a shift to a new and higher set point for appetite. Close inspection of the body mass records reveal that this regulatory change must have occurred suddenly, perhaps within a single 24-hr period.

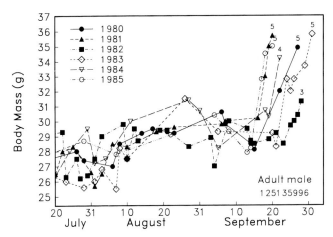

FIGURE 11.8.   Changes in body mass of an adult male *oriantha* during six seasons from the time that molt began to when premigratory fattening and migration occurred. Numerals indicate fat class on the last capture of the season.

This insight on the switch to hyperphagia is different from the one that might be gathered from perusing the records of body mass in captives. In them mass appears to increase much more gradually than in the wild birds. There are several reasons for this: captives tend to put on fat in the presence of *ad libitum* food, even before they are hyperphagic; they have traditionally been weighed only at weekly or, at the most, semiweekly intervals; and, despite asynchronies in their schedules, their body mass changes have usually been presented collectively as means. In combination, these factors tend to portray mass gain in hyperphagic birds as being more gradual than it actually is (King et al. 1965, Morton et al. 1973). Much the same method of presenting body mass changes has also obscured how suddenly appetite is re-set in hibernators as they prepare metabolically for hibernation (Morton 1975; Mrosovsky 1975, 1976).

In recent years there has been an attempt to discover if food intake in White-crowned Sparrows is affected by various metabolites and hormones. In many of these experiments feeding activity was either undisturbed or inhibited. Cholecystokinin injections, for example, suppressed food intake (Richardson et al. 1993). In another set of experiments, feeding was unaffected by manipulations of carbohydrate metabolism and it decreased after plasma lipids were elevated through administrations of insulin and glucagon (Boswell et al. 1995). Unlike mammals, White-crowned Sparrows do not increase food intake in response to carbohydrate utilization and they appear to be more sensitive to signals from lipid metabolism than to those from carbohydrate metabolism (Boswell et al. 1996). At least one promising result has been obtained, however, and it typifies the type of information needed for understanding how environmental signals can be transduced to sudden increases in appetite. Richardson et al. (1995) found that neuropeptide Y (a member of the pancreatic peptide family that is widely distributed in the vertebrate brain) stimulated feeding when injected into the third ventricle of *gambelii*. The feeding response occurred on both short and long photoperiods, although sensitivity to neuropeptide Y appeared to be greater when the birds were being held on long days. At some time in the future it may be possible to monitor the

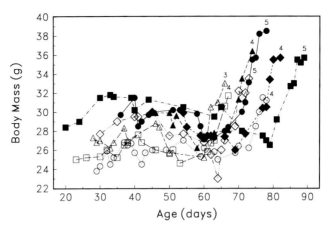

FIGURE 11.9.   Changes in body mass of four male (solid symbols) and four female (open symbols) *oriantha* juveniles according to their age (in days). Numbers indicate fat class on the last capture of the season.

brain chemistry of migrants, such as *oriantha* and *gambelii,* as they transit from normal, homeostatic weight regulation to hyperphagia. Changes in neurochemical activity at that time should help us to understand how such large shifts in appetite and weight regulation can occur so quickly in migrants.

Body mass increased in *oriantha* juveniles until they reached adult size at about four weeks of age. They then completed the postjuvenal molt and eventually became hyperphagic and fattened. Data from eight juveniles (four males and four females) whose birth dates were known, and that had multiple captures, show that their fattening response had the same configuration as the one observed in adults, an abrupt inception, preceded by a slight decrease in mass that occurred at the end of molt (Fig. 11.9). The average gain per day, as a percent of initial body mass, was 2.3 to 2.6% in both juveniles and adults (Table 11.3). One exceptional juvenile male went from 26.5 to 30.4 g in 22.5 hr, a 14.7% increase. Fat classes in these frequently handled birds was usually 4 or 5 (see Table 6.3) on the day they were last captured (Figs. 11.8, 11.9).

Onset of the fattening response was not age-specific in juveniles and varied in occurrence from about 55 to 90 days of age. Mean duration of the response was eight or nine days, no matter the age or sex (Table 11.3). Females were about

TABLE 11.3.   DURATION OF AUTUMNAL PREMIGRATORY FATTENING PERIOD IN *Oriantha* AND AVERAGE GAIN IN BODY MASS PER DAY (IN G AND AS % OF INITIAL BODY MASS)

	Duration of fattening period (d)			Gain in body mass per day (g)	Gain per day (% of initial body mass)
	Mean	SD	N		
Juveniles					
Males	9.29	2.84	103	0.66	2.3
Females	8.59	3.25	73	0.68	2.6
Adults					
Males	9.05	3.31	74	0.69	2.4
Females	8.22	2.88	46	0.61	2.3

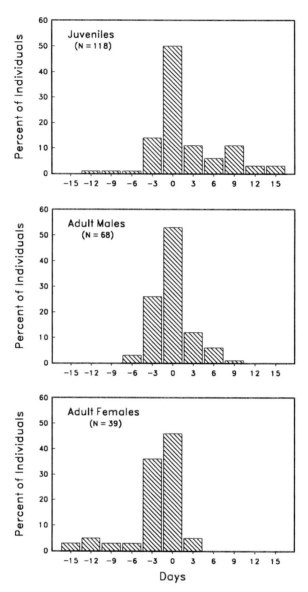

FIGURE 11.10.   Onset of premigratory fattening in *oriantha* in relation to the end of molt. Negative numbers indicate days of molt remaining, day 0 equals end of molt, positive numbers indicate number of days molt had been completed before fattening began.

10% smaller than males and they tended to top out at lower masses, 32–34 g vs. 36–38 g, although individuals of both sexes and age groups were known occasionally to exceed these levels by 2 g or more.

The inflection point in the curve showing when body mass began to increase abruptly—the onset of premigratory fattening—occurred in most *oriantha,* juveniles and adults alike, just about the time when molt was being completed (Fig. 11.10). There were some cases, as in adult females rearing fledglings late in the season, where the two functions overlapped by as much as two weeks. Conversely, molt had also been completed for about two weeks in a few juveniles before fattening began (Fig. 11.10). Still, fattening began in most birds when molt was ending and overlap between these two functions was not extensive. Molt termination itself is probably not utilized to regulate fattening onset because the two have been separated experimentally by Lindström et al. (1994). They found that simulation of autumn conditions, achieved by advancing the photoperiod by one month, did not affect molt dynamics in captive Bluethroats (*Luscinia svecica*), but fat deposition was shifted. It began early, right in the middle of molt in the experimental birds, rather than at the end, as is usual in this high latitude migrant.

Frequently retrapped, hyperphagic *oriantha* disappeared about the time their fat scores had reached class 4 or 5. Only occasionally did one in this completely fattened condition remain on the study area for even a day or two (see examples in Fig. 11.9).

MIGRATION DEPARTURE

The precise moment that any of the birds in this study began their autumnal flight to wintering areas was unknown. Yet this time could be deduced to within a day or two from frequently trapped individuals because, as stated above, they were seldom recaptured after reaching a peak mass. They fattened and left. This would seem to be a highly suitable response because birds should not depart until well supplied with energy reserves, nor should they linger, once appropriately obese, since fat reserves are costly to maintain (Hurly 1992).

Migration dynamics were obtained during seven years wherein trapping (using seed for bait) was conducted three to five days a week through the time in October when all *oriantha* had disappeared from the study area. As a result, migration departure dates were determined for 241 juveniles and 199 adults. Their frequency of departures, according to calendar date, occurred in approximately normal distributions for both age classes (Fig. 11.11). There was no difference in migration schedule for males and females within the two age classes, but juveniles, on average, did leave 3.2 d earlier than adults (Morton and Pereyra 1994). The earliest departure was 8 September and the latest was 23 October. Both of these birds were juveniles. The range in departure dates was 45 d for juveniles and 37 d for adults, with most of the variation being traceable to interannual differences in reproductive schedules. Departure was delayed about one day for every two days that nesting had been delayed earlier in the summer by environmental conditions such as a persisting snow cover. Over the seven-year period, mean departure date varied by about 14 d in juveniles and eight d in adults. Consistent with the differential of 3.2 d mentioned above, mean departure date of juveniles was earlier than that of adults in six of the seven years.

Departures did not follow a predictable, repetitive pattern. In some years their frequencies resembled a normal distribution, in others it was bimodal or multimodal. One year a mass exodus occurred just ahead of a fierce snowstorm. Usually, though, there was fair weather when individuals set off and the number of birds visiting seed-baited traps dwindled steadily through time.

Mean age of juveniles at their time of departure was 76.7 d (SD = 7.2 d, N = 43). It ranged from 64 to 98 d and appeared to have no central tendency (Morton and Pereyra 1994). This ability of individuals barely two months of age to fatten and migrate at the regular time, rather than being delayed into late

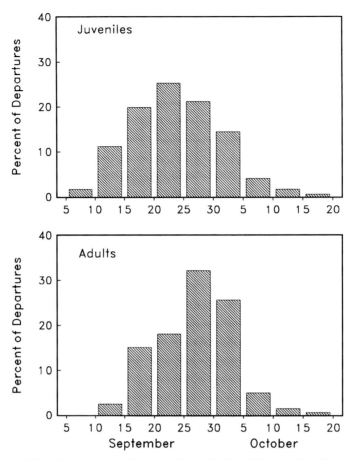

FIGURE 11.11.   Migration departure schedules of juvenile (N = 241) and adult (N = 199) *oriantha*; seven yr of data.

October or early November, can be tied to the earlier observation that late-born young appear to be stimulated by decreasing daylengths to begin molting at an early age.

An overview of migration departure dates for the various age classes in the population shows that although juveniles tended to migrate ahead of adults, age was not a determining factor among adults of either sex (ANOVA $F_{5, 122} = 1.08$, $P = 0.38$ for males; $F_{4, 75} = 0.13$, $P = 0.97$ for females; Table 11.4).

THE STIMULUS FOR MIGRATION

The preceding data show clearly that *oriantha* did not tarry on the breeding meadows once they had fattened. Upon achieving what must have been energy reserves sufficient for their southward journey they departed, probably individually or in small flocks because dates of last captures were usually well spread out.

According to current wisdom, the urge to migrate in autumn is the expression of a genetically controlled circannual rhythm that is phased by the photoperiod so as to maintain its long-term accuracy (Gwinner 1971, 1977b, 1986, 1990, 1996;

TABLE 11.4. Julian Dates for Migration Departure and Body Mass at Departure in *Oriantha*, According to Year of Age

	Males					Females				
	Departure date		Body mass (g)			Departure date		Body mass (g)		
Age	Mean	SD	Mean	SD	N	Mean	SD	Mean	SD	N
0[a]	266.8	7.4	34.4	2.4	140	267.7	7.7	31.6	2.1	101
1	270.2	6.7	35.1	1.8	60	269.7	6.7	31.7	1.9	48
2	269.1	5.6	35.0	2.0	37	271.7	5.2	31.8	1.8	21
3	273.8	6.2	35.5	2.8	13	263.0	0.0	32.4	0.0	1
4	271.3	5.3	34.4	1.9	9	270.6	9.2	32.0	1.7	5
5	268.0	4.2	32.4	2.6	2	274.0	0.0	30.7	0.0	1
6	267.5	6.4	35.9	1.3	2	—	—	—	—	—

[a] Juveniles.

King and Farner 1974; Berthold 1975, 1988; Gauthreaux 1996). So strong is this rhythm that captives kept lean by food deprivation will still show intense nocturnal locomotor activity, or *Zugunruhe,* the behavioral analog of migratory movement that is exhibited by individuals restrained in cages (King and Farner 1963, Lofts et al. 1963, Gwinner 1968, Berthold 1977). Pertinent to the present study is an older idea, one which proposes that achievement of a favorable migratory condition or disposition (in this case, being obese) could cause the release of migration behavior (Farner 1955a). Coalescing these ideas with the *oriantha* data leads me to suggest that an endogenous rhythm is involved in both the metabolic preparation for migration and in the propensity for migration behavior to be expressed, but the stimulus for beginning the journey itself is provided in free-living birds by the acquisition of appropriate amounts of stored fat. This could be facilitated, for example, by feedback from fat depots or from levels of circulating lipids.

Other than fattening, metabolic preparation for migration might also involve increasing the oxygen carrying abilities of the blood (important for skeletal muscle function during migration flights) through synthesis of additional erythrocytes. Wingfield and Farner (1980) found, for example, that hematocrit (packed erythrocyte volume) increased from about 52 to 57% during vernal migration in *gambelii,* a long-distance migrant, but did not increase in *pugetensis,* a short-distance migrant. *Oriantha,* a medium-distance migrant, had high hematocrits (57 to 59%) upon arrival at Tioga Pass and these then decreased and remained stable through the summer nesting period. Hematocrit dropped again during molt, in late July and August, to about 49%, then increased in late September to about 55% (Fig. 11.12). Some of this late-season increase was probably due to restoration of premolt plasma volumes, but increased erythropoietic activity could have been contributing as well. Interestingly, Lee (2000) discovered that hematocrit varies with photoperiod. It averaged 51% in *oriantha* held on short days (8L:16D) and 54% in those held on long days (16L:8D).

STOPOVER MIGRANTS AND THE MIGRATION SCHEDULE

In seven years TPM was trapped regularly during the fall months until all *oriantha* had disappeared. Other *Zonotrichia* that were stopping over during southward migration were also captured during that time. Nearly all of these were *gambelii* (which sometimes joined with *oriantha* to form mixed flocks), but a few

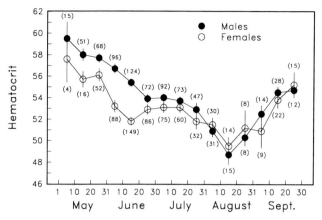

FIGURE 11.12.   Seasonal changes in hematocrit of adult *oriantha* at Tioga Pass. Means ± 1 SE; sample sizes in parentheses.

Golden-crowned Sparrows were also handled in most years and once a Harris's Sparrow. No *oriantha* were captured in autumn passage. Apparently those that summered to the north flew beyond Tioga Pass before stopping.

First captures of the season for stopover *gambelii* ranged between 7 and 17 September, with the mean date being 11 September. Dates of last captures for the season ranged between 5 and 23 October, with the mean being 11 October (Morton and Pereyra 1987). During September and October, therefore, both *oriantha* and *gambelii* appeared regularly in traps although from early October onward the majority of those captured each day were *gambelii* (Fig. 11.13). During their stopover period, which decreased in duration from an average of 7.6 d in early September to 2.5 d in late October, about 70% of the *gambelii* being trapped showed an increase in fat class and body mass. In many of the retrapped individuals a phase of rapid weight gain occurred that averaged about 0.4 g per d (Fig. 11.14).

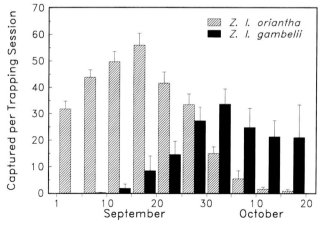

FIGURE 11.13.   Mean number of *oriantha* and *gambelii* captured per trapping session on TPM in September and October during seven yr (1979–1985). Number of trapping sessions per five-day interval during those seven years ranged from six to 27. Bars show mean (+1 SE).

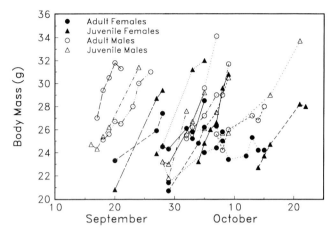

FIGURE 11.14.   Body mass changes in *gambelii* retrapped during stopover periods on TPM.

Several points that are relevant to the migration biology of White-crowned Sparrows can be made at this juncture. Data from the stopover birds (*gambelii*) show that hyperphagia persisted beyond the initial episode of fattening that preceded departure from breeding areas. And, like individuals launching from summering areas, they seldom lingered once they had fattened. In other words, the initial migration movement, and those that occurred subsequently as the migration unfolded, bore close resemblance to one another when their pre-flight and departure characteristics were compared. Finally, the fact that close relatives of *oriantha* routinely stopped over on the study area well into October suggests that adequate food for a fattening response was still present on TPM after most of the *oriantha* had departed. Why not use this extra cushion of time to prolong the breeding season and produce more offspring? The answer must be that survival is poor in late-hatched young and, perhaps, in adults that must provide care for them. Insects, the primary food needed for nestling growth and nutrition, became scarce in the fall, and although seeds of grasses and sedges were often abundant, they may have been only adequate for putting on fat. In addition, ambient temperatures dropped sharply in September and October, especially nocturnal ones (Table 1.1), and molting birds, with their diminished thermoregulatory capacities, would undoubtedly have been stressed by such low temperatures. Another factor is that the frequency of potentially debilitating storms began to increase (Table 9.1). When such storms occurred they had an effect on the propensity of *gambelii* to stay in the high altitude meadows. For example, in 1984 the autumnal weather was very mild, and a total of 507 *gambelii* was captured on TPM. In 1982, on the other hand, a series of storms began in late September and only 66 *gambelii* were taken. This is not to say that survival of *gambelii* was affected in 1982. In early October of that year we surveyed the brushy thickets and weed patches that occur along the Great Basin-Sierra Nevada interface and found them there in substantial numbers. It appears that *gambelii* utilize the ripe grasses and sedges of the high elevation meadows during autumnal stopovers and if a major storm moves in they simply drop to lower elevations and continue on with their migration. But molting *oriantha* have reduced mobility and probably could not easily exercise this option. They would have to remain and endure the bad weather (one post-molt adult male was known to have spent the day of 11 September in lower Lee Vining Canyon, following a snowstorm in the previous night). It seems, then, that the timing of autumnal migration in *oriantha* has evolved with a built-in margin of safety. They become refractory and complete the season-ending functions of molt and fattening before the frequency of bad weather begins to increase. By the time the first powerful winter storms strike the high mountain breeding areas they have already departed for Mexico thereby improving the likelihood of their continued survival and participation in subsequent reproductive efforts.

CHAPTER 12: Concluding Remarks

The primary purpose of this study, including the publications stemming from it, has been to enlarge our understanding of avian migration and reproductive biology. Ideally, the data and conclusions will apply not only to White-crowned Sparrows summering in the subalpine, but also to many other species by disclosing details of natural history and life history that will prove to be shared in common. The data should thus be useful for comparative purposes and for identifying new avenues of research. And they should also help to reveal some of the principles that underlie environmental adaptation.

One principle that seems to have emerged is that challenges posed by environmental variation often can be met with existing behavioral and physiological responses; adaptation occurs through flexibility rather than through acquisition of new abilities or mechanisms. Furthermore, and undoubtedly due to their differing biological roles, strategies adopted by males and females to cope with these challenges may differ.

An example was in the way gonadal development occurred in relation to migration schedule and to snow conditions at the breeding area (Chapter 5). Testicular enlargement continued for about a month after males had reached Tioga Pass but ovaries remained small, barely above wintertime size, and did not achieve maximal mass until the first ovulation. About 75% of testicular growth and more than 90% of ovarian growth was post-migrational. This helped to minimize the mass being transported during migration but did not appear to compromise function in males because their early-season plasma testosterone levels were high and they were fertile. In most years post-arrival gonadal developmental proceeded quickly in both sexes but if snow cover prevented nesting, physiological flexibility was displayed by females in that further ovarian growth was inhibited. And ovaries could remain in what appeared to be an undeveloped, arrested condition for six weeks or more. This energetically efficient response did not seem to compromise reproductive capabilities of females, however, because if nesting sites were provided by investigators or became available naturally they were able to begin laying within only a few days. If storms occurred before nesting was under way members of both sexes ceased efforts to acquire mates and territories in favor of a temporary move to lower altitude where conditions were milder.

Once the nesting season was in progress, another highly adaptive response that directly affected reproductive success and that required large adjustments in both physiology and behavior occurred when nesting was interrupted. Almost immediately endocrine pathways were reactivated, courtship was renewed, and females built a new nest and re-acquired enough nutrients to begin laying. Modal elapsed time for this complete sequence to occur was only 5 d and, if necessary, it could be repeated as many as four times in a season.

Additional behavioral flexibility was exhibited by females when snow cover was persistent in that their choice of nest sites was altered (Chapter 10). In light snow years as few as 10% of nests were built above ground in pines and willows, but in heavy snow years when open ground with places to hide nests were scarce up to 70% of nests were placed above ground. This helped to minimize the seasonal delay in nesting onset, which was important because the longer nesting was delayed the shorter the period available for renesting attempts and the fewer young produced.

Another principle is that adaptive responses can have costs; they may involve various kinds of trade-offs. For example, building nests in elevated sites can lessen delays caused by persistent snow cover, but females incubating in those nests weigh 5% less than those with ground nests, probably because they must combat an increase in convective cooling by producing more heat through shivering. Also, according to our thinking, a single, efficient regulatory process acts to regulate both clutch size (via termination of laying) and onset of incubation. Hatching asynchrony results from this process and it is a cost because it can sometimes facilitate unnecessary mortality in nestlings. Another possible trade-off, not yet explored in wild birds, is that accelerated molt, such as the one that allows females nesting late in the season to catch up with other adults, may compromise survival because quickly grown plumage is of poorer quality (see Dawson et al. 2000).

Along with revealing underlying principles of environmental adaptation, such as the two mentioned above, this study has also shown that experience counts for very little in passerine reproduction: there was no effect of age on egg size, clutch size, clutch volume, or number of fledglings produced (reproductive success). Perhaps the latter should be expected because the modal number of broods fledged, both annually and per lifetime, was one. There must be strong selection for maximal reproductive performance by yearlings. Only two age-related effects were found. One was that between-year breeding dispersal decreased with age, and the other was that incubation period was shorter if females were at least three years old. Interestingly, these phenomena appear to be related. Decreased dispersal by older females may signal their attainment of a favored nesting location. One expression of this optimal condition could be increased foraging efficiency, which, in turn, permits increased attentiveness and a shortened incubation period.

These are a few examples of how *oriantha* responded to high altitude conditions and they help to distinguish the relative roles of environmental factors, such as photoperiod, that act as initial predictive information from those, such as nutritional plane and availability of nesting sites, that act as supplementary information. These examples also serve to remind us that dividing physiology and behavior into separate categories is more a matter of convenience than reality. In truth, the more we learn about the lives of organisms and the ways they react to ecological conditions, the clearer it becomes that the two act together in complementary, reciprocal fashion and are often functionally inseparable.

Many possibilities for additional research arise from the *oriantha* data. One of the more interesting, and possibly intractable, ones is the cause and effect relationship that occurs in hatching asynchrony. We have hypothesized that asynchrony is an epiphenomenon, an unselected by-product of a mechanism that has evolved to turn off a physiological phase of reproduction (egg laying) while simultaneously turning on a behavioral one (full-time attentiveness). The competitive inequalities in siblings that stem from a staggered hatching pattern imperil the smallest chick(s) and adaptation to this problem may occur in at least three ways: (1) females minimize the hatching spread by maintaining high levels of attentiveness during the hatching period, even though they lose considerable body mass in the process (Chapter 6); (2) the last egg is the clutch tends to be relatively large, thereby producing a chick that is better able to compete with its older siblings (Chapter 7); and (3) from other studies, yolk testosterone concentrations increase with laying order (Schwabl 1993, Lipar et al. 1999), which may also help last-hatched young to compete. Like many of these questions that involve evolutionary history, ultimate causation is inferred from proximate results, and the reason asynchrony developed in the first place may never be settled to everyone's satisfaction. Nonetheless, investigations of the regulatory processes that occur toward the end of the ovulatory sequence, when clutch size is determined, are likely to produce important new information (see, for example, Sockman et al. 2000).

Investigations of how habitat quality and mate quality affect settlement patterns of females and their choices of nesting area over a lifetime should also be enlightening, especially when coupled with paternity data. Intrasexual aggression appears to be an important component of this site selection-breeding dispersal interplay and the straightforward method of trapping with decoys (Chapter 3) would seem to be a useful approach for measuring levels of aggression during territory acquisition and defense in both sexes.

There are many other results from the Tioga work which suggest that additional inquiry may be in order. For example, we expected that red blood cell synthesis would be stimulated by exposure to high altitude conditions, thereby causing hematocrits to increase during the summer. In fact, the opposite occurred, and the relative contributions of various underlying factors that could be responsible, such as changes in water balance and hemopoiesis, are unknown. Some fundamental adjustment in circulation dynamics related to migration biology seems to be occurring, however.

Another regulatory system worthy of a better look, and one that has potential for broad applicability in vertebrates, is the shift to hyperphagia that occurs at the onset of premigratory fattening. This change in food intake appears to be abrupt and massive and migratory birds should, therefore, be good models or preparations for detecting the mechanisms underlying appetite regulation.

The field observations also indicate that great opportunities exist for discovering metabolic costs of reproduction not only for broad categories, such as egg laying, incubation, and feeding nestlings, but also for times that could be crucial for survival or for when energy balance may be in jeopardy because of conflicting or overlapping functions. What happens to energy balance, for example, when pre-breeding altitudinal movements occur, when nesting sequences are disrupted by storms, or when molting begins during the parental phase? How stressed are females when incubating in above-ground nests, when their attempts to hatch out the last eggs in the clutch conflict with self maintenance, when they are engaged simultaneously in building replacement nests and preparing to ovulate, or when they are performing all care of offspring by themselves? There is no need to continue along these lines. Hopefully, thoughtful young scientists will come to their own conclusions about the data and hypotheses presented in this monograph and will be stimulated to design and pursue follow-up investigations of their own.

ACKNOWLEDGMENTS

Above all others, I must express my appreciation to the dozens of Occidental College students who labored alongside me in every phase of this study. Thanks people for all the traps you carried, the nests you found, the records you kept, and the bad weather and mosquitos and other hardships (even the mouse-generated "raisins" in the oatmeal) that you shrugged aside. Thanks for your ideas and inspirations, your enthusiasm and friendship, and for making it all fun. Doug Burns, John Crandall, Galen Morton, Linda Peterson, Keith Sockman, and Josie Weisbach deserve special mention for their help with data compilation and analysis. Any errors, including interpretations, are surely mine. I have also benefited greatly over the years from collaborations with scientists from other institutions. To Luis Baptista, Cindy Carey, Tom Hahn, Cindy Kagarise Sherman, Paul Sherman, Wes Weathers, and John Wingfield, thanks for your help and for everything you've taught me. In addition, the manuscript was greatly improved by many thoughtful suggestions and constructive criticisms from Greg Ball, Tom Hahn, Chris Norment, Bill Searcy, Glenn Walsberg, and the editor, John Rotenberry. Because of them it became more focused, accurate, and coherent. Finally, I am grateful to my wife, Maria Elena Pereyra, for her constant encouragement, contribution of artwork, and guidance of this unreformed Luddite through the daunting maze of modern statistical, word-processing, reference-management, and graphics software packages. Thanks Malena, I couldn't have finished this without you.

LITERATURE CITED

ABLE, K. P., AND V. P. BINGMAN. 1987. The development of orientation and navigation behavior in birds. Quarterly Review of Biology 62:1–29.

ADKINS-REGAN, E. 1995. Predictors of fertilization in the Japanese Quail, *Coturnix japonica*. Animal Behaviour 50:1405–1415.

AEBISCHER, A., N. PERRIN, M. KRIEG, J. STUDER, AND D. R. MEYER. 1996. The role of territory choice, mate choice and arrival date on breeding success in the Savi's Warbler *Locustella luscinioides*. Journal of Avian Biology 27:143–152.

AFTON, A. D. 1979. Incubation temperature of the Northern Shoveler. Canadian Journal of Zoology 57:1052–1056.

ALATALO, R. V., L. GUSTAFSSON, AND A. LUNDBERG. 1984. Why do young passerine birds have shorter wings than older birds? Ibis 126:410–415.

ALERSTAM, T. 1990. Bird Migration. Cambridge University Press, New York, NY.

AMERICAN ORNITHOLOGISTS' UNION. 1998. Check-list of North American Birds, 7th edition. American Ornithologists' Union, Washington, D.C.

AMUNDSEN, T., AND T. SLAGSVOLD. 1991. Hatching asynchrony: facilitating adaptive or maladaptive brood reduction? Acta XX Congressus Internationalis Ornithologici 20: 1707–1719.

ARNOLD, T. W., F. C. ROHWER, AND F. ARMSTRONG. 1987. Egg viability, nest predation, and adaptive significance of clutch size in prairie ducks. American Naturalist 130:643–653.

ASCHOFF, J. 1955. Jahresperiodik der Fortpflanzung bei Warmblütern. Studium Generale 8:742–776.

ASKENMO, C., AND U. UNGER. 1986. How to be double-brooded: trends and timing of breeding performance in the Rock Pipit. Ornis Scandinavica 17:237–244.

AUSTIN, G. T. 1976. Behavioral adaptations of the Verdin to the desert. Auk 93:245–262.

BAERENDS, G. P. 1959. The ethological analysis of incubation behaviour. Ibis 101:357–368.

BAILEY, R. E. 1952. The incubation patch of passerine birds. Condor 54:121–136.

BAKER, J. R. 1938a. The evolution of breeding seasons. Pp. 167–177 *in* G. R. DeBeer (editor). Evolution. Oxford University Press, Oxford, UK.

BAKER, J. R. 1938b. The relation between latitude and breeding seasons in birds. Proceedings of the Zoological Society, London (A) 108:557–582.

BAKER, M. C. 1983. The behavioral response of female Nuttall's White-crowned Sparrows to male song of natal and alien dialects. Behavioral Ecology and Sociobiology 12:309–315.

BAKER, M. C., L. R. MEWALDT, AND R. M. STEWART. 1981. Demography of White-crowned Sparrows (*Zonotrichia leucophrys nuttalli*). Ecology 62:636–644.

BAKER, M. C., AND D. B. THOMPSON. 1985. Song dialects of White-crowned Sparrows: historical processes inferred from patterns of geographic variation. Condor 87:127–141.

BALDA, R. P., G. WEISENBERGER, AND M. STRAUSS. 1970. White-crowned Sparrow (*Zonotrichia leucophrys*) breeding in Arizona. Auk 87:809.

BALL, G. F. 1991. Endocrine mechanisms and the evolution of avian parental care. Acta XX Congressus Internationalis Ornithologici 20:984–991.

BALL, G. F. 1993. The neural integration of environmental information by seasonally breeding birds. American Zoologist 33:185–199.

BALL, G. F., AND T. P. HAHN. 1997. GnRH neuronal systems in birds and their relation to the control of seasonal reproduction. Pp. 325–342 *in* I. S. Parhar and Y. Sakuma (editors). GnRH neurons: Gene to behavior. Brain Shuppan, Tokyo, Japan.

BANCROFT, G. T. 1984. Patterns of variation in size of Boat-tailed Grackle *Quiscalus major* eggs. Ibis 126:496–509.

BANKS, R. C. 1959. Development of nestling White-crowned Sparrows in central coastal California. Condor 61:96–109.

BANKS, R. C. 1964. Geographic variation in the White-crowned Sparrow, *Zonotrichia leucophrys*. University of California Publications in Zoology 70:1–123.

BAPTISTA, L. F. 1975. Song dialects and demes in sedentary populations of the White-crowned Sparrow (*Zonotrichia leucophrys nuttalli*). University of California Publications in Zoology 105:1–52.

BAPTISTA, L. F. 1977. Geographic variation in song and dialects of the Puget Sound White-crowned Sparrow. Condor 79:356–370.

BAPTISTA, L. F. 1985. The functional significance of song sharing in the White-crowned Sparrow. Canadian Journal of Zoology 63:1741–1752.

BAPTISTA, L. F., AND J. R. KING. 1980. Geographical variation in song and song dialects of montane White-crowned Sparrows. Condor 82:267–284.

BAPTISTA, L. F., AND M. L. MORTON. 1982. Song dialects and mate selection in montane White-crowned Sparrows. Auk 99:537–547.

BAPTISTA, L. F., AND M. L. MORTON. 1988. Song learning in montane White-crowned Sparrows: from whom and when. Animal Behaviour 36:1753–1764.

BAPTISTA, L. F., P. W. TRAIL, B. B. DEWOLFE, AND M. L. MORTON. 1993. Singing and its functions in female White-crowned Sparrows. Animal Behaviour 46:511–524.

BARBA, E., J. A. GIL-DELGADO, AND J. S. MONROS. 1995. The costs of being late: consequences of delaying Great Tit *Parus major* first clutches. Journal of Animal Ecology 64:642–651.

BARRENTINE, C. D., M. W. LINCOLN, C. E. CORCHRAN, AND P. M. WALTERS. 1993. Wing-length change in the first postnuptial molt of Gambel's White-crowned Sparrows. North American Bird Bander 18:148–150.

BARRETT, R. T. 1980. Temperature of Kittiwake *Rissa tridactyla* eggs and nests during incubation. Ornis Scandinavica 11:50–59.

BART, J., AND A. TORNES. 1989. Importance of monogamous male birds in determining reproductive success. Behavioral Ecology and Sociobiology 24:109–116.

BÉDARD, J., AND G. LAPOINTE. 1984. Banding returns, arrival times, and site fidelity in the Savannah Sparrow. Wilson Bulletin 96:196–205.

BÉDARD, J., AND G. LAPOINTE. 1985. Influence of parental age and season on Savannah Sparrow reproductive success. Condor 87:106–110.

BERGLUND, A., C. MAGNHAGEN, A. BISAZZA, B. KONIG, AND F. HUNTINGFORD. 1993. Female-female competition over reproduction. Behavioral Ecology 4:184–187.

BERTHOLD, P. 1969. Uber Populationsunterschiede im Gonadenzyklus europaischer *Sturnus vulgaris, Fringilla coelebs, Erithacus rubecula* und *Phylloscopus collybita* und deren Ursachen. Zoologisch Jahrbuch Systematik 96:491–557.

BERTHOLD, P. 1975. Migration: control and metabolic physiology. Pp. 77–124 *in* D. S. Farner and J. R. King (editors). Avian Biology. Vol. 5. Academic Press, New York, NY.

BERTHOLD, P. 1977. Über die Entwicklung von Zugunruhe vei der Gartengrasmücke (*Sylvia borin*) bei verhinderter Fettdeposition. Vogelwarte 29:113–116.

BERTHOLD, P. 1988. The control of migration in European warblers. Acta XIX Congressus Internationalis Ornithologici 1:215–249.

BERTHOLD, P., E. GWINNER, AND H. KLEIN. 1970. Vergleichende Untersuchungen der Jugendentwicklung eines ausgeprägten Zugvogels, *Sylvia borin,* und eines weniger ausgeprägten Zugvogels, *S. atricapilla.* Vogelwarte 25:297–331.

BIEBACH, H. 1979. Energetik des Brütens beim Star (*Sturnus vulgaris*). Journal fur Ornithologie 120:121–138.

BIJLSMA, R. 1982. Breeding season, clutch size and breeding success in the Bullfinch *Pyrrhula pyrrhula.* Ardea 70:25–30.

BILLINGS, W. D., AND L. C. BLISS. 1959. An alpine snowbank environment and its effects on vegetation, plant development, and productivity. Ecology 40:388–397.

BIRKHEAD, T. L. 1987. Sperm competition in birds. Trends in Ecology and Evolution 2: 268–272.

BIRKHEAD, T. R. 1992. Sperm storage and the fertile period in the Bengalese Finch. Auk 109:620–625.

BIRKHEAD, T. R. 1996. Mechanisms of sperm competition in birds. American Scientist 84: 254–262.

BIRKHEAD, T. R., AND A. P. MØLLER. 1992. Sperm competition in birds. Academic Press, London, UK.

BLACKBURN, T. M. 1991. An interspecific relationship between egg size and clutch size in birds. Auk 108:973–977.

BLANCHARD, B. D. 1941. The White-crowned sparrows (*Zonotrichia leucophrys*) of the Pacific seaboard: environment and annual cycle. University of California Publications in Zoology 46:1–178.

BLANCHARD, B. D. 1942. Migration in Pacific Coast White-crowned Sparrows. Auk 59: 47–63.

BLEM, C. R. 1990. Avian energy storage. Current Ornithology 7:59–100.

BÖHM, C., AND A. LANDMANN. 1995. Nistplatzwahl, Neststandort und Nestbau beim Wasserpieper (*Anthus spinoletta*). Journal fur Ornithologie 136:1–16.

BOERSMA, P. D., AND N. T. WHEELWRIGHT. 1979. Egg neglect in the procellariformes: reproductive adaptations in the Fork-tailed Storm-Petrel. Condor 81:157–165.

BOLLINGER, E. K., AND T. A. GAVIN. 1989. The effects of site quality on breeding-site fidelity in Bobolinks. Auk 106:584–594.

BOOTH, D. T., AND R. S. SEYMOUR. 1987. Effect of eggshell thinning on water vapor conductance of Malleefowl eggs. Condor 89:453–459.

BOSWELL, T., M. RAMENOFSKY, R. D. RICHARDSON, R. J. SEELEY, J. C. WINGFIELD, AND S. C. WOODS. 1996. Regulation of food intake by metabolic fuels in migratory birds. Poster, VI International Symposium on Avian Endocrinology, Chateau Lake Louise, Alberta, Canada.

BOSWELL, T., R. D. RICHARDSON, R. J. SEELEY, M. RAMENOFSKY, J. C. WINGFIELD, M. I. FRIEDMAN, AND S. C. WOODS. 1995. Regulation of food intake by metabolic fuels in White-crowned Sparrows. American Journal of Physiology 269:R1462–R1468.

BOYCE, M. S., AND C. M. PERRINS. 1987. Optimizing Great Tit clutch size in a fluctuating environment. Ecology 68:142–153.

BRISKIE, J. V. 1992. Copulation patterns and sperm competition in the polygynandrous Smith's Longspur. Auk 109:563–575.

BRISKIE, J. V., AND S. G. SEALY. 1990. Variation in size and shape of Least Flycatcher eggs. Journal of Field Ornithology 61:180–191.

VON BRÖMSSEN, A., AND C. JANSSON. 1980. Effects of food addition to Willow Tit *Parus montanus* and Crested Tit *P. cristatus* at the time of breeding. Ornis Scandinavica 11: 173–178.

BROOKE, M. D. 1979. Differences in the quality of territories held by Wheatears (*Oenanthe oenanthe*). Journal of Animal Ecology 48:21–32.

BROWN, C. R., AND M. B. BROWN. 1999a. Fitness components associated with clutch size in Cliff Swallows. Auk 116:467–486.

BROWN, C. R., AND M. B. BROWN. 1999b. Fitness components associated with laying date in the Cliff Swallow. Condor 101:230–245.

BULMER, M. G., AND C. M. PERRINS. 1973. Mortality in the Great Tit *Parus major*. Ibis 115:277–281.

BYRKJEDAL, I. 1980. Nest predation in relation to snow-cover—a possible factor influencing the start of breeding in shorebirds. Ornis Scandinavica 11:249–252.

BYRKJEDAL, I., AND J. KÅLÅS. 1985. Seasonal variation in egg size in Golden Plover *Pluvialis apricaria* and Dotterel *Charadrius morinellus* populations. Ornis Scandinavica 16: 108–112.

CALDER, W. A. 1971. Temperature relationships and mating of the Calliope Hummingbird. Condor 73:314–321.

CAREY, C., S. D. GARBER, E. L. THOMPSON, AND F. C. JAMES. 1983. Avian reproduction over an altitudinal gradient. II. Physical characteristics and water loss of eggs. Physiological Zoology 56:340–352.

CAREY, C., AND M. L. MORTON. 1976. Aspects of circulatory physiology of montane and lowland birds. Comparative Biochemistry and Physiology 54A:61–74.

CAREY, M. 1990. Effects of brood size and nestling age on parental care by male Field Sparrows (*Spizella pusilla*). Auk 107:580–586.

CATCHPOLE, C., B. LEISLER, AND H. WINKLER. 1985. Polygyny in the Great Reed Warbler, *Acrocephalus arundinaceus*: a possible case of deception. Behavioral Ecology and Sociobiology 16:285–291.

CAVITT, J. F., AND C. F. THOMPSON. 1997. Mass loss in breeding House Wrens: effects of food supplements. Ecology 78:2512–2523.

CHABOT, B. F., AND W. D. BILLINGS. 1972. Origins and ecology of the Sierran alpine flora and vegetation. Ecological Monographs 42:163–199.

CHARNOV, E. L., AND J. R. KREBS. 1974. On clutch size and fitness. Ibis 116:217–219.

CHILGREN, J. D., AND W. A. DEGRAW. 1977. Some blood characteristics of White-crowned Sparrows during molt. Auk 94:169–171.

CHILTON, G., M. C. BAKER, C. D. BARRENTINE, AND M. A. CUNNINGHAM. 1995. White-crowned Sparrow (*Zonotrichia leucophrys*). *In* A. Poole and F. Gill (editors). The Birds of North America, No. 183. The Academy of Natural Sciences, Philadelphia, PA, and American Ornithologists' Union, Washington, D.C.

CHILTON, G., M. R. LEIN, AND L. F. BAPTISTA. 1990. Mate choice by female White-crowned Sparrows in a mixed-dialect population. Behavioral Ecology and Sociobiology 27:223–227.

CLARK, A. B., AND D. S. WILSON. 1981. Avian breeding adaptations: hatching asynchrony, brood reduction, and nest failure. Quarterly Review of Biology 56:253–277.

CLARKE, J. A., AND R. E. JOHNSON. 1992. The influence of spring snow depth on White-tailed Ptarmigan breeding success in the Sierra Nevada. Condor 94:622–627.

CLUTTON-BROCK, T. H. 1984. Reproductive effort and terminal investment in iteroparous animals. American Naturalist 123:212–228.

COCKREM, J. F. 1995. Timing of seasonal breeding in birds, with particular reference to New Zealand birds. Reproduction, Fertility and Development 7:1–19.

COLEMAN, R. M., AND R. D. WHITTALL. 1990. Variation in egg weight in the Bengalese Finch (*Lonchura striata* var. *domestica*). Canadian Journal of Zoology 68:272–275.

COLLIAS, E. C. 1984. Egg measurements and coloration throughout life in the Village Weaverbird, *Ploceus cucullatus.* Proceedings of the 5th Pan-African Ornithological Congress 5:461–475.

COLLIAS, E. C. 1993. Inheritance of egg-color polymorphism in the Village Weaver (*Ploceus cucullatus*). Auk 110:683–692.

COLLIAS, N. E. 1997. On the origin and evolution of nest building by passerine birds. Condor 99:253–270.

COLLIAS, N. E., AND E. C. COLLIAS. 1984. Nest building and bird behavior. Princeton University Press, Princeton, NJ.

COMMON, R. H., R. S. MATHUR, S. MULAY, AND G. O. HENNEBERRY. 1968. Distribution patterns of *in vivo* conversion products of injected estradiol-17β-4^{14}C and estrone-4^{14}C in the urines of the non-laying and laying hen. Canadian Journal of Biochemistry and Physiology 47:539–545.

CONDER, P. 1989. The Wheatear. Christopher Helm, London, UK.

CORTOPASSI, A. J., AND L. R. MEWALDT. 1965. The circumannual distribution of White-crowned Sparrows. Bird-Banding 36:141–169.

CRAWFORD, R. D. 1977. Breeding biology of year-old and older female Red-Winged and Yellow-headed blackbirds. Wilson Bulletin 29:73–80.

CRISTOL, D. A., AND T. S. JOHNSEN. 1994. Spring arrival, aggression and testosterone in female Red-winged Blackbirds (*Agelaius phoeniceus*). Auk 111:210–214.

CUSTER, T. W., AND F. A. PITELKA. 1977. Demographic features of a Lapland Longspur population near Barrow, Alaska. Auk 94:505–525.

DAAN, S., C. DIJKSTRA, R. DRENT, AND T. MEIJER. 1988. Food supply and the annual timing of avian reproduction. Acta XIX Congressus Internationalis Ornithologici 19:392–407.

DAAN, S., C. DIJKSTRA, AND J. M. TINBERGEN. 1990. Family planning in the Kestrel (*Falco tinnunculus*): the ultimate control of covariation of laying date and clutch size. Behaviour 114:83–114.

DARLEY, J. A., D. M. SCOTT, AND N. K. TAYLOR. 1971. Territorial fidelity of catbirds. Canadian Journal of Zoology 49:1465–1478.

DARLEY, J. A., D. M. SCOTT, AND N. K. TAYLOR. 1977. Effects of age, sex, and breeding success on site fidelity of Gray Catbirds. Bird-Banding 48:145–151.

DAVIES, N. B. 1985. Cooperation and conflict among Dunnocks, *Prunella modularis,* in a variable mating system. Animal Behaviour 33:628–648.

DAVIES, N. B. 1992. Dunnock behaviour and social evolution. Oxford University Press, Oxford.

DAVIES, N. B., AND A. LUNDBERG. 1985. The influence of food on time budgets and timing of breeding of the Dunnock *Prunella modularis.* Ibis 127:100–110.

DAVIS, D. E. 1955. Breeding biology of birds. Pp. 264–308 *in* A. Wolfson (editor). Recent studies in avian biology University of Illinois Press, Urbana, IL.

DAWSON, A. 1989. The involvement of thyroxine and daylength in the development of photorefractoriness in European Starlings. Journal of Experimental Zoology 249:68–75.

DAWSON, A. 1991. Photoperiodic control of testicular regression and moult in male House Sparrows *Passer domesticus.* Ibis 133:312–316.

DAWSON, A. 1993. Thyroidectomy progressively renders the reproductive system of starlings (*Sturnus vulgaris*) unresponsive to changes in daylength. Journal of Endocrinology 139:51–55.

DAWSON, A., AND A. R. GOLDSMITH. 1982. Prolactin and gonadotrophin secretion in wild starlings (*Sturnus vulgaris*) during the annual cycle and in relation to nesting, incubation and rearing young. General and Comparative Endocrinology 48:213–221.

DAWSON, A., S. A. HINSLEY, P. N. FERNS, R. H. C. BONSER, AND L. ECCLESTON. 2000. Rate of moult affects feather quality: a mechanism linking current reproductive effort to future survival. Proceedings of the Royal Society, London (B) 267:2093–2098.

DAWSON, A., AND F. J. MCNAUGHTON. 1992. Puberty in European Starlings: can nestlings perceive daylength? Ornis Scandinavica 23:209–213.

DAWSON, A., AND P. J. SHARP. 1998. The role of prolactin in the development of reproductive photorefractoriness and postnuptial molt in the European Starling (*Sturnus vulgaris*). Endocrinology 139:485–490.

DAWSON, W. R., AND J. W. HUDSON. 1970. Birds. Pp. 224–302 *in* G. C. Whittow (editor). Comparative physiology of thermoregulation: invertebrates and nonmammalian vertebrates. Vol. 1. Academic Press, New York, NY.

DEAN, A. M. 1998. The molecular anatomy of an ancient adaptive event. American Scientist 86:26–37.

DEEVEY, E. S., JR. 1947. Life tables for natural populations of animals. Quarterly Review of Biology 22:283–314.

DEGRAW, W. A., AND M. D. KERN. 1985. Changes in the blood and plasma volume of Harris' Sparrows during postnuptial molt. Comparative Biochemistry and Physiology 81A:889–893.

DE LAET, J. F., AND A. A. DHONDT. 1989. Weight loss of the female during the first brood as a factor influencing second brood initiation in Great Tits *Parus major* and Blue Tits *P. caeruleus.* Ibis 131:281–289.

DESANTE, D. F., AND L. F. BAPTISTA. 1989. Factors affecting the termination of breeding in Nuttall's White-crowned Sparrows. Wilson Bulletin 101:120–124.

DE STEVEN, D. 1980. Clutch size, breeding success, and parental survival in the Tree Swallow (*Iridoprocne bicolor*). Evolution 34:278–291.

DEVICHE, P., J. C. WINGFIELD, AND P. J. SHARP. 2000. Year-class differences in the reproductive system, plasma prolactin and corticosterone concentrations, and onset of prebasic molt in male Dark-eyed Juncos (*Junco hyemalis*) during the breeding season. General and Comparative Endocrinology 118:425–435.

DEWOLFE, B. B., AND L. F. BAPTISTA. 1995. Singing behavior, song types on their wintering grounds and the question of leap-frog migration in Puget Sound White-crowned Sparrows. Condor 97:376–389.

DEWOLFE, B. B., AND R. H. DEWOLFE. 1962. Mountain White-crowned Sparrows in California. Condor 64:378–389.

DEWOLFE, B. B., G. W. WEST, AND L. J. PEYTON. 1973. The spring migration of Gambel's Sparrows through southern Yukon Territory. Condor 75:43–59.

DHONDT, A. A. 1989a. Blue Tit. Pp. 15–33 *in* I. Newton (editor). Lifetime reproduction in birds Academic Press, San Diego, CA.

DHONDT, A. A. 1989b. The effect of old age on the reproduction of Great Tits *Parus major* and Blue Tits *P. caeruleus.* Ibis 131:268–280.

DIXON, C. 1978. Breeding biology of the Savannah Sparrow on Kent Island. Auk 95:235–246.

DRENT, R. H. 1972. Adaptive aspects of physiology of incubation. Acta XV Congressus Internationalis Ornithologici 15:255–280.

DRENT, R. H. 1975. Incubation. Pp. 333–420 in D. S. Farner and J. R. King (editors). Avian biology. Vol. 5. Academic Press, New York, NY.

DRENT, R. H., AND S. DAAN. 1980. The prudent parent: energetic adjustments in avian breeding. Ardea 68:225–252.

DUFTY, A. J. 1989. Testosterone and survival: a cost of aggressiveness? Hormones and Behavior 23:185–193.

DUNLOP, E. B. 1910. On incubation. British Birds 4:137–145.

DUNN, E. H. 1975. The timing of endothermy in the development of altricial birds. Condor 77:288–293.

DUNN, E. H. 1976. The relationship between brood size and age of effective homeothermy in nestling House Wrens. Wilson Bulletin 88:478–482.

DUNN, E. H. 1979. Age of effective homeothermy in nestling Tree Swallows according to brood size. Wilson Bulletin 91:455–457.

DUNN, J. L., K. L. GARRETT, AND J. K. ALDERFER. 1995. White-crowned Sparrow subspecies: identification and distribution. Birding 27:182–200.

DUNN, P. O., AND S. J. HANNON. 1991. Intraspecific competition and the maintenance of monogamy in Tree Swallows. Behavioral Ecology 2:258–266.

DUNNET, G. 1991. Long-term studies of birds. Ibis 133(Suppl. 1):1–2.

ECKHARDT, R. C. 1977. Effects of a late spring storm on a Dusky Flycatcher population. Auk 94:362.

EDWARDS, J. S. 1972. Arthropod fallout on Alaskan snow. Arctic and Alpine Research 4:167–176.

EDWARDS, J. S. 1987. Arthropods of alpine aeolian ecosystems. Annual Review of Entomology 32:163–179.

EDWARDS, J. S., AND P. C. BANKO. 1976. Arthropod fallout and nutrient transport: a quantitative study of Alaskan snowpatches. Arctic and Alpine Research 8:237–245.

EHRLICH, P. R., D. E. BREEDLOVE, P. F. BRUSSARD, AND M. A. SHARP. 1972. Weather and the "regulation" of subalpine population. Ecology 53:243–247.

ELLIOTT, J. A., AND B. D. GOLDMAN. 1981. Seasonal reproduction: photoperiodism and biological clocks. Pp. 377–423 in N. T. Adler (editor). Neuroendocrinology of reproduction. Plenum Press, New York, NY.

EL-WAILLY, A. 1966. Energy requirements for egg-laying and incubation in the Zebra Finch, Taeniopygia castanotis. Condor 68:582–594.

ENS, B. J. 1992. The social prisoner. Ph.D. dissertation. Rijksuniversiteit, Groningen, The Netherlands.

EVANS, F. C. 1985. In praise of natural history. Bulletin of the Ecological Society of America 66:455–460.

EVANS OGDEN, L. J., AND B. J. M. STUTCHBURY. 1996. Constraints on double brooding in a Neotropical migrant, the Hooded Warbler. Condor 98:736–744.

EWALD, P. W., AND S. ROHWER. 1982. Effects of supplemental feeding on timing of breeding, clutch-size and polygyny in Red-winged Blackbirds Agelaius phoeniceus. Journal of Animal Ecology 51:429–450.

FALLS, J. B., AND J. G. KOPACHENA. 1994. White-throated Sparrow (Zonotrichia albicollis). In A. Poole and F. Gill (editors). The Birds of North America, No. 128. The Academy of Natural Sciences, Philadelphia, PA, and American Ornithologists' Union, Washington, D.C.

FARACI, F. M. 1991. Adaptations to hypoxia in birds: how to fly high. Annual Reviews in Physiology 53:59–70.

FARNER, D. S. 1955a. The annual stimulus for migration: experimental and physiologic aspects. Pp. 198–237 in A. Wolfson (editor). Recent studies in avian biology University of Illinois Press, Urbana, IL.

FARNER, D. S. 1955b. Birdbanding in the study of population dynamics. Pp. 397–448 in

A. Wolfson (editor). Recent studies in avian biology University of Illinois Press, Urbana, IL.

FARNER, D. S. 1958a. Breeding population of *Zonotrichia leucophrys gambelii* in the northern Cascade Mountains of Washington. Condor 60:196.

FARNER, D. S. 1958b. Incubation and body temperatures of the Yellow-eyed Penguin. Auk 75:248–262.

FARNER, D. S. 1958c. Photoperiodism in animals with special reference to avian testicular cycles. Biological Colloquium, Oregon State College 19:17–29.

FARNER, D. S. 1964. The photoperiodic control of reproductive cycles in birds. American Scientist 52:137–156.

FARNER, D. S. 1975. Photoperiodic controls in the secretion of gonadotropins in birds. American Zoologist 15(Suppl.):117–135.

FARNER, D. S. 1983. Some recent advances in avian physiology. Journal of the Yamashina Institute of Ornithology 15:97–140.

FARNER, D. S. 1986. Generation and regulation of annual cycles in migratory passerine birds. American Zoologist 26:493–501.

FARNER, D. S., R. S. DONHAM, K. S. MATT, P. S. MATTOCKS, JR., M. C. MOORE, AND J. C. WINGFIELD. 1983. The nature of photorefractoriness. Pp. 149–166 *in* S.-I. Mikami, K. Homma, and M. Wada (editors). Avian endocrinology: environmental and ecological perspectives. Japan Scientific Societies Press, Tokyo, Japan, and Springer Verlag, New York, NY.

FARNER, D. S., R. S. DONHAM, AND M. C. MOORE. 1981. Induction of testicular development in House Sparrows, *Passer domesticus,* and White-crowned Sparrows, *Zonotrichia leucophrys gambelii* with very long days and continuous light. Physiological Zoology 54: 372–378.

FARNER, D. S., R. S. DONHAM, M. C. MOORE, AND R. A. LEWIS. 1980. The temporal relationship between the cycle of testicular development and molt in the White-crowned Sparrow, *Zonotrichia leucophrys gambelii.* Auk 97:63–75.

FARNER, D. S., AND B. K. FOLLETT. 1966. Light and other environmental factors affecting avian reproduction. Journal of Animal Science 25(Suppl.):90–115.

FARNER, D. S., AND B. K. FOLLETT. 1979. Reproductive periodicity in birds. Pp. 829–872 *in* J. W. Barrington (editor). Hormones and evolution. Vol. 2. Academic Press, New York, NY.

FARNER, D. S., B. K. FOLLETT, J. R. KING, AND M. L. MORTON. 1966. A quantitative examination of ovarian growth in the White-crowned Sparrow. Biological Bulletin 130: 67–75.

FARNER, D. S., AND R. A. LEWIS. 1971. Photoperiodism and reproductive cycles in birds. Pp. 325–370 *in* A. C. Giese (editor). Photophysiology: current topics in photochemistry and photobiology. Vol. 6. Academic Press, New York, NY.

FARNER, D. S., AND R. A. LEWIS. 1973. Field and experimental studies of the annual cycles of White-crowned Sparrows. Journal of Reproduction and Fertility 1973(Suppl. 19):35–50.

FARNER, D. S., AND L. R. MEWALDT. 1955. The natural termination of the refractory period in the White-crowned Sparrow. Condor 57:112–116.

FARNER, D. S., AND A. C. WILSON. 1957. A quantitative examination of testicular growth in the White-crowned Sparrow. Biological Bulletin 113:254–267.

FJELDSÅ, F. 1991. The activity of birds during snow-storms in high-level woodlands in Peru. Bulletin of the British Ornithological Club 111:4–11.

FLINT, P. L., AND J. B. GRAND. 1996. Variation in egg size of the Northern Pintail. Condor 98:162–165.

FOLLETT, B. K. 1984. Birds. Pp. 283–350 *in* G. E. Lamming (editor). Marshall's physiology of reproduction, 4th edition. Vol. 1. Churchill Livingstone, Edinburgh, UK.

FOLLETT, B. K., D. S. FARNER, AND P. W. MATTOCKS. 1975. Luteinizing hormone in the plasma of White-crowned Sparrows (*Zonotrichia leucophrys gambelii*) during artificial photostimulation. General and Comparative Endocrinology 26:126–134.

FOSTER, M. S. 1975a. The overlap of molting and breeding in some tropical birds. Condor 77:304–314.

FOSTER, M. S. 1975b. Temporal patterns of resource allocation and life history phenomena. Florida Scientist 38:129–139.

FOX, A. D., I. S. FRANCIS, J. MADSEN, AND J. M. STROUD. 1987. The breeding biology of the Lapland Bunting *Calcarius lapponicus* in West Greenland during two contrasting years. Ibis 129:541–552.

FRANSSON, T., AND S. JAKOBSSON. 1998. Fat storage in male Willow Warblers in spring: do residents arrive lean or fat? Auk 115:759–763.

FREED, L. A. 1981. Loss of mass in breeding wrens: stress or adaptation? Ecology 62: 1179–1186.

FREEMAN-GALLANT, C. R. 1998. Fitness consequences of male parental care in Savannah Sparrows. Behavioral Ecology 9:486–492.

FREER, V. 1979. Factors affecting site tenacity in New York Bank Swallows. Bird-Banding 50:349–357.

FRETWELL, S. D. 1972. Populations in a seasonal environment. Princeton University Press, Princeton, NJ.

FRIEDMANN, H., L. GRISCOM, AND R. T. MOORE. 1950. Distributional check-list of the birds of Mexico. Pacific Coast Avifauna No. 29. Cooper Ornithological Club, Berkeley, CA.

GATES, J. E. 1979. Avian nest placement in relation to plant height. Jack-Pine Warbler 57: 191–198.

GAUTHREAUX, S. A., JR. 1978. The ecological significance of behavioural dominance. Pp. 17–54 *in* P. P. G. Bateson and P. H. Klopfer (editors). Perspectives in ethology. Vol. 3. Plenum Press, London, UK.

GAUTHREAUX, S. A., JR. 1996. Bird migration: methodologies and major research trajectories (1945–1995). Condor 98:442–453.

GAVIN, T. A., AND E. K. BOLLINGER. 1988. Reproductive correlates of breeding-site fidelity in Bobolinks (*Dolichonyx oryzivorus*). Ecology 69:96–103.

GESSAMAN, J. A., AND G. L. WORTHEN. 1982. The effect of weather on avian mortality. Utah State University Printing Service, Logan, Utah.

GODFREY, W. E. 1965. Review of "Geographic variation in the White-crowned Sparrow *Zonotrichia leucophrys*" by R.C. Banks. Auk 82:510–511.

GOLDSMITH, A. R. 1982. Plasma concentration of prolactin during incubation and parental feeding throughout repeated breeding cycles in canaries (*Serinus canarius*). Journal of Endocrinology 94:51–59.

GOLDSMITH, A. R., AND T. J. NICHOLLS. 1984. Thyroidectomy prevents the development of photorefractoriness and the associated rise in plasma prolactin in starlings. General and Comparative Endocrinology 54:256–263.

GOWATY, P. A., AND W. C. BRIDGES. 1991. Behavioral, demographic, and environmental correlates of extrapair fertilizations in eastern bluebirds, *Sialia sialis*. Behavioral Ecology 2:339–350.

GOWATY, P. A., AND J. H. PLISSNER. 1987. Association of male and female American Robins (*Turdus migratorius*) during the breeding season: paternity assurance by sexual access or mate-guarding. Wilson Bulletin 99:56–62.

GRAHAM, R. W., M. A. GRAHAM, E. K. SCHROEDER, E. ANDERSON, A. D. BARNOSKY, J. A. BURNS, C. S. CHURCHER, D. K. GRAYSON, R. D. GUTHRIE, C. R. HARINGTON, G. T. JEFFERSON, L. D. MARTIN, H. G. MCDONALD, R. E. MORLAN, H. A. SEMKEN, S. D. WEBB, L. WERDELIN, AND M. C. WILSON. 1996. Spatial response of mammals to late quaternary environmental fluctuations. Science 272:1601–1606.

GRATTO, C. L., R. I. G. MORRISON, AND F. COOKE. 1985. Philopatry, site tenacity, and mate fidelity in the Semipalmated Sandpiper. Auk 102:16–24.

GRAYSON, D. K. 1993. The desert's past: a natural history of the Great Basin. Smithsonian Institution Press, Washington, D.C.

GREEN, G. H., J. J. D. GREENWOOD, AND C. S. LLOYD. 1977. The influence of snow conditions on the date of breeding of wading birds in north-east Greenland. Journal of Zoology 183:311–328.

GREENWOOD, P. J. 1980. Mating systems, philopatry and dispersal in birds and mammals. Animal Behaviour 28:1140–1162.

GREENWOOD, P. J., AND P. H. HARVEY. 1982. The natal and breeding dispersal of birds. Annual Review of Ecology and Systematics 13:1–21.

GREENWOOD, P. J., P. H. HARVEY, AND C. M. PERRINS. 1979. Mate selection in the Great Tit *Parus major* in relation to age, status and natal dispersal. Ornis Fennica 56:75–86.

GREIG-SMITH, P. W., C. J. FEARE, E. M. FREEMAN, AND P. L. SPENCER. 1988. Causes and consequences of egg-size variation in the European Starling *Sturnus vulgaris*. Ibis 130: 1–10.

GRIGGS, R. F. 1938. Timberlines in the northern Rocky Mountains. Ecology 19:548–564.

GRINNELL, J. 1928. Notes on the systematics of west American birds. III. Condor 30:185–189.

GWINNER, E. 1968. Circannuale Periodik als Grundlage des jahreszeitilichen Funktionswandels bei Zugvögeln. Untersuchungen am Fitis (*Phylloscopus trochilus*) und am Waldlaubsänger (*P. sibilatrix*). Journal fur Ornithologie 109:70–95.

GWINNER, E. 1971. A comparative study of circannual rhythms in warblers. Pp. 405–427 *in* M. Menaker (editor). Biochronometry. National Academy of Science, Washington, D.C.

GWINNER, E. 1975. Die circannuale Periodik der Fortpflanzungsaktivitat beim Star (*Sturnus vulgaris*) unter dem Einfluss gleich- und andersgeschlechtiger Artgenossen. Zeitschrift fur Tierpsychologie 38:34–43.

GWINNER, E. 1977a. Circannual rhythms in bird migration. Annual Review of Ecology and Systematics 8:381–405.

GWINNER, E. 1977b. Photoperiodic synchronization of circannual rhythms in the European Starling (*Sturnus vulgaris*). Naturwissenschaften 64:44.

GWINNER, E. 1986. Circannual rhythms. Vol. 18. Zoophysiology. Springer Verlag, New York, NY.

GWINNER, E. 1990. Circannual rhythms in bird migration: control of temporal patterns and interactions with photoperiod. Pp. 257–268 *in* E. Gwinner (editor). Bird migration Springer Verlag, Berlin, Germany.

GWINNER, E. 1996. Circadian and circannual programmes in avian migration. Journal of Experimental Biology 199:39–48.

GWINNER, E., AND J. DITTAMI. 1985. Photoperiodic responses in temperate zone and equatorial stonechats: a contribution to the problem of photoperiodism in tropical organisms. Pp. 279–294 *in* B. K. Follett, S. Ishii, and A. Chandola (editors). The endocrine system and the environment. Japan Scientific Societies Press, Tokyo, Japan, and Springer Verlag, New York, NY.

GWINNER, E., S. KÖNIG, AND C. S. HALEY. 1995. Genetic and environmental factors influencing clutch size in equatorial and temperate zone Stonechats (*Saxicola torquata axillaris* and *S. t. rubicola*): an experimental study. Auk 112:748–755.

HAFTORN, S. 1978a. Egg-laying and regulation of egg temperature during incubation in the Goldcrest *Regulus regulus*. Ornis Scandinavica 9:2–21.

HAFTORN, S. 1978b. Energetics of incubation by the Goldcrest *Regulus regulus* in relation to ambient air temperatures and geographic distribution of the species. Ornis Scandinavica 9:22–30.

HAFTORN, S. 1979. Incubation and regulation of egg temperature in the Willow Tit *Parus montanus*. Ornis Scandinavica 10:220–234.

HAFTORN, S. 1981. Incubation during the egg-laying period in relation to clutch-size and other aspects of reproduction in the Great Tit *Parus major*. Ornis Scandinavica 12:169–185.

HAFTORN, S. 1986. Clutch size, intraclutch egg size variation, and breeding strategy in the Goldcrest *Regulus regulus*. Journal fur Ornithologie 127:291–301.

HAFTORN, S. 1988. Incubating female passerines do not let the egg temperature fall below the 'physiological zero temperature' during their absences from the nest. Ornis Scandinavica 19:97–110.

HAHN, T. P., AND G. F. BALL. 1995. Changes in brain GnRH associated with photorefractoriness in House Sparrows (*Passer domesticus*). General and Comparative Endocrinology 99:349–363.

HAHN, T. P., T. BOSWELL, J. C. WINGFIELD, AND G. F. BALL. 1997. Temporal flexibility in avian reproduction: patterns and mechanisms. Current Ornithology 14:39–80.

HAHN, T. P., AND M. L. MORTON. 1995. Repetitive altitudinal migrations before breeding by Mountain White-crowned Sparrows, *Zonotrichia leucophrys oriantha.* American Zoologist 35:86A.

HAHN, T. P., J. SWINGLE, J. C. WINGFIELD, AND M. RAMENOFSKY. 1992. Adjustments of the prebasic molt schedule in birds. Ornis Scandinavica 23:314–321.

HALL, M. R., AND A. R. GOLDSMITH. 1983. Factors affecting prolactin secretion during breeding and incubation in the domestic duck (*Anas platyrhynchos*). General and Comparative Endocrinology 49:270–276.

HANKINSON, M. D. 1999. Male House Sparrows behave as if a fertilization window exists. Auk 116:1141–1144.

HARBISON, H., D. A. NELSON, AND T. P. HAHN. 1999. Long-term persistence of song dialects in the Mountain White-crowned Sparrow. Condor 101:133–148.

HARDY, J. L., D. R. ROBERTS, AND R. C. BANKS. 1965. The composition of a wintering population of White-crowned Sparrows in Kern County, California. Condor 67:90–91.

HARMESON, J. P. 1974. Breeding ecology of the Dickcissel. Auk 91:348–349.

HARRIS, M. O., AND F. W. TUREK. 1982. Photoperiodic control of the timing of testicular regression in White-throated Sparrows. General and Comparative Endocrinology 46:124–129.

HAUKIOJA, E. 1969. Weights of Reed Buntings (*Emberiza schoeniclus*) during summer. Ornis Fennica 46:13–21.

HAUKIOJA, E. 1970. Clutch size of the Reed Bunting *Emberiza schoeniclus.* Ornis Fennica 47:101–135.

HAUKIOJA, E. 1971. Short-distance dispersal in the Reed Bunting *Emberiza schoeniclus.* Ornis Fennica 48:45–67.

HAYES, J. P., J. R. SPEAKMAN, AND P. A. RACEY. 1992. The contributions of local heating and reducing exposed surface area to the energetic benefits of huddling by short-tailed field voles (*Microtus agrestis*). Physiological Zoology 65:742–762.

HAYS, H. 1969. Differential survival among nestling Red-winged Blackbirds after a storm. Auk 86:563–564.

HEBERT, P. N., AND S. G. SEALY. 1992. Onset of incubation in Yellow Warblers: a test of the hormonal hypothesis. Auk 109:249–255.

HEISE, G. 1970. Zur Brutbiologie des Seggenrohrsangers (*Acrocephalus paludicola*). Journal fur Ornithologie 111:54–67.

HEMBORG, C. 1999a. Annual variation in the time of breeding and moulting in male and female Pied Flycatchers *Ficedula hypoleuca.* Ibis 141:226–232.

HEMBORG, C. 1999b. Sexual differences in moult-breeding overlap and female reproductive costs in Pied Flycatchers, *Ficedula hypoleuca.* Journal of Animal Ecology 68:429–436.

HENDRICKS, P. 1991. Repeatability of size and shape of American Pipit eggs. Canadian Journal of Zoology 69:2624–2628.

HENDRICKS, P., AND C. J. NORMENT. 1992. Effects of a severe snowstorm on subalpine and alpine populations of nesting American Pipits. Journal of Field Ornithology 63:331–338.

HENDRICKS, P., AND C. J. NORMENT. 1994. Hatchability of American Pipit eggs in the Beartooth Mountains, Wyoming. Wilson Bulletin 106:392–399.

HERLUGSON, C. J. 1981. Nest site selection in Mountain Bluebirds. Condor 83:252–255.

HILL, B. G., AND R. LEIN. 1985. The non-song vocal repertoire of the White-crowned Sparrow. Condor 87:327–335.

HILL, D. P., AND S. G. SEALY. 1994. Desertion of nests parasitized by cowbirds: have Clay-coloured Sparrows evolved an anti-parasite defence? Animal Behaviour 48:1063–1070.

HILL, G. E. 1986. Severe aggression between female Black-headed Grosbeaks. Wilson Bulletin 98:486–488.

HILLSTROM, L., AND K. OLSSON. 1994. Advantages of hatching synchrony in the Pied Flycatcher *Ficedula hypoleuca.* Journal of Avian Biology 25:205–214.

HINDE, R. A. 1962. Temporal relations of brood patch development in domesticated canaries. Ibis 104:90–97.

HOBSON, K. A., AND S. G. SEALY. 1990. Female song in the Yellow Warbler. Condor 92: 259–261.

HOCHACHKA, W. M., J. N. M. SMITH, AND P. ARCESE. 1989. Song sparrow. Pp. 135–152 *in* I. Newton (editor). Lifetime reproduction in birds. Academic Press, London, UK.

HÖGSTEDT, G. 1980. Evolution of clutch size in birds: adaptive variation in relation to territory quality. Science 210:1148–1150.

HÖGSTEDT, G. 1981. Should there be a positive or negative correlation between survival of adults in a bird population and their clutch size? American Naturalist 118:568–571.

HÖTKER, H. 1989. Meadow pipit. Pp. 119–133 *in* I. Newton (editor). Lifetime reproduction in birds. Academic Press, London, UK.

HOLBERTON, R. L., J. D. PARRISH, AND J. C. WINGFIELD. 1996. Modulation of the adreno-cortical stress response in neotropical migrants during autumn migration. Auk 113:558–564.

HORVATH, E. G., AND K. A. SULLIVAN. 1988. Facultative migration in Yellow-eyed Juncos. Condor 90:482–484.

HORVÁTH, O. 1964. Seasonal differences in Rufous Hummingbird nest height and their relation to nest climate. Ecology 45:235–241.

HOWARTH, B. 1974. Sperm storage as a function of the female reproductive tract. Pp. 237–270 *in* A. D. Johnson and C. E. Foley (editors). The oviduct and its functions. Academic Press, New York, NY.

HOWE, H. F. 1976. Egg size, hatching asynchrony, sex, and brood reduction in the Common Grackle. Ecology 57:1195–1207.

HOWE, H. F. 1978. Initial investment, clutch size, and brood reduction in the Common Grackle (*Quiscalus quiscula*). Ecology 59:1109–1122.

HOYT, D. F. 1979. Practical methods of estimating volume and fresh weight of bird eggs. Auk 96:73–77.

HOYT, D. F., D. VLECK, AND C. M. VLECK. 1978. Metabolism of avian embryos: ontogeny and temperature effects in the Ostrich. Condor 80:265–271.

HUBBARD, J. D. 1978. Breeding biology and reproductive energetics of the Mt. White-crowned Sparrow in Colorado. Ph.D. dissertation. University of Colorado, Boulder, CO.

HUGGINS, R. A. 1941. Egg temperatures of wild birds under natural conditions. Ecology 22:148–157.

HURLY, T. A. 1992. Energetic reserves of Marsh Tits (*Parus palustris*): food and fat storage in response to variable food supply. Behavioral Ecology 3:181–188.

HUSSELL, D. J. T. 1972. Factors affecting clutch size in arctic passerines. Ecological Monographs 42:317–364.

HUSSELL, D. J. T., AND T. E. QUINNEY. 1987. Food abundance and clutch size of Tree Swallows *Tachycineta bicolor*. Ibis 129:243–258.

IMMELMANN, K. 1971. Ecological aspects of periodic reproduction. Pp. 341–512 *in* D. S. Farner and J. R. King (editors). Avian biology. Vol. 1. Academic Press, New York, NY.

IMMELMANN, K. 1973. Role of the environment in reproduction as source of "predictive" information. Pp. 121–157 *in* D. S. Farner (editor). Breeding biology of birds. National Academy of Sciences, Washington, D.C.

IRVING, L., AND J. KROG. 1956. Temperature during development of birds in arctic nests. Physiological Zoology 29:195–205.

JÄRVINEN, A. 1991. Proximate factors affecting egg volume in subarctic hole-nesting passerines. Ornis Fennica 68:99–104.

JÄRVINEN, A. 1994. Global warming and egg size of birds. Ecography 17:108–110.

JÄRVINEN, A., AND M. PRYL. 1989. Egg dimensions of the Great Tit *Parus major* in southern Finland. Ornis Fennica 66:69–74.

JÄRVINEN, A., AND R. A. VÄISÄNEN. 1983. Egg size and related reproductive traits in a southern passerine *Ficedula hypoleuca* breeding in an extreme northern environment. Ornis Scandinavica 14:253–262.

JÄRVINEN, A., AND J. YLIMAUNU. 1986. Intraclutch egg-size variation in birds: physiological responses of individuals to fluctuations in environmental conditions. Auk 103:235–237.

JEHL, J. R., JR., AND D. J. T. HUSSELL. 1966. Effects of weather on reproductive success of birds at Churchill, Manitoba. Journal of the Arctic Institute of North America 19: 185–190.

JOHNSON, A. W. 1967. The birds of Chile. Vol. 2. Platt Establecimientos Gráficos S.A., Buenos Aires, Argentina.

JOHNSTON, R. F., AND R. C. FLEISCHER. 1981. Overwinter mortality and sexual size dimorphism in the House Sparrow. Auk 98:503–511.

JONES, H. G., J. W. POMEROY, D. A. WALKER, AND R. A. WHARTON. 1994. Snow ecology: a report on a new initiative. Bulletin of the Ecological Society of America 75:29–31.

JONES, I. L. 1994. Mass changes of Least Auklets *Aethia pusilla* during the breeding season: evidence for programmed loss of mass. Journal of Animal Ecology 63:71–78.

JONES, R. E. 1971. The incubation patch of birds. Biological Review 46:315–339.

JONSSON, P. 1994. Responses of female Great Tits *Parus major* to photoperiodic stimulation and the presence of a male. Ornis Svecica 4:41–47.

KAISER, A. 1992. Fat deposition and theoretical flight range of small autumn migrants in southern Germany. Bird Study 39:96–110.

KASHKIN, V. V. 1961. Heat exchange of bird eggs during incubation. Biophysica 6:97–107.

KEMPENAERS, B., AND B. C. SHELDON. 1996. Why do male birds not discriminate between their own and extra-pair offspring? Animal Behavior Monographs 51:1165–1173.

KENDEIGH, S. C. 1949. Effect of temperature and season on energy resources of the English Sparrow. Auk 66:113–127.

KENDEIGH, S. C. 1952. Parental care and its evolution in birds. Illinois Biological Monographs 22:1–358.

KENDEIGH, S. C. 1963. Thermodynamics of incubation in the House Wren, *Troglodytes aedon*. Acta XIII Congressus Internationalis Ornithologici 13:884–904.

KERN, M. D. 1979. Seasonal changes in the reproductive system of the female White-crowned Sparrow, *Zonotrichia leucophrys gambelii*, in captivity and in the field. Cell and Tissue Research 202:379–398.

KERN, M. D. 1984. Racial differences in nests of White-crowned Sparrows. Condor 86: 455–466.

KERN, M. D., R. J. COWIE, AND M. YEAGER. 1992. Water loss, conductance, and structure of eggs of Pied Flycatchers during egg laying and incubation. Physiological Zoology 65:1162–1187.

KETTERSON, E. D., AND V. NOLAN, JR. 1976. Geographic variation and its climatic correlates in the sex ratio of eastern-wintering Dark-eyed Juncos (*Junco hyemalis*). Ecology 57: 679–693.

KETTERSON, E. D., AND V. NOLAN, JR. 1992. Hormones and life histories: an integrative approach. American Naturalist 140 (Supplement):S33–S62.

KING, J. R. 1961a. The bioenergetics of vernal premigratory fat deposition in the White-crowned Sparrow. Condor 63:128–142.

KING, J. R. 1961b. On the regulation of vernal premigratory fattening in the White-crowned Sparrow. Physiological Zoology 34:145–157.

KING, J. R. 1972. Adaptive periodic fat storage by birds. Acta XV Congressus Internationalis Ornithologici 15:200–217.

KING, J. R., AND D. S. FARNER. 1959. Premigratory changes in body weight and fat in wild and captive male White-crowned Sparrows. Condor 61:315–324.

KING, J. R., AND D. S. FARNER. 1963. The relationship of fat deposition to Zugunruhe and migration. Condor 65:200–223.

KING, J. R., AND D. S. FARNER. 1965. Studies of fat deposition in migratory birds. Annals of the New York Academy of Sciences 131:422–440.

KING, J. R., AND D. S. FARNER. 1974. Biochronometry and bird migration: general perspective. Pp. 625–629 *in* L. E. Scheving, F. Halberg, and J. E. Pauly (editors). Chronobiology. Igaku Shoin Ltd., Tokyo, Japan.

KING, J. R., D. S. FARNER, AND M. L. MORTON. 1965. The lipid reserves of White-crowned Sparrows on the breeding ground in central Alaska. Auk 82:236–252.

KING, J. R., B. K. FOLLETT, D. S. FARNER, AND M. L. MORTON. 1966. Annual gonadal cycles and pituitary gonadotropins in *Zonotrichia leucophrys gambelii*. Condor 68:476–487.

KING, J. R., AND J. HUBBARD. 1981. Comparative patterns of nestling growth in White-crowned Sparrows. Condor 83:362–369.

KING, J. R., S. A. MAHONEY, C. S. MAXWELL, AND L. R. MEWALDT. 1976. Additional records of Mountain White-crowned Sparrows parasitized by the Brown-headed Cowbird. Auk 93:389–390.

KING, J. R., AND L. R. MEWALDT. 1987. The summer biology of an unstable insular population of White-crowned Sparrows in Oregon. Condor 89:549–565.

KING, J. R., AND M. E. MURPHY. 1985. Periods of nutritional stress in the annual cycles of endotherms: fact or fiction? American Zoologist 25:955–964.

KLICKA, J., AND R. M. ZINK. 1997. The importance of recent ice ages in speciation: a failed paradigm. Science 277:1666–1669.

KLIMKIEWICZ, M. K., AND A. G. FUTCHER. 1987. Longevity records of North American birds: Coerebinae through Estrildidae. Journal of Field Ornithology 58:318–333.

KLOMP, H. 1970. The determination of clutch-size in birds. Ardea 58:1–124.

KNAPTON, R. W. 1979. Breeding ecology of the Clay-colored Sparrow. Living Bird 17:137–158.

KOENIG, W. D. 1982. Ecological and social factors affecting hatchability of eggs. Auk 99:526–536.

KREBS, C. J. 1972. Ecology: the experimental analysis of distribution and abundance. Harper and Row, New York, NY.

KREBS, C. J. 1991. The experimental paradigm and long-term population studies. Ibis 133(Suppl. 1):3–8.

KROODSMA, D. E., AND R. PICKERT. 1980. Environmentally dependent sensitive periods for avian vocal learning. Nature 288:477–479.

KROODSMA, D. E., M. C. BAKER, L. F. BAPTISTA, AND L. PETRINOVICH. 1985. Vocal "dialects" in Nuttall's White-crowned Sparrow. Current Ornithology 2:103–133.

KUENZEL, W. J., AND C. W. HELMS. 1967. Obesity produced in a migratory bird by hypothalamic lesions. BioScience 17:395–396.

KUENZEL, W. J., AND C. W. HELMS. 1970. Hyperphagia, polydipsia, and other effects of hypothalamic lesions in the White-throated Sparrow, *Zonotrichia albicollis*. Condor 72:66–75.

KULESZA, G. 1990. An analysis of clutch-size in New World passerine birds. Ibis 132:407–422.

LACK, D. 1947. The significance of clutch-size. Ibis 89:302–352.

LACK, D. 1954. The natural regulation of animal numbers. Oxford University Press, Oxford, UK.

LACK, D. 1956. Further notes on the breeding biology of the Swift *Apus apus*. Ibis 98:606–617.

LACK, D. 1966. Population studies of birds. Oxford University Press, Oxford, UK.

LACK, D. 1968. Ecological adaptations for breeding in birds. Methuen, London, UK.

LAMPE, H. M., AND M. C. BAKER. 1994. Behavioural response to song playback by male and female White-crowned Sparrows of two subspecies. Bioacoustics 5:171–185.

LAVERS, N. 1974. Three more cases of White-crowned Sparrows parasitized by Brown-headed Cowbirds. Auk 91:829–830.

LAWTON, M. F., AND R. O. LAWTON. 1980. Nest-site selection in the Brown Jay. Auk 97:631–633.

LEE, S. 2000. Habitat preference and photoperiod-induced physiological changes in Mountain White-crowned Sparrows. B.A. thesis. Princeton University, Princeton, NJ.

LEECH, S. M., AND M. L. LEONARD. 1997. Begging and the risk of predation in nestling birds. Behavioral Ecology 8:644–646.

LEHRMAN, D. S. 1961. Hormonal regulation of parental behavior in birds and infrahuman mammals. Pp. 1268–1382 *in* W. C. Young (editor). Sex and internal secretions, 3rd edition. Williams and Wilkins, Baltimore, MD.

LEHRMAN, D. S., AND R. P. WORTIS. 1960. Previous breeding experience and hormone-induced incubation behavior in the Ring Dove. Science 132:1667–1668.

LEIN, M. R. 1979. Song pattern of the Cypress Hills population of White-crowned Sparrows. Canadian Field-Naturalist 93:272–275.

LEIN, M. R., AND K. W. CORBIN. 1990. Song and plumage phototypes in a contact zone between subspecies of the White-crowned Sparrow (*Zonotrichia leucophrys*). Canadian Journal of Zoology 68:2625–2629.

LEONARD, M. L. 1990. Polygyny in Marsh Wrens: asynchronous settlement as an alternative to the polygyny-threshold model. American Naturalist 136:446–458.

LEWIS, R. A. 1975a. Reproductive biology of the White-crowned Sparrow. II. Environmental control of reproductive and associated cycles. Condor 77:111–124.

LEWIS, R. A. 1975b. Reproductive biology of the White-crowned Sparrow (*Zonotrichia leucophrys pugetensis* Grinnell). I. Temporal organization of reproductive and associated cycles. Condor 77:46–59.

LEWIS, R. A., AND D. S. FARNER. 1973. Temperature modulation of photoperiodically induced vernal phenomena in White-crowned Sparrows (*Zonotrichia leucophrys*). Condor 75:279–286.

LEWIS, R. A., AND J. F. S. ORCUTT. 1971. Social behavior and avian sexual cycles. Scientia 65:447–472.

LIFJELD, J. T., P. O. DUNN, AND D. F. WESTNEAT. 1994. Sexual selection by sperm competition in birds: male-male competition or female choice? Journal of Avian Biology 25:244–250.

LIKER, A., AND T. SZEKELY. 1997. Aggression among female lapwings, *Vanellus vanellus*. Animal Behaviour 54:797–802.

LILL, A. 1979. Nest inattentiveness and its influence on development of the young in the Superb Lyrebird. Condor 81:225–231.

LINDÉN, M., AND A. P. MØLLER. 1989. Cost of reproduction and covariation of life history traits in birds. Trends in Ecology and Evolution 4:367–372.

LINDSTEDT, S. L., AND W. A. CALDER. 1976. Body size and longevity in birds. Condor 78:91–94.

LINDSTRÖM, A., S. DAAN, AND G. H. VISSER. 1994. The conflict between moult and migratory fat deposition: a photoperiodic experiment with Bluethroats. Animal Behaviour 48:1173–1181.

LIPAR, J. L., E. D. KETTERSON, AND V. NOLAN, JR. 1999. Intraclutch variation in testosterone content of Red-winged Blackbird eggs. Auk 116:231–235.

LÖHRL, H. 1959. Zur Frage des Zeitpunktes einer Pragung auf die Heimatregion beim Halsbandschnapper (*Ficedula albicollis*). Journal fur Ornithologie 100:132–140.

LOFTS, B., A. J. MARSHALL, AND A. WOLFSON. 1963. The experimental demonstration of pre-migration activity in the absence of fat deposition in birds. Ibis 105:99–105.

LOFTS, B., AND R. K. MURTON. 1968. Photoperiodic and physiological adaptations regulating avian breeding cycles and their ecological significance. Journal of Zoology 155:327–394.

LOZANO, G. A., S. PERREAULT, AND R. E. LEMON. 1996. Age, arrival date and reproductive success of male American Redstarts *Setophaga ruticilla*. Journal of Avian Biology 27:164–170.

LYON, B. E., AND R. D. MONTGOMERIE. 1987. Ecological correlates of incubation feeding: a comparative study of high arctic finches. Ecology 68:713–722.

LYON, B. E., R. D. MONTGOMERIE, AND L. D. HAMILTON. 1987. Male parental care and monogamy in Snow Buntings. Behavioral Ecology and Sociobiology 20:377–382.

MACDOUGALL-SHACKLETON, E. A. 2001. Song dialects, mate choice, and population structure in Mountain White-crowned Sparrows (*Zonotrichia leucophrys oriantha*). Ph.D. dissertation. Princeton University, Princeton, New Jersey.

MACDOUGALL-SHACKLETON, E. A., AND R. J. ROBERTSON. 1998. Confidence of paternity and paternal care by Eastern Bluebirds. Behavioral Ecology 9:201–205.

MACDOUGALL-SHACKLETON, S. A., E. A. MACDOUGALL-SHACKLETON, AND T. P. HAHN. 2001. Physiological and behavioural responses of female Mountain White-crowned Sparrows to natal- and foreign-dialect songs. Canadian Journal of Zoology 79:1–9.

MAGRATH, R. D. 1990. Hatching asynchrony in altricial birds. Biological Review 65:587–622.

MAGRATH, R. D. 1992. Seasonal changes in egg-mass within and among clutches of birds:

general explanations and a field study of the Blackbird *Turdus merula.* Ibis 134:171–179.

MANEY, D. L., T. P. HAHN, S. J. SCHOECH, P. J. SHARP, M. L. MORTON, AND J. C. WINGFIELD. 1999. Effects of ambient temperature on photo-induced prolactin secretion in three subspecies of White-crowned Sparrows, *Zonotrichia leucophrys.* General and Comparative Endocrinology 113:445–456.

MARCHAND, P. J. 1987. Life in the cold. University Press of New England, Hanover, NH.

MARLER, P. 1970. A comparative approach to vocal learning: song development in White-crowned Sparrows. Journal of Comparative and Physiological Psychology 71:1–25.

MARLER, P., AND M. TAMURA. 1962. Song "dialects" in three populations of White-crowned Sparrows. Condor 64:368–377.

MARSH, R. L., AND W. R. DAWSON. 1982. Substrate metabolism in seasonally acclimatized American Goldfinches. American Journal of Physiology 242:R563–R569.

MARSH, R. L., AND W. R. DAWSON. 1989. Avian adjustments to cold. Pp. 206–253 *in* L. C. H. Wang (editor). Advances in comparative and environmental physiology 4: animal adaptation to cold. Springer Verlag, Berlin, Germany.

MARSHALL, A. J. 1960. The role of the internal rhythm of reproduction in the timing of avian breeding seasons, including migration. Acta XII Congressus Internationalis Ornithologici 12:475–482.

MARSHALL, A. J. 1961. Breeding seasons and migration. Pp. 307–339 *in* A. J. Marshall (editor). Biology and comparative physiology of birds. Vol. 2. Academic Press, New York, NY.

MARTIN, T. E., AND J. J. ROPER. 1988. Nest predation and nest-site selection of a western population of the Hermit Thrush. Condor 90:51–57.

MARZLUFF, J. M., AND R. P. BALDA. 1992. The Pinyon Jay. Academic Press, London, UK.

MAXWELL, C. S., AND J. R. KING. 1976. The oxygen consumption of the Mountain White-crowned Sparrow (*Zonotrichia leucophrys oriantha*) in relation to air temperature. Condor 78:569–570.

MCGILLIVRAY, W. B. 1981. Climatic influences on productivity in the House Sparrow. Wilson Bulletin 93:196–206.

MCGILLIVRAY, W. B., AND E. C. MURPHY. 1984. Sexual differences in longevity of House Sparrows at Calgary, Alberta. Wilson Bulletin 96:456–458.

MCKINNEY, F., K. M. CHENG, AND D. J. BRUGGERS. 1984. Sperm competition in apparently monogamous birds. Pp. 523–545 *in* R. L. Smith (editor). Sperm competition and the evolution of animal mating systems. Academic Press, Orlando, FL.

MCNAUGHTON, F. J., A. DAWSON, AND A. R. GOLDSMITH. 1992. Juvenile photorefractoriness in Starlings, *Sturnus vulgaris,* is not caused by long days after hatching. Proceedings of the Royal Society, London (B) 248:123–128.

MEAD, P. S. 1983. Egg volume and hatching in the Mountain White-crowned Sparrow. M.A. thesis. Occidental College, Los Angeles, CA.

MEAD, P. S., AND M. L. MORTON. 1985. Hatching asynchrony in the Mountain White-crowned Sparrow (*Zonotrichia leucophrys oriantha*): a selected or incidental trait? Auk 102:781–792.

MEAD, P. S., M. L. MORTON, AND B. E. FISH. 1987. Sexual dimorphism in egg size and implications regarding facultative manipulation of sex in Mountain White-crowned Sparrows. Condor 89:798–803.

MEIER, A. H., AND A. C. RUSSO. 1985. Circadian organization of the avian annual cycle. Current Ornithology 2:303–343.

MEIJER, T., C. DEERENBERG, S. DAAN, AND C. DIJKSTRA. 1992. Egg-laying and photorefractoriness in the European Kestrel *Falco tinnunculus.* Ornis Scandinavica 23:405–410.

MELTOFTE, H. 1983. Arrival and pre-nesting period of the snow bunting *Plectrophenax nivalis* in East Greenland. Polar Research 1:185–198.

MERILA, J., AND D. A. WIGGINS. 1997. Mass loss in breeding Blue Tits: the role of energetic stress. Journal of Animal Ecology 66:452–460.

MERKLE, M. S., AND R. M. R. BARCLAY. 1996. Body mass variation in breeding Mountain Bluebirds *Sialia currucoides*: evidence of stress or adaptation for flight? Journal of Animal Ecology 65:401–413.

MEWALDT, L. R., S. S. KIBBY, AND M. L. MORTON. 1968. Comparative biology of Pacific coastal White-crowned Sparrows. Condor 60:14–30.

MEWALDT, L. R., AND J. R. KING. 1978. Latitudinal variation of postnuptial molt in Pacific coast White-crowned Sparrows. Auk 95:168–179.

MEWALDT, L. R., AND J. R. KING. 1986. Estimation of sex ratio from wing-length in birds when sexes differ in size but not coloration. Journal of Field Ornithology 57:155–167.

MIDDLETON, A. L. A. 1979. Influence of age and habitat on reproduction by the American Goldfinch. Ecology 60:418–432.

MØLLER, A. P. 1991. Ectoparasite loads affect optimal clutch size in swallows. Functional Ecology 5:351–359.

MØLLER, A. P., AND T. R. BIRKHEAD. 1991. Frequent copulations and mate guarding as alternative paternity guards in birds: a comparative study. Behaviour 118:170–186.

MONTGOMERIE, R. D. 1988. Seasonal patterns of mate guarding in Lapland Longspurs. Acta XIX Congressus Internationalis Ornithologici 19:442–453.

MOORE, M. C. 1982. Hormonal response of free-living male White-crowned Sparrows to experimental manipulation of female sexual behavior. Hormones and Behavior 16:323–329.

MOORE, M. C. 1983. Effect of female sexual displays on the endocrine physiology and behaviour of male White-crowned Sparrows, Zonotrichia leucophrys. Journal of Zoology 199:137–148.

MOORE, M. C. 1984. Changes in territorial defense produced by changes in circulating levels of testosterone: a possible hormonal basis for mate-guarding behavior in White-crowned Sparrows. Behaviour 88:215–226.

MOORE, M. C., R. S. DONHAM, AND D. S. FARNER. 1982. Physiological preparation for autumnal migration in White-crowned Sparrows. Condor 84:410–419.

MOORE, M. C., H. SCHWABL, AND D. S. FARNER. 1983. Biochronometry of testicular regression in White-crowned Sparrows (Zonotrichia leucophrys gambelii). Journal of Comparative Physiology 153:489–494.

MORENO, J. 1991. Body-mass variation in breeding Northern Wheatears: a field experiment with supplementary food. Condor 91:178–186.

MORENO, J., L. GUSTAFSSON, A. CARLSON, AND T. PÄRT. 1991. The cost of incubation in relation to clutch-size in the Collared Flycatcher Ficedula albicollis. Ibis 133:186–193.

MORENO, J., S. MERINO, J. POTTI, A. DELEON, AND R. RODRIGUEZ. 1999. Maternal energy expenditure does not change with flight costs or food availability in the Pied Flycatcher (Ficedula hypoleuca): costs and benefits for nestlings. Behavioral Ecology and Sociobiology 46:244–251.

MORTON, G. A., AND M. L. MORTON. 1990. Dynamics of postnuptial molt in free-living Mountain White-crowned Sparrows. Condor 92:813–828.

MORTON, M. L. 1967. Diurnal feeding patterns in White-crowned Sparrows, Zonotrichia leucophrys gambelii. Condor 69:491–512.

MORTON, M. L. 1975. Seasonal cycles of body weights and lipids in Belding ground squirrels. Bulletin of the Southern California Academy of Sciences 74:128–143.

MORTON, M. L. 1976. Adaptive strategies of Zonotrichia breeding at high latitude or high altitude. Acta XVI Congressus Internationalis Ornithologici 16:322–336.

MORTON, M. L. 1977. Relationship of reproductive cycle to environmental conditions and energy stores in White-crowned Sparrows at high altitude. Proceedings of the American Philosophical Society 121:377–382.

MORTON, M. L. 1978. Snow conditions and the onset of breeding in the Mountain White-crowned Sparrow. Condor 80:285–289.

MORTON, M. L. 1979. Fecal sac ingestion in the Mountain White-Crowned Sparrow. Condor 81:72–77.

MORTON, M. L. 1984. Sex and age ratios in wintering White-crowned Sparrows. Condor 86:85–87.

MORTON, M. L. 1991. Postfledging dispersal of Green-tailed Towhees to a subalpine meadow. Condor 93:466–468.

MORTON, M. L. 1992a. Control of postnuptial molt in the Mountain White-crowned Sparrow: a perspective from field data. Ornis Scandinavica 23:322–327.

MORTON, M. L. 1992b. Effects of sex and birth date on premigration biology, migration schedules, return rates and natal dispersal in the Mountain White-crowned Sparrow. Condor 94:117–133.

MORTON, M. L. 1994a. Comparison of reproductive timing to snow conditions in wild onions and White-crowned Sparrows at high altitude. Great Basin Naturalist 54:371–375.

MORTON, M. L. 1994b. Hematocrits in montane sparrows in relation to reproductive schedule. Condor 96:119–126.

MORTON, M. L. 1997. Natal and breeding dispersal in the Mountain White-crowned Sparrow *Zonotrichia leucophrys oriantha*. Ardea 85:145–154.

MORTON, M. L., AND N. ALLAN. 1990. Effects of snowpack and age on reproductive schedules and testosterone levels in male White-crowned Sparrows in a montane environment. Pp. 235–249 *in* M. Wada, S. Ishii, and C. G. Scanes (editors). Endocrinology of birds: molecular to behavioral. Japan Scientific Societies Press, Tokyo, Japan, and Springer Verlag, New York, NY.

MORTON, M. L., AND C. CAREY. 1971. Growth and the development of endothermy in the Mountain White-crowned Sparrow (*Zonotrichia leucophrys oriantha*). Physiological Zoology 44:177–189.

MORTON, M. L., J. HORSTMANN, AND C. CAREY. 1973. Body weights and lipids of summering Mountain White-crowned Sparrows in California. Auk 90:83–93.

MORTON, M. L., J. HORSTMANN, AND J. OSBORN. 1972a. Reproductive cycle and nesting success of the Mountain White-crowned Sparrow (*Zonotrichia leucophrys oriantha*) in the central Sierra Nevada. Condor 74:152–163.

MORTON, M. L., J. E. OREJUELA, AND S. M. BUDD. 1972b. The biology of immature Mountain White-crowned Sparrows (*Zonotrichia leucophrys oriantha*) on the breeding ground. Condor 74:423–430.

MORTON, M. L., AND M. E. PEREYRA. 1985. The regulation of egg temperatures and attentiveness patterns in the Dusky Flycatcher (*Empidonax oberholseri*). Auk 102:25–37.

MORTON, M. L., AND M. E. PEREYRA. 1987. Autumn migration of Gambel's White-crowned Sparrow through Tioga Pass, California. Journal of Field Ornithology 58:6–21.

MORTON, M. L., AND M. E. PEREYRA. 1994. Autumnal migration departure schedules in Mountain White-crowned Sparrows. Condor 96:1020–1029.

MORTON, M. L., M. E. PEREYRA, AND L. F. BAPTISTA. 1985. Photoperiodically induced ovarian growth in the White-crowned Sparrow (*Zonotrichia leucophrys gambelii*) and its augmentation by song. Comparative Biochemistry and Physiology 80A:93–97.

MORTON, M. L., L. E. PETERSON, D. M. BURNS, AND N. ALLAN. 1990. Seasonal and age-related changes in plasma testosterone levels in Mountain White-crowned Sparrows. Condor 92:166–173.

MORTON, M. L., AND P. W. SHERMAN. 1978. Effects of a spring snowstorm on behavior, reproduction and survival of Belding's ground squirrels. Canadian Journal of Zoology 56:2578–2590.

MORTON, M. L., K. W. SOCKMAN, AND L. E. PETERSON. 1993. Nest predation in the Mountain White-crowned Sparrow. Condor 95:72–82.

MORTON, M. L., M. W. WAKAMATSU, M. E. PEREYRA, AND G. A. MORTON. 1991. Postfledging dispersal, habitat imprinting, and philopatry in a montane, migratory sparrow. Ornis Scandinavica 22:98–106.

MORTON, M. L., AND D. E. WELTON. 1973. Postnuptial molt and its relation to reproductive cycle and body weight in Mountain White-crowned Sparrows (*Zonotrichia leucophrys oriantha*). Condor 75:184–189.

MOSS, R., AND A. WATSON. 1982. Heritability of egg size, hatch weight, body weight, and viability in Red Grouse (*Lagopus lagopus scoticus*). Auk 99:683–686.

MROSOVSKY, N. 1975. The amplitude and period of circannual cycles of body weight in golden-mantled ground squirrels with medial hypothalamic lesions. Brain Research 99:97–116.

MROSOVSKY, N. 1976. Lipid programmes and life strategies in hibernators. American Zoologist 16:685–697.

MULDER, B. S., B. B. SCHULTZ, AND P. W. SHERMAN. 1978. Predation on vertebrates by Clark's Nutcracker. Condor 80:449–451.

MURPHY, E. C. 1978. Seasonal variation in reproductive output of House Sparrows: the determination of clutch size. Ecology 59:1189–1199.

MURPHY, E. C., AND E. HAUKIOJA. 1986. Clutch size in nidicolous birds. Current Ornithology 4:141–180.

MURPHY, M. T. 1986. Body size and condition, timing of breeding, and aspects of egg production in Eastern Kingbirds. Auk 103:465–476.

MURRAY, B. G., JR. 1992. The evolutionary significance of lifetime reproductive success. Auk 167:167–172.

MURRAY, B. G., JR. 1994. Effect of selection for successful reproduction on hatching synchrony and asynchrony. Auk 111:806–813.

NELSON, D. A., AND P. MARLER. 1994. Selection-based learning in bird song development. Proceedings of the National Academy of Sciences, U.S.A. 91:10498–10501.

NELSON, D. A., P. MARLER, AND M. L. MORTON. 1996. Overproduction in song development: an evolutionary correlate with migration. Animal Behaviour 51:1127–1140.

NELSON, D. A., P. MARLER, AND A. PALLERONI. 1995. A comparative approach to vocal learning: intraspecific variation in the learning process. Animal Behaviour 50:83–97.

NEWTON, I. 1989a. Introduction. Pp. 1–11 in I. Newton (editor). Lifetime reproduction in birds Academic Press, San Diego, CA.

NEWTON, I. 1989b. Synthesis. Pp. 441–469 in I. Newton (editor). Lifetime Reproduction in Birds Academic Press, San Diego, CA.

NICE, M. M. 1937. Studies in the life history of the Song Sparrow, I. Transactions of the Linnaean Society of New York 4:1–246.

NICE, M. M. 1938. The biological significance of bird weights. Bird-Banding 9:1–11.

NICHOLLS, T. J., A. R. GOLDSMITH, AND A. DAWSON. 1988. Photorefractoriness in birds and comparison with mammals. Physiological Reviews 68:133–176.

NILSSON, J.-Å. 1989. Causes and consequences of natal dispersal in the marsh tit, *Parus palustris*. Journal of Animal Ecology 58:619–636.

NILSSON, L. 1983. Laying of replacement clutches in the Willow Warbler *Phylloscopus trochilus* in Lapland, Sweden. Ornis Scandinavica 14:48–50.

NOLAN, V., JR. 1978. The ecology and behavior of the Prairie Warbler *Dendroica discolor*. Ornithological Monographs 26:1–595.

NOLAN, V., JR., E. D. KETTERSON, C. ZIEGENFUS, D. P. CULLEN, AND C. R. CHANDLER. 1992. Testosterone and avian life histories: effects of experimentally elevated testosterone on prebasic molt and survival in male Dark-eyed Juncos. Condor 94:364–370.

NORBERG, R. A. 1981. Temporary weight decrease in breeding birds may result in more fledged young. American Naturalist 118:838–850.

NORMENT, C. J. 1992. Comparative breeding biology of Harris' Sparrows and Gambel's White-crowned Sparrows in the Northwest Territories, Canada. Condor 94:954–975.

NORMENT, C. J. 1993. Nest-site characteristics and nest predation in Harris' Sparrows and White-crowned Sparrows in the Northwest Territories, Canada. Auk 110:769–777.

NORMENT, C. J. 1994. Breeding site fidelity in Harris' Sparrows, *Zonotrichia querula* in the Northwest Territories. Canadian Field-Naturalist 108:234–236.

NORMENT, C. J., AND M. E. FULLER. 1997. Breeding-season frugivory by Harris' Sparrows (*Zonotrichia querula*) and White-crowned Sparrows (*Zonotrichia leucophrys*) in a low-arctic ecosystem. Canadian Journal of Zoology 75:670–679.

NORMENT, C. J., AND S. A. SHACKLETON. 1993. Harris' Sparrow (*Zonotrichia querula*). In A. Poole and F. Gill (editors). The Birds of North America, No. 64. The Academy of Natural Sciences, Philadelphia, PA, and American Ornithologists' Union, Washington, D.C.

NORMENT, C. J., P. HENDRICKS, AND R. SANTONOCITO. 1998. Golden-crowned Sparrow (*Zonotrichia atricapilla*). In A. Poole and F. Gill (editors). The Birds of North America, No. 352. The Academy of Natural Sciences, Philadelphia, PA, and American Ornithologists' Union, Washington, D.C.

NORRIS, R. A., AND F. S. L. WILLIAMSON. 1955. Variation in relative heart size of certain passerines with increase in altitude. Wilson Bulletin 67:78–83.

NUR, N. 1988. The cost of reproduction in birds: an examination of the evidence. Ardea 76:155–168.

OAKESON, B. B. 1954. The Gambel's Sparrow at Mountain Village, Alaska. Auk 71:351–365.

OJANEN, M. 1979. Effect of a cold spell on birds in northern Finland in May 1968. Ornis Fennica 56:148–155.

OJANEN, M., M. ORELL, AND R. A. VÄISÄNEN. 1979. Role of heredity in egg size variation in the Great Tit *Parus major* and the Pied Flycatcher *Ficedula hypoleuca*. Ornis Scandinavica 10:22–28.

OJANEN, M., M. ORELL, AND R. A. VÄISÄNEN. 1981. Egg size variation within passerine clutches: effects of ambient temperature and laying sequence. Ornis Fennica 58:93–108.

O'NEILL, J. P., AND T. A. PARKER, III. 1978. Responses of birds to a snowstorm in the Andes of southern Peru. Wilson Bulletin 90:446–449.

OPPENHEIMER, S. D., M. E. PEREYRA, AND M. L. MORTON. 1996. Egg laying in Dusky Flycatchers and White-crowned Sparrows. Condor 98:428–430.

OREJUELA, J. E., AND M. L. MORTON. 1975. Song dialects in several populations of Mountain White-crowned Sparrows (*Zonotrichia leucophrys oriantha*) in the Sierra Nevada. Condor 77:145–153.

ORIANS, G. H. 1969. On the evolution of mating systems in birds and mammals. American Naturalist 103:589–603.

ORIANS, G. H. 1980. Marsh-nesting blackbirds. Princeton University Press, Princeton, NJ.

OSTLER, W. K., K. T. HARPER, K. B. MCKNIGHT, AND D. C. ANDERSON. 1982. The effects of increasing snowpack on a subalpine meadow in the Uinta Mountains, Utah, U.S.A. Arctic and Alpine Research 14:203–214.

OTTO, C. 1979. Environmental factors affecting egg weight within and between colonies of Fieldfare *Turdus pilaris*. Ornis Scandinavica 10:111–116.

OWEN, H. E. 1976. Phenological development of herbaceous plants in relation to snowmelt date. Pp. 323–341 *in* H. W. Steinhoff and J. D. Ives (editors). San Juan Ecology Project, Final Report: Ecological impacts of snowpack augmentation in the San Juan Mountains, Colorado. Colorado State University Publications, Fort Collins, CO.

PALADINO, F. V. 1986. Transient nocturnal hypothermia in White-crowned Sparrows. Ornis Scandinavica 17:78–79.

PAPP, R. P. 1978. A nival aeolian ecosystem in California. Arctic and Alpine Research 10:117–131.

PARISH, D. M. B., AND J. C. COULSON. 1998. Parental investment, reproductive success and polygyny in the lapwing, *Vanellus vanellus*. Animal Behaviour 56:1161–1167.

PÄRT, T., AND L. GUSTAFSON. 1989. Breeding dispersal in the Collared Flycatcher (*Ficedula albicollis*): possible causes and reproductive consequences. Journal of Animal Ecology 58:305–320.

PARTRIDGE, L. 1989. Lifetime reproductive success and life-history evolution. Pp. 421–440 *in* I. Newton (editor). Lifetime reproduction in birds. Academic Press, San Diego, CA.

PATTIE, D. L. 1977. Population levels and bioenergetics of arctic birds on Truelove Lowland. Pp. 413–436 *in* L. C. Bliss (editor). Truelove Lowland, Devon Island: a high arctic ecosystem. University of Alberta Press, Edmonton, Alberta.

PAYNE, R. B. 1969. Overlap of breeding and molting schedules in a collection of African birds. Condor 71:140–145.

PAYNE, R. B. 1972. Mechanisms and control of molt. Pp. 103–155 *in* D. S. Farner and J. R. King (editors). Avian biology. Vol. 2. Academic Press, New York, NY.

PAYNE, R. B. 1989. Indigo Bunting. Pp. 154–172 *in* I. Newton (editor). Lifetime reproduction in birds. Academic Press, San Diego, CA.

PAYNE, R. B., AND L. L. PAYNE. 1993. Breeding dispersal in Indigo Buntings: circumstances and consequences for breeding success and population structure. Condor 95:1–24.

PEREYRA, M. E. 1998. Effects of environment and endocrine function on control of reproduction in a high elevation tyrannid. Ph.D. dissertation. Northern Arizona University, Flagstaff, AZ.

PEREYRA, M. E., AND M. L. MORTON. 2001. Nestling growth and thermoregulatory development in subalpine Dusky Flycatchers. Auk 118:116–136.

PERRINS, C. M. 1979. British tits. Collins, London, UK.

PERRINS, C. M. 1996. Eggs, egg formation and the timing of breeding. Ibis 138:2–15.

PERRINS, C. M., AND P. J. JONES. 1975. The inheritance of clutch size in the Great Tit. Condor 76:225–229.

PERRINS, C. M., AND R. H. MCCLEERY. 1989. Laying dates and clutch size in the Great Tit. Wilson Bulletin 101:236–253.

PETRINOVICH, L., AND T. L. PATTERSON. 1978. Polygyny in the White-crowned Sparrow (*Zonotrichia leucophrys*). Condor 80:99–100.

PETRINOVICH, L., AND T. L. PATTERSON. 1981. The responses of White-crowned Sparrows to songs of different dialects and subspecies. Zeitschrift fur Tierpsychologie 57:1–14.

PETTIFOR, R. A. 1993. Brood-manipulation experiments. I. The number of offspring surviving per nest in Blue Tits (*Parus caeruleus*). Journal of Animal Ecology 62:131–144.

PIELOU, E. C. 1991. After the ice age: the return of life to glaciated North America. University of Chicago Press, Chicago, IL.

PLESZCZYNSKA, W. K. 1978. Microgeographic prediction of polygyny in the Lark Bunting. Science 201:935–937.

PLISSNER, J. H., AND P. A. GOWATY. 1996. Patterns of natal dispersal, turnover and dispersal costs in Eastern Bluebirds. Animal Behaviour 51:1307–1322.

POWER, H. W., E. D. KENNEDY, L. C. ROMAGNANO, M. P. LOMBARDO, A. S. HOFFENBERG, P. C. STOUFFER, AND T. R. MCGUIRE. 1989. The parasitism insurance hypothesis: why starlings leave space for parasitic eggs. Condor 91:753–765.

PRESTON, F. W., AND R. T. NORRIS. 1947. Nesting heights of breeding birds. Ecology 28:241–273.

PRINZINGER, V. R., K. HUND, AND G. HOCHSIEDER. 1979. Brutund Bebrütungstemperatur am Beispiel von Star (*Sturnus vulgaris*) und Mehlschwalbe (*Delichon urbica*): Zwei Bebrütungsparameter mit inverser Tagesperiodik. Vogelwelt 5:18–188.

PULLIAINEN, E. 1978. Influence of heavy snowfall in June 1977 on the life of birds in NE Finnish Forest Lapland. Aquilo Series in Zoology 18:1–4.

PUSEY, A. E. 1987. Sex-biased dispersal and inbreeding avoidance in birds and mammals. Trends in Ecology and Evolution 2:295–299.

QUINN, M. S., AND G. L. HOLROYD. 1992. Asynchronous polygyny in the House Wren (*Troglodytes aedon*). Auk 109:192–195.

RAHN, H., AND A. AR. 1974. The avian egg: incubation time and water loss. Condor 76:147–152.

RAND, A. L. 1948. Glaciation, an isolating factor in speciation. Evolution 2:314–321.

RAND, A. L. 1961. Wing length as an indicator of weight: a contribution. Bird-Banding 32:71–79.

RAND, W. M. 1973. A stochastic model of the temporal aspect of breeding strategies. Theoretical Biology 40:337–351.

REID, W. V. 1988. Age correlations within pairs of breeding birds. Auk 105:278–285.

RICHARDSON, M. I. 1997. An investigation of parasite-host interactions between two haematozoa, *Haemoproteus* and *Plasmodium,* and Mountain White-crowned Sparrows (*Zonotrichia leucophrys oriantha*). B.A. thesis. Princeton University, Princeton, NJ.

RICHARDSON, R. D., T. BOSWELL, B. D. RAFFETY, R. J. SEELEY, J. C. WINGFIELD, AND S. C. WOODS. 1995. NPY increases food intake in White-crowned Sparrows: effect in short and long photoperiods. American Journal of Physiology 268:R1418–R1422.

RICHARDSON, R. D., T. BOSWELL, S. C. WEATHERFORD, J. C. WINGFIELD, AND S. C. WOODS. 1993. Cholecystokinin octapeptide decreases food intake in White-crowned Sparrows. American Journal of Physiology 264:R852–R856.

RICHTER, W. 1984. Nestling survival and growth in the Yellow-headed Blackbird, *Xanthocephalus xanthocephalus.* Ecology 65:597–608.

RICKLEFS, R. E. 1967. A graphical method of fitting equations to growth curves. Ecology 48:978–983.

RICKLEFS, R. E. 1968. Patterns of growth in birds. Ibis 110:419–451.

RICKLEFS, R. E. 1969. An analysis of nesting mortality in birds. Smithsonian Contributions in Zoology 9:1–48.

RICKLEFS, R. E. 1973. Patterns of growth in birds. II. Growth rate and mode of development. Ibis 115:177–201.

RICKLEFS, R. E. 1974. Energetics of reproduction in birds. Pp. 152–297 *in* R. A. Paynter (editor). Avian energetics. Vol. 15. Nuttall Ornithological Club, Cambridge, MA.

RICKLEFS, R. E. 1982. Some considerations on sibling competition and avian growth rates. Auk 99:141–147.

RICKLEFS, R. E. 1993. Sibling competition, hatching asynchrony, incubation period, and lifespan in altricial birds. Current Ornithology 11:199–275.

RICKLEFS, R. E., AND D. J. T. HUSSELL. 1984. Changes in adult mass associated with the nesting cycle in the European Starling. Ornis Scandinavica 15:155–161.

RITCHISON, G. 1986. The singing behavior of female Northern Cardinals. Condor 88:156–159.

ROBINSON, J. E., AND B. K. FOLLETT. 1982. Photoperiodism in Japanese Quail: the termination of seasonal breeding by photorefractoriness. Proceedings of the Royal Society, London (B) 215:95–116.

ROBINSON, K. D., AND J. T. ROTENBERRY. 1991. Clutch size and reproductive success of House Wrens rearing natural and manipulated broods. Auk 108:277–284.

ROFSTAD, G., AND J. SANDVIK. 1985. Variation in egg size of the Hooded Crow *Corvus corone cornix.* Ornis Scandinavica 16:38–44.

ROHWER, F. C. 1988. Inter- and intraspecific relationships between egg size and clutch size in waterfowl. Auk 105:161–176.

ROONEEM, T. M., AND R. J. ROBERTSON. 1996. The potential to lay replacement clutches by Tree Swallows. Condor 99:228–231.

ROSENBERG, N. J. 1974. Microclimate: the biological environment. John Wiley and Sons, New York, NY.

ROSS, H. A. 1980. The reproductive rates of yearling and older Ipswich Sparrows, *Passerculus sandwichensis princeps.* Canadian Journal of Zoology 58:1557–1563.

ROST, R. 1992. Hormones and behaviour: a comparison of studies on seasonal changes in song production and testosterone plasma levels in the Willow Tit *Parus montanus.* Ornis Fennica 69:1–6.

ROTHSTEIN, S. I. 1973. Variation in the incidence of hatching failure in the Cedar Waxwing and other species. Condor 75:164–169.

ROWE, L., D. LUDWIG, AND D. SCHLUTER. 1994. Time, condition, and the seasonal decline of avian clutch size. American Naturalist 143:698–722.

RUNFELDT, S., AND J. C. WINGFIELD. 1985. Experimentally prolonged sexual activity in female sparrows delays termination of reproductive activity in their untreated mates. Animal Behaviour 33:403–410.

RYDÉN, O. 1978. Egg weight in relation to laying sequence in a south Swedish urban population of the Blackbird *Turdus merula.* Ornis Scandinavica 9:172–177.

SAETHER, B.-E. 1988. Pattern of covariation between life-history traits of European birds. Nature 331:616–617.

SAETHER, B.-E. 1990. Age-specific variation in reproductive performance of birds. Current Ornithology 7:251–283.

SALT, W. R. 1966. A nesting study of *Spizella pallida.* Auk 83:274–281.

SAMSON, F. B. 1976a. Pterylosis and molt in Cassin's Finch. Condor 78:505–511.

SAMSON, F. B. 1976b. Territory, breeding density, and fall departure in Cassin's Finch. Auk 93:477–497.

SANSUM, E. L., AND J. R. KING. 1976. Long-term effects of constant photoperiods on testicular cycles of White-crowned Sparrows (*Zonotrichia leucophrys gambelii*). Physiological Zoology 49:406–416.

SCHAFFER, W. M. 1974. Optimal reproductive effort in fluctuating environments. American Naturalist 108:783–790.

SCHULZE-HAGEN, K., B. LEISLER, T. R. BIRKHEAD, AND A. DYRCZ. 1995. Prolonged copulation, sperm reserves and sperm competition in the Aquatic Warbler *Acrocephalus paludicola.* Ibis 137:85–91.

SCHWABL, H. 1993. Yolk is a source of maternal testosterone for developing birds. Proceedings of the National Academy of Sciences, U.S.A. 90:11446–11450.

SCHWABL, H., AND E. KRINER. 1991. Territorial aggression and song of male European Robins (*Erithacus rubecula*) in autumn and spring: effects of antiandrogen treatment. Hormones and Behavior 25:180–194.

SCOTT, D., AND W. D. BILLINGS. 1964. Effects of environmental factors on standing crop and production of alpine tundra. Ecological Monographs 34:243–270.

SEALY, S. G. 1975. Influence of snow on egg-laying in auklets. Auk 92:528–538.

SEALY, S. G., J. V. BRISKIE, AND G. C. BIERMANN. 1986. Deaths of female passerine birds on their nests while incubating. Journal of Field Ornithology 57:315–317.

SEARCY, W. A. 1979. Female choice of mates: a general model for birds and its application to Red-winged Blackbirds (*Agelaius phoeniceus*). American Naturalist 114:77–100.

SEARCY, W. A. 1984. Song repertoire size and female preferences in song sparrows. Behavioral Ecology and Sociobiology 14:281–286.

SEARCY, W. A. 1988. Do female Red-winged Blackbirds limit their own breeding densities? Ecology 69:85–95.

SEARCY, W. A., AND K. YASUKAWA. 1995. Polygyny and sexual selection in Red-winged Blackbirds. Princeton University Press, Princeton, NJ.

SHARP, P. J. 1980. Female reproduction. Pp. 435–454 *in* A. Epple and M. H. Stetson (editors). Avian endocrinology. Academic Press, New York, NY.

SHERMAN, P., AND M. L. MORTON. 1988. Extra-pair fertilizations in Mountain White-crowned Sparrows. Behavioral Ecology and Sociobiology 22:413–420.

SHERRY, D. F., N. MROSOVSKY, AND J. A. HOGAN. 1980. Weight loss and anorexia during incubation in birds. Journal of Comparative and Physiological Psychology 94:89–98.

SILVERIN, B., AND A. GOLDSMITH. 1984. The effects of modifying incubation on prolactin secretion in free-living Pied Flycatchers. General and Comparative Endocrinology 55: 239–244.

SILVERIN, B., M. KIKUCHI, AND S. ISHII. 1997. Seasonal changes in follicle-stimulating hormone in free-living Great Tits. General and Comparative Endocrinology 108:366–373.

SKOWRON, C., AND M. KERN. 1980. The insulation in nests of selected North American songbirds. Auk 97:816–824.

SKUTCH, A. F. 1976. Parent birds and their young. University of Texas Press, Austin, TX.

SLAGSVOLD, T. 1981. Clutch size and population stability in birds: a test of hypotheses. Oecologia 49:213–217.

SLAGSVOLD, T. 1993. Female-female aggression and monogamy in Great Tits *Parus major*. Ornis Scandinavica 24:155–158.

SLAGSVOLD, T., T. AMUNDSEN, S. DALE, AND H. LAMPE. 1992. Female-female aggression explains polyterritoriality in male Pied Flycatchers. Animal Behaviour 43:397–407.

SLAGSVOLD, T., AND J. T. LIFJELD. 1988. Ultimate adjustment of clutch size to parental feeding capacity in a passerine bird. Ecology 69:1918–1922.

SLAGSVOLD, T., AND J. T. LIFJELD. 1989. Hatching asynchrony in birds: the hypothesis of sexual conflict over parental investment. American Naturalist 134:239–253.

SLAGSVOLD, T., AND J. T. LIFJELD. 1990. Influence of male and female quality on clutch size in tits (*Parus* spp.). Ecology 71:1258–1266.

SLAGSVOLD, T., AND J. T. LIFJELD. 1994. Polygyny in birds: the role of competition between females for male parental care. American Naturalist 143:59–94.

SLAGSVOLD, T., J. SANDVIK, G. ROFSTAD, Ö. LORENTSEN, AND M. HUSBY. 1984. On the adaptive value of intraclutch egg-size variation in birds. Auk 101:685–697.

SMITH, J. N. M., AND P. ARCESE. 1989. How fit are floaters? Consequences of alternative territorial behaviors in a nonmigratory sparrow. American Naturalist 133:830–845.

SMITH, K. G., AND D. C. ANDERSEN. 1982. Food, predation, and reproductive ecology of the Dark-eyed Junco in northern Utah. Auk 99:650–661.

SMITH, K. G., AND D. C. ANDERSEN. 1985. Snowpack and variation in reproductive ecology of a montane ground-nesting passerine, *Junco hyemalis*. Ornis Scandinavica 16:8–13.

SMITH, S. M. 1991. The Black-capped Chickadee: behavioral ecology and natural history. Cornell University Press, Ithaca, NY.

SMITH, S. M. 1995. Age-specific survival in breeding Black-capped Chickadees (*Parus atricapillus*). Auk 112:840–846.

SNOW, D. W. 1958. The breeding of the Blackbird *Turdus merula* at Oxford. Ibis 100:1–30.

SOCKMAN, K. W., AND T. P. HAHN. 1996. Roost-site selection in the Mountain White-crowned Sparrow. American Zoologist 36:94A.

SOCKMAN, K. W., AND H. SCHWABL. 1999. Daily estradiol and progesterone levels relative to laying and onset of incubation in canaries. General and Comparative Endocrinology 114:257–268.

SOCKMAN, K. W., H. SCHWABL, AND P. J. SHARP. 2000. The role of prolactin in the regulation of clutch size and onset of incubation behavior in the American Kestrel. Hormones and Behavior 38:168–176.

SOGGE, M. K., M. D. KERN, R. KERN, AND C. VAN RIPER, III. 1991. Growth and development of thermoregulation in nestling San Miguel Island Song Sparrows. Condor 93: 773–776.

SOKOLOV, L. V. 1991. Philopatry and dispersal of birds. Proceeding of the Zoological Institute, Russia 230:1–232.

SOTHERLAND, P. R., G. C. PACKARD, T. L. TAIGEN, AND T. J. BOARDMAN. 1980. An altitudinal cline in conductance of Cliff Swallow (*Petrochelidon pyrrhonota*) eggs to water vapor. Auk 97:177–185.

STEARNS, S. C. 1992. The evolution of life histories. Oxford University Press, New York, NY.

STERNBERG, H. 1989. Pied Flycatcher. Pp. 55–74 *in* I. Newton (editor). Lifetime reproduction in birds. Academic Press, San Diego, CA.

STEVENS, L. 1996. Avian biochemistry and molecular biology. Cambridge University Press, Cambridge, UK.

STEWART, I. F. 1963. Variation of wing length with age. Bird Study 10:1–9.

STOLESON, S. H., AND S. R. BEISSINGER. 1995. Hatching asynchrony and the onset of incubation in birds, revisited: when is the critical period? Current Ornithology 12:199–270.

STOREY, C. R. 1976. Some effects of manipulation of daily photoperiod on the rate of onset of a photorefractory state in canaries (*Serinus canarius*). General and Comparative Endocrinology 30:204–208.

STURKIE, P. D., AND W. J. MUELLER. 1976. Reproduction in the female and egg production. Pp. 302–330 *in* P. D. Sturkie (editor). Avian physiology, 3rd edition. Springer Verlag, New York, NY.

SUAREZ, F. 1991. Influencias ambientales en la variacion del tamaño, forma y peso de los huevos de la Collalba Rubia (*Oenanthe hispanica*). Doñana, Acta Vertebrata 18:39–49.

SULLIVAN, K. A., AND W. W. WEATHERS. 1992. Brood size and thermal environment influence field metabolism of nestling Yellow-eyed Juncos. Auk 109:112–118.

SUTTON, G. M. 1935. The juvenal plumage and postjuvenal molt in several species of Michigan sparrows. Cranbrook Institute of Science Bulletin 3:1–36.

SWAN, L. E. 1952. Some environmental conditions influencing life at high altitudes. Ecology 33:109–111.

SWANSON, D. L. 1995. Seasonal variation in thermogenic capacity of migratory Warbling Vireos. Auk 112:870–877.

SZÉKELY, T., J. N. WEBB, A. I. HOUSTON, AND J. M. MCNAMARA. 1996. An evolutionary approach to offspring desertion in birds. Current Ornithology 13:271–330.

TAYLOR, L. R. 1989. Objective and experiment in long-term research. Pp. 20–70 *in* G. E. Likens (editor). Long-term studies in ecology. Springer Verlag, New York, NY.

TAYLOR, W. P. 1912. Field notes on amphibians, reptiles and birds of northern Humboldt County, Nevada, with a discussion of some of the faunal features of the region. University of California Publications in Zoology 7:319–436.

THOMPSON, L. S. 1978. Species abundance and habitat relations of an insular montane avifauna. Condor 80:1–14.

THOMSON, A. L. 1950. Factors determining the breeding season of birds: an introductory review. Ibis 92:173–184.

TINBERGEN, J. M., AND S. DAAN. 1990. Family planning in the Great Tit (*Parus major*): optimal clutch size as integration of parent and offspring fitness. Behaviour 114:161–190.

TOMPA, F. S. 1962. Territorial behavior: the main controlling factor of a local Song Sparrow population. Auk 79:687–697.

TRIVERS, R. L. 1972. Parental investment and sexual selection. Pp. 136–179 in B. Campbell (editor). Sexual selection and the descent of man, 1871–1971. Aldine-Atherton, Chicago, IL.

TRIVERS, R. L., AND D. E. WILLARD. 1973. Natural selection of parental ability to vary the sex ratio of offspring. Science 179:90–91.

UNDERHILL, L. G., R. P. PRYS-JONES, R. J. DOWSETT, P. HERROELEN, D. N. JOHNSON, M. R. LAWN, S. C. NORMAN, D. J. PEARSON, AND A. J. TREE. 1992. The biannual primary moult of Willow Warblers Phylloscopus trochilus in Europe and Africa. Ibis 134:286–297.

VAN BALEN, J. H. 1967. The significance of variations in body weight and wing length in the Great Tit, Parus major. Ardea 55:1–59.

VAN BALEN, J. H. 1979. Observations on the post-fledging dispersal of the Pied Flycatcher, Ficedula hypoleuca. Ardea 67:134–137.

VANDER WERF, E. 1992. Lack's clutch size hypothesis: an examination of the evidence using meta-analysis. Ecology 73:1699–1705.

VAN NOORDWIJK, A. J., J. H. VAN BALEN, AND W. SCHARLOO. 1980. Heritability of ecologically important traits in the Great Tit. Ardea 68:193–203.

VEGA RIVERA, J. H., W. J. MCSHEA, J. H. RAPPOLE, AND C. A. HAAS. 1999. Postbreeding movements and habitat use of adult Wood Thrushes in northern Virginia. Auk 116:458–466.

VERBEEK, N. A. M. 1970. Breeding ecology of the Water Pipit. Auk 87:425–451.

VERBEEK, N. A. M. 1988. Development of a stable body temperature and growth rates in nestlings of three ground nesting passerines in alpine tundra. Journal fur Ornithologie 129:449–456.

VERBEEK, N. A. M. 1995. Body temperature and growth of nestling Northwestern Crows, Corvus caurinus. Canadian Journal of Zoology 73:1019–1023.

VERBOVEN, N., AND S. VERHULST. 1996. Seasonal variation in the incidence of double broods: the date hypothesis fits better than the quality hypothesis. Journal of Animal Ecology 65:264–273.

VERHULST, S., AND R. A. HUT. 1996. Post-fledging care, multiple breeding and the costs of reproduction in the Great Tit. Animal Behavior Monographs 51:957–966.

VERNER, J. 1964. Evolution of polygamy in the Long-billed Marsh Wren. Evolution 18:252–261.

VINUELA, J. 1997. Adaptation vs. constraint: intraclutch egg-mass variation in birds. Journal of Animal Ecology 66:781–792.

VLECK, C. M. 1981a. Energetic cost of incubation in the Zebra Finch. Condor 83:229–237.

VLECK, C. M. 1981b. Hummingbird incubation: female attentiveness and egg temperature. Oecologia 51:199–205.

VLECK, C. M., AND G. J. KENAGY. 1980. Embryonic metabolism of the Fork-tailed Storm-Petrel: physiological patterns during prolonged and interrupted incubation. Physiological Zoology 53:32–42.

WALKINSHAW, L. H. 1939. Nesting of the Field Sparrow and survival of the young. Bird-Banding 10:107–114.

WALSBERG, G. E. 1981. Nest-site selection and the radiative environment of the Warbling Vireo. Condor 83:86–88.

WALSBERG, G. E., AND J. R. KING. 1978. The heat budget of incubating Mountain White-crowned Sparrows (Zonotrichia leucophrys oriantha) in Oregon. Physiological Zoology 51:92–103.

WASSERMAN, F. E. 1980. Territorial behavior in a pair of White-throated Sparrows. Wilson Bulletin 92:74–87.

WEATHERHEAD, P. J., AND M. R. L. FORBES. 1994. Natal philopatry in passerine birds: genetic or ecological influences? Behavioral Ecology 5:426–433.

WEATHERS, W. W., AND K. A. SULLIVAN. 1989. Nest attentiveness and egg temperature in the Yellow-eyed Junco. Condor 91:628–633.

WEATHERS, W. W., AND K. A. SULLIVAN. 1991. Growth and energetics of nestling Yellow-eyed Juncos. Condor 93:138–146.

WEAVER, T. 1974. Ecological effects of weather modification: effects of late snowmelt on *Festuca idahoensis* Elmer meadows. American Midland Naturalist 92:346–356.

WEAVER, T., AND D. COLLINS. 1977. Possible effects of weather modification (increased snowpack) on *Festuca idahoensis* meadows. Journal of Range Management 30:451–456.

WEEDEN, J. S. 1966. Diurnal rhythm of attentiveness of incubating female Tree Sparrows (*Spizella arborea*) at a northern latitude. Auk 83:368–388.

WERSCHKUL, D. F., AND J. A. JACKSON. 1979. Sibling competition and avian growth rates. Ibis 121:97–102.

WESTNEAT, D. F. 1988. Male parental care and extrapair copulations in the Indigo Bunting. Auk 105:149–160.

WESTNEAT, D. F., AND P. W. SHERMAN. 1993. Parentage and the evolution of parental behavior. Behavioral Ecology 4:66–77.

WESTNEAT, D. F., P. W. SHERMAN, AND M. L. MORTON. 1990. The ecology and evolution of extra-pair copulations in birds. Current Ornithology 7:331–369.

WHEELWRIGHT, N. T., AND P. D. BOERSMA. 1979. Egg chilling and the thermal environment of the Fork-tailed Storm-Petrel (*Oceanodroma furcata*) nest. Physiological Zoology 52:231–239.

WHEELWRIGHT, N. T., C. B. SCHULTZ, AND P. J. HODUM. 1992. Polygyny and male parental care in Savannah Sparrows: effects on female fitness. Behavioral Ecology and Sociobiology 31:279–289.

WHEELWRIGHT, N. T., G. TRUSSELL, J. P. DEVINE, AND R. ANDERSON. 1994. Sexual dimorphism and population sex ratios in juvenile Savannah Sparrows. Journal of Field Ornithology 65:520–529.

WHITE, F. N., AND J. L. KINNEY. 1974. Avian incubation. Science 186:107–115.

WHITMORE, R. C., J. A. MOSHER, AND H. H. FROST. 1977. Spring migrant mortality during unseasonable weather. Auk 94:778–781.

WHITMORE, R. C., AND R. C. WHITMORE. 1997. Late fall and early spring bird observations for Mulegé, Baja California Sur, Mexico. Great Basin Naturalist 57:131–141.

WIGGINS, D. A. 1990. Sources of variation in egg mass of Tree Swallows *Tachycineta bicolor*. Ornis Scandinavica 21:157–160.

WILEY, R. H., AND M. S. WILEY. 1980. Spacing and timing in the nesting ecology of a tropical blackbird: comparison of populations in different environments. Ecological Monographs 50:153–178.

WILLIAMS, J. B. 1996. Energetics of avian incubation. Pp. 375–416 *in* C. Carey (editor). Avian energetics and nutritional ecology. Chapman and Hall, New York, NY.

WILLIAMS, J. B., AND H. HANSELL. 1981. Bioenergetics of captive Belding's Savannah Sparrows. Comparative Biochemistry and Physiology 69:783–787.

WILLIAMS, J. B., AND K. A. NAGY. 1984. Validation of the doubly labeled water technique for measuring energy metabolism in Savannah Sparrows. Physiological Zoology 57:325–328.

WILLIAMS, J. B., AND A. PRINTS. 1986. Energetics of growth in nestling Savannah Sparrows: a comparison of doubly labeled water and laboratory estimates. Condor 88:74–83.

WILLIAMS, T. D. 1994. Intraspecific variation in egg size and egg composition in birds: effects on offspring fitness. Biological Review 68:35–59.

WILSON, F. E., AND R. S. DONHAM. 1988. Daylength and control of seasonal reproduction in male birds. Pp. 101–120 *in* M. H. Stetson (editor). Processing of environmental information in vertebrates. Springer Verlag, Berlin, Germany.

WILSON, F. E., AND B. K. FOLLETT. 1974. Plasma and pituitary luteinizing hormone in intact and castrated Tree Sparrows (*Spizella arborea*) during a photoinduced gonadal cycle. General and Comparative Endocrinology 23:82–93.

WILSON, F. E., AND B. D. REINERT. 1993. The thyroid and photoperiodic control of seasonal reproduction in American Tree Sparrows (*Spizella arborea*). Journal of Comparative Physiology B 163:563–573.

WILSON, F. E., AND B. D. REINERT. 1995. A one-time injection of thyroxine programmed seasonal reproduction and postnuptial molt in chronically thyroidectomized male American Tree Sparrows *Spizella arborea* exposed to long days. Journal of Avian Biology 26:225–233.

WILSON, F. E., AND B. D. REINERT. 1998. Effect of withdrawing long days from male American Tree Sparrows (*Spizella arborea*): implications for understanding thyroid-dependent programming of seasonal reproduction and postnuptial molt. Biology of Reproduction 58:15–19.

WILTSCHKO, W., AND R. WILTSCHKO. 1978. A theoretical model for migratory orientation and homing in birds. Oikos 30:177–187.

WINGFIELD, J. C. 1980. Fine temporal adjustment of reproductive functions. Pp. 367–389 *in* A. Epple and M. H. Stetson (editors). Avian endocrinology. Academic Press, New York, NY.

WINGFIELD, J. C. 1983. Environmental and endocrine control of avian reproduction: an ecological approach. Pp. 265–288 *in* S.-I. Mikami, K. Homma, and M. Wada (editors). Avian endocrinology: environmental and ecological perspectives. Japan Scientific Societies Press, Tokyo, Japan, and Springer Verlag, New York, NY.

WINGFIELD, J. C. 1984a. Androgens and mating systems: testosterone-induced polygyny in normally monogamous birds. Auk 101:665–671.

WINGFIELD, J. C. 1984b. Environmental and endocrine control of reproduction in the Song Sparrow, *Melospiza melodia.* General and Comparative Endocrinology 56:406–416.

WINGFIELD, J. C. 1984c. Influence of weather on reproduction. Journal of Experimental Zoology 232:589–594.

WINGFIELD, J. C. 1985. Short term changes in plasma levels of hormones during establishment and defense of a breeding territory in male Song Sparrows, *Melospiza melodia.* Hormones and Behavior 19:174–187.

WINGFIELD, J. C. 1993. Control of testicular cycles in the Song Sparrow, *Melospiza melodia melodia*: interaction of photoperiod and an endogenous program? General and Comparative Endocrinology 92:388–401.

WINGFIELD, J. C., G. F. BALL, A. J. DUFTY, R. E. HEGNER, AND M. RAMENOFSKY. 1987. Testosterone and aggression in birds. American Scientist 75:603–608.

WINGFIELD, J. C., AND D. S. FARNER. 1978a. The annual cycle of plasma irLH and steroid hormones in feral populations of the White-crowned Sparrow, *Zonotrichia leucophrys gambelii.* Biology of Reproduction 19:1046–1056.

WINGFIELD, J. C., AND D. S. FARNER. 1978b. The endocrinology of a natural breeding population of the White-crowned Sparrow (*Zonotrichia leucophrys pugetensis*). Physiological Zoology 51:188–205.

WINGFIELD, J. C., AND D. S. FARNER. 1979. Some endocrine correlates of renesting after loss of clutch or brood in the White-Crowned Sparrow, *Zonotrichia leucophrys gambelii.* General and Comparative Endocrinology 38:322–331.

WINGFIELD, J. C., AND D. S. FARNER. 1980. Control of seasonal reproduction in temperate-zone birds. Progress in Reproductive Biology 5:62–101.

WINGFIELD, J. C., AND D. S. FARNER. 1993. Endocrinology of reproduction in wild species. Pp. 163–327 *in* D. S. Farner, J. R. King, and K. C. Parkes (editors). Avian biology. Vol. 9. Academic Press, San Diego, CA.

WINGFIELD, J. C., AND A. R. GOLDSMITH. 1990. Plasma levels of prolactin and gonadal steroids in relation to multiple-brooding and renesting in free-living populations of the Song Sparrow, *Melospiza melodia.* Hormones and Behavior 24:89–103.

WINGFIELD, J. C., AND T. P. HAHN. 1994. Testosterone and territorial behaviour in sedentary and migratory sparrows. Animal Behaviour 47:77–89.

WINGFIELD, J. C., T. P. HAHN, R. LEVIN, AND P. HONEY. 1992. Environmental predictability and control of gonadal cycles in birds. Journal of Experimental Zoology 261:214–231.

WINGFIELD, J. C., T. P. HAHN, M. WADA, L. B. ASTHEIMER, AND S. SCHOECH. 1996. Interrelationship of day length and temperature on the control of gonadal development, body mass, and fat score in White-crowned Sparrows, *Zonotrichia leucophrys gambelii.* General and Comparative Endocrinology 101:242–255.

WINGFIELD, J. C., T. P. HAHN, M. WADA, AND S. J. SCHOECH. 1997. Effects of day length and temperature on gonadal development, body mass, and fat depots in White-crowned

Sparrows, *Zonotrichia leucophrys pugetensis.* General and Comparative Endocrinology 107:44–62.

WINGFIELD, J. C., R. E. HEGNER, A. J. DUFTY, AND G. F. BALL. 1990. The "challenge hypothesis": theoretical implications for patterns of testosterone secretion, mating systems, and breeding strategies. American Naturalist 136:829–846.

WINGFIELD, J. C., AND G. J. KENAGY. 1991. Natural regulation of reproductive cycles. Pp. 181–241 *in* P. K. T. Pang and M. P. Schreibman (editors). Vertebrate endocrinology: fundamentals and biomedical implications. Vol. 4, Part B, Reproduction. Academic Press, San Diego, CA.

WINGFIELD, J. C., D. L. MANEY, C. W. BREUNER, J. D. JACOBS, S. LYNN, M. RAMENOFSKY, AND R. D. RICHARDSON. 1998. Ecological bases of hormone-behavior interactions: the "emergency life history stage". American Zoologist 38:191–206.

WINGFIELD, J. C., M. C. MOORE, AND D. S. FARNER. 1983. Endocrine responses to inclement weather in naturally breeding populations of White-Crowned Sparrows (*Zonotrichia leucophrys pugetensis*). Auk 100:56–62.

WINGFIELD, J. C., AND M. RAMENOFSKY. 1997. Corticosterone and facultative dispersal in response to unpredictable events. Ardea 85:155–166.

WINGFIELD, J. C., AND M. WADA. 1989. Changes in plasma levels of testosterone during male-male interactions in the Song Sparrow, *Melospiza melodia*: time course and specificity of response. Journal of Comparative Physiology A 166:189–194.

WINKLER, D. W., AND P. E. ALLEN. 1995. Effects of handicapping on female condition and reproduction in Tree Swallows (*Tachycineta bicolor*). Auk 112:737–747.

WINKLER, D. W., AND P. E. ALLEN. 1996. The seasonal decline in Tree Swallow clutch size: physiological constraint or strategic adjustment? Ecology 77:922–932.

WITSCHI, E. 1961. Sex and secondary sexual characters. Pp. 115–168 *in* A. J. Marshall (editor). Biology and comparative physiology of birds. Vol. 2. Academic Press, New York, NY.

WITTENBERGER, J. F. 1976. The ecological factors selecting for polygyny in altricial birds. American Naturalist 110:779–799.

WITTENBERGER, J. F. 1982. Factors affecting how male and female Bobolinks apportion parental investments. Condor 84:22–39.

WOLFSON, A. 1954. Sperm storage at lower-than-body temperature outside the body cavity in some passerine birds. Science 120:68–71.

WOODBURN, R. J. W., AND C. M. PERRINS. 1997. Weight change and the body reserves of female Blue Tits, *Parus caeruleus,* during the breeding season. Journal of Zoology 243: 789–802.

WOOLFENDEN, G. E., AND J. W. FITZPATRICK. 1984. The Florida Scrub Jay. Princeton University Press, Princeton, NJ.

YAMAGISHI, S. 1981. Effect of parents' age class on breeding success of the Meadow Bunting *Emberiza cioides* (Aves: Emberizidae). Japanese Journal of Ecology 31:117–119.

ZAMORA, R. 1990. Importancia de los neveros como sustrato de alimentacion para los passeriformes de alta montaña. Doñana, Acta Vertebrata 17:57–66.

ZERBA, E., AND L. F. BAPTISTA. 1980. Courtship feeding in some emberizine finches. Wilson Bulletin 92:245–246.

ZERBA, E., AND M. L. MORTON. 1983a. Dynamics of incubation in Mountain White-crowned Sparrows. Condor 85:1–11.

ZERBA, E., AND M. L. MORTON. 1983b. The rhythm of incubation from egg laying to hatching in Mountain White-crowned Sparrows. Ornis Scandinavica 14:188–197.

ZINK, R. M. 1982. Patterns of genic and morphologic variation among sparrows in the genera *Zonotrichia, Melospiza, Junco,* and *Passerella.* Auk 99:632–649.

ZINK, R. M., D. L. DITTMAN, AND W. L. ROOTES. 1991. Mitochondrial DNA variation and the phylogeny of *Zonotrichia.* Auk 108:578–584.